Yours is a
Precious Witness

Memoirs of Jews and Catholics in Wartime Italy

Margherita Marchione

PAULIST PRESS
New York/Mahwah, N.J.

Acknowledgments: The author is indebted to Reverend Robert A. Graham for his guidance, to Robert Allerot for computer assistance, to Sister Filomena Di Carlo for secretarial work, to Clement Anzul, Shirley Horner, Sy Rotter, and Joan Messner Epstein for their encouragement. She expresses appreciation for financial help received from David Jurist, Arthur McGinnis, N. Larry Paragano, Frank Visceglia and other Catholic and Jewish friends who supported this project.

Photo credits: pp. ix, 35 (top), 185—Property of the Religious Teachers Filippini, Morristown, N.J.; p. 3—*L'Osservatore Romano,* Città del Vaticano; pp. 10, 12, 124—*Storia degli ebrei italiani sotto il fascismo* by Renzo De Felice, copyright © 1961 by Giulio Einaudi Editore, S.p.A., Torino, Italy; pp. 18, 62, 188—United States Holocaust Memorial Museum, Washington, D.C.; pp. 35 (bottom), 36—*Roma città prigioniera* by Cesare DeSimone, copyright © 1994, Gruppo Ugo Mursia Editore, S.p.A., Milano, Italy; p. 38—American Jewish Joint Distribution Committee, courtesy of United States Holocaust Memorial Museum, Washington, D.C.; pp. 48, 58–61, 97, 105–108, 133–136, 182–184—Monumenti Musei e Gallerie Pontificie, Città del Vaticano; p. 186—YIVO Institute for Jewish Research, courtesy of United States Holocaust Memorial Museum, Washington, D.C.

Library of Congress Cataloging-in-Publication Data

Marchione, Margherita.
    Yours is a precious witness— : memoirs of Jews and Catholics in wartime Italy / by Margherita Marchione.
       p. cm.
    Includes bibliographical references and index.
    ISBN 0-8091-0485-7 (alk. paper)
    1. Jews—Persecutions—Italy. 2. Holocaust, Jewish (1939–1945)—Italy. 3. Righteous Gentiles in the Holocaust—Italy. 4. World War, 1939–1945—Jews—Rescue—Italy. 5. Pius XII, Pope, 1876–1958—Relations with Jews. 6. Catholic Church—Italy—History—20th century. 7. World War, 1939–1945—Catholic Church. 8. Italy—Ethnic relations. I. Title.
DS135.I8M25   1997
940.53´18´0945—dc20   96-35039
                                                    CIP

Published by Paulist Press
997 Macarthur Boulevard
Mahwah, New Jersey 07430

Printed and bound in the
United States of America

To Reverend Robert A. Graham, S.J.,
whose friendship I will always treasure!

Contents

PART III

Pope Pius XII

In his first encyclical, *Summi Pontificatus* (1939), Pope Pius XII clearly, if implicitly, condemned the Nazis: "The spirit of violence and of discord brings indescribable suffering on mankind. Do We need to give assurance that Our paternal heart is close to all Our children in compassionate love, and especially to the afflicted, the oppressed, the persecuted?"

Foreword

---

*I*t is time to look at the story of Pope Pius XII. No longer can one speak of his *silence* for which he has long been criticized. His words and actions during the German occupation of Italy and throughout World War II deserve to be re-evaluated. His was a language of *action*.

Italian citizens saved the lives of thousands of Jewish men, women, and children from 1943 to 1945. Catholic priests and nuns housed Jewish people sometimes for months and years. Only with Vatican approval could they disregard the strict regulations regarding access to lay persons in cloistered areas of convents and monasteries. They obeyed when word came to open their doors for those who, if captured by the Nazis, would have been sent to concentration camps. They had the moral courage to risk their own lives.

Several members of the Religious Teachers Filippini alone cared for 114 Jewish men, women, and children. Their stories were known to Sister Margherita Marchione—educator, historian, author, and herself an American member of the Religious Teachers Filippini. In November of 1994, she convinced Sy Rotter, producer of *Documentaries International*, to interview several of her Italian counterparts. She added much more of her own research and interviews of others who actually hid their Jewish friends and neighbors and gathered their stories in this book, *Yours Is a Precious Witness*.

These survivors of the Holocaust and their rescuers in Italy help establish the truth about the assistance given by the Catholic Church. This documentation of their stories encourages the reader to look beyond the superficial treatment afforded to Pope Pius XII. It will provoke historians to take a more profound look at the facts. Hopefully, posterity will cease to perpetuate unfounded calumnies and misrepresentations. Among the living Vatican collaborators are Cardinal Paolo

Dezza, Cardinal Paolo Palazzini, Monsignor John Patrick Carroll-Abbing, Monsignor Hugh O'Flaherty, and others who participated in saving the Jews from deportation.

This isn't the first time Sister Margherita has been passionate about shedding light on a subject. She was director of the Philip Mazzei research project at Fairleigh Dickinson University and spent ten years writing about his little-known contributions to the history of the United States. Philip Mazzei was a neighbor and friend of Thomas Jefferson who called him a "Zealous Whig." He became Virginia's agent in Europe (1779), founded the Constitutional Society of 1784, and wrote four volumes of history on the Colonies (1788). Marchione's research produced a collection of 3,000 documents, including letters to and from the first five presidents of the United States. To honor Mazzei's 250th anniversary, she obtained American and Italian commemorative stamps.

Sister Margherita's undying dedication to this book will change so much of the negative conception that has fed bigotry, hatred, and misunderstanding between two peoples and between nations around the world. Unrelentingly Sister Margherita has never given up her quest for the absolute facts so that they can be presented to mankind. Her simple, beautiful, dignified ways are an inspiration to all of us. She is hard-working and persistent. Thank goodness these stories have at last been told. Now we must share them.

If more people were like Sister Margherita we would have a world with much more love in it; hatred and prejudices would not exist as they do today.

David Jurist

Pope John Paul II

Kneeling in the Brzezinka concentration camp, Pope John Paul II said: "I kneel on this Golgotha of the contemporary world, on these tombs, many without names, similar to the tomb of the Unknown Soldier. I come to pray with you and to give testimony to the world about what constitutes, in our times, the greatness and wretchedness of man; his victory and his defeat." (June 7, 1979)

Prologue

Marking the fiftieth anniversary of the end of World War II, Pope John Paul II celebrated Mass in St. Peter's Basilica, June 11, 1995. With him were clerics who had been prisoners, two Polish bishops who had been interned at Dachau, and the bishops of Hiroshima and Nagasaki, where atomic bombs were dropped in August of 1945.

The Nazi concentration camp at Dachau, a small town twelve miles from Munich, was liberated by American soldiers in the Rainbow Division. The U.S. troops found 35,000 inmates crammed into a facility prepared for 5,000; many were dying. Among the liberators was eighteen-year-old mortarman Leonard Bachmann from St. Paul-Minneapolis, who received the Bronze Star.

His experience at Dachau, of "what man could do to his brother," led directly to his decision to become a priest. In 1948, Bachmann entered the Missionary Servants of the Most Holy Trinity.

Father Bachmann noted recently that half of the 2,800 priests who were prisoners died in Dachau. He joined Cardinal Friedrich Wetter of Munich and celebrated the Mass in commemoration of the fiftieth anniversary of the Liberation. He recalled the words of Cardinal Wetter: "Even when we see no grave around us, we are standing on the largest priest cemetery in the world."

Among the priests who survived the Nazi horrors was Father Raphael Nienaltowski, a Capuchin, who was one of the Polish prisoners at Dachau. He was twenty-six years old when he became the subject of "deadly medical experiments by the Nazis." When the Allies arrived he was near death, but the American medics saved his life. After the war he remained in Germany, helping the estimated 2 million displaced Poles. He later came to the United States and lived in New Jersey where he died in 1993.

At the June 1995 anniversary Mass, Pope John Paul II prayed for the war's victims and denounced continuing conflicts around the globe. On the sufferings in the Nazi concentration camps, he stated: "To keep alive the memory of what happened is not only an historical necessity but a moral one. We must not forget!"

These words inspired the author to interview several members of the Religious Teachers Filippini who lived in Rome during World War II. During these interviews, as well as during her research in Rome, she was told repeatedly that, "at the request of Pope Pius XII, doors of convents and monasteries were opened to save the Jews when the Nazis occupied Italy." Notwithstanding the risks involved, priests and nuns opened their doors and compassionately cared for their guests.[1]

Rome was full of refugees. Long before the October 16, 1943, raid on the Roman Jews, convents were taking in refugees, Jews or non-Jews, as well as soldiers and anti-Fascists. The Pontiff's wishes were implemented through normal channels, i.e., the Congregation for Religious and the Vicariat which was under the jurisdiction of Cardinal Marchetti-Salvagiani and of Bishop Luigi Traglia.

In those days especially, the Vicariat necessarily was in constant contact with the Pope himself, even by telephone. "Directives" were given orally because, under the German occupation, archives (and not just Jewish) were subject to Gestapo raids.

Robert A. Graham, S.J., Vatican historian, encouraged the author to continue her research when he wrote, "Yours is a precious witness."[2] Neither a research project nor a history of the Holocaust, the book is a record of memories—*a precious witness*—that pays homage to both survivors and rescuers in Italy.

This book, *Yours Is a Precious Witness,* is an effective vehicle for the study of Holocaust victims and the appreciation of courageous Christian rescuers. It honors those heroes and heroines who hid Jews in attics, cellars, and barns, providing food and clothing, false papers, and money for escape. They were compassionate men and women who performed acts of heroism, risking prison and deportation for their own families, even death.

The roots of the Jewish community in Italy—the oldest community in Europe—had remained unsevered for 2,000 years despite periods of intolerance and persecution. The Jews in Piedmont considered themselves among the founding fathers of the Italian state. With the unification of Italy in 1870, Jews from the ghettos joined the middle class and helped finance growing industries. Thus a Jewish upper middle class or aristocracy was created.

In a small population of 47,000, they became generals, cabinet ministers, and prime ministers. Practicing religion privately and unobtrusively, Jews blended physically as well as linguistically with Italians. Gradually some lost contact with their roots. The Jews' sense of national and religious identity influenced the decision of most Italian Jews to remain in Italy.

For fifty years, the oral history of Italian Jews and their rescuers has remained virtually untapped. It includes the many priests and nuns who served and continue to serve humanity. Theirs was a contribution to the diversity of the Jewish experience during World War II, especially in Italy.

Italian Jews found both material aid and moral comfort in the Catholic Church. Interviews with survivors and rescuers show that the Church was not a silent accomplice to the Holocaust of the Jews.

It is hoped that this book will add to the texture of the lives of Italian Jews and, with a profoundly human dimension, provide a missing part of Italian social history. *Yours Is a Precious Witness* offers a paradoxical mixture of benevolence and betrayal, persecution and rescue of a community caught up in the totalitarianism and cruelty of anti-Semitism.

Jews and Fascists coexisted in Italy. The Italian Jews found a safe and comfortable home in a society where they were respected. No one could believe that there were concentration camps for the organized extermination of human beings. It was a "terrible shock" to Jews and Italians who staunchly refused to cooperate with the Nazis.

Yours Is a Precious Witness will perpetuate the legacy of these brave people. It is indeed a debt to honor the Christian rescuers in Italy who risked their lives to save Jews during the Holocaust. It is an expression of gratitude toward Pope Pius XII, and the men and women, including priests and nuns, whose altruistic behavior and moral courage saved so many refugees.

The book is not a historical analysis of World War II. Rather it is an *apologia* in defense of Pope Pius XII, who could not take a public stand against the Nazis without endangering the lives of other human beings. Facts and documents will dispel the unwarranted accusations of some authors who continue to condemn His Holiness.

Many critics have interpreted Pope Pius XII's "silence" as "indifference" or "cowardice." This is not so. He was a fearless religious leader who was also a great statesman. He had to follow a course of action, or of inaction, which one or other of the warring nations would misunderstand or exploit. His words would receive a political interpretation in which the religious aspects would be completely lost and, from the Papacy's point of view, no good would be accomplished.

These memoirs link Jews and Catholics together as they express their solidarity. They help to bridge differences, not perpetuate the tragic horrors of the Holocaust. Virtually every leader in the world was guilty of inaction and complicity while, behind the scenes, the Pope worked to save all who could be saved.

The Church was founded with a mission that transcends politics and is subject to no earthly power. Despite the enormous pressures that governments exerted on the Papacy, Pius XII consistently adhered to the fundamental concept that the Church is "in the world but not of it." In all his actions, the Pope was guided by religious and humanitarian motives.[3]

In a letter dated February 5, 1996, Anthony L. Capitani, a U.S. Army chaplain, stated: "Your book about Pope Pius XII's efforts on behalf of the Jews in World War II is timely, factual, and fascinating. From my first audience with him, I found that he had a warm personality despite the far away and scholarly appearance his glasses gave him. Throughout the years I felt sorry for the shabby way certain press and public figures disparaged him in those turbulent times, especially since the Vatican was often the only conduit between POWs and news to their families.

"Some people have a myopic view of history and an extremely poor sense of reality, especially the difficult times German Catholics experienced and the senseless harm and futility of any public act of excommunication upon any psychopath. Under the circumstances Pius XII followed the best course available to him and stayed free of useless Western propaganda cheap shots.

"All war is essentially murder whether it is conducted by direct shooting or dropping napalm and bombs from the skies upon a hopeless mix of civilian and military population. I think history will vindicate Pius XII during that fearsome and troublesome era."

No one denies that historically Jews had been marginalized in European culture. Nazi policy sought the extermination not only of Jews but also of non-Jewish peoples as well. However, since World

War II there has been a revolution in the attitude of the Catholic Church in its acknowledgment of the Judaic roots of Christianity and its repudiation of anti-Semitism. Indeed, there has been a resurgence of mutual understanding and fraternal dialogue.

Repeatedly, Pope John Paul II has defended Pope Pius XII, recalling "how deeply he felt about the tragedy of the Jewish people, and how hard and effectively he worked to assist them during the Second World War."[4]

This exposition heralds all dedicated rescuers and recounts some heroic deeds. It should help eliminate the false interpretations of Pope Pius XII's motives found in a number of books on the Holocaust, some of which seem designed to ignore the truth and regenerate bigotry and hatred. It should not be difficult for the reader to formulate his or her own conclusions.

The stories of rescuers and survivors have relevance to events in today's world where racial and religious intolerance continue to threaten international peace.

Margherita Marchione

Varese: May, 1944. Jews captured by the SS.

Part I

The first page of the "Declaration on Race" in Mussolini's own handwriting. (September, 1938)

A. Introduction

1. Historical Background

*A*fter centuries of foreign domination, Italy was finally united under the House of Savoy in 1870, and the total emancipation of Jews was achieved.

Jews had contributed to the struggle for freedom; they were educated and had obtained prominent positions in all fields; fifty Jewish generals served in the Italian army in World War I. Their contributions were in business, banking, and insurance, as well as in education, the arts, and literature. They participated in government; some joined the Fascist movement; others were anti-Fascists who understood the danger of an authoritarian government. Italian Jews retained their Jewishness and a deep respect for Jewish ethical concepts, their culture, their heritage. This did not diminish their love for Italy.

In June 1940, Benito Mussolini joined Hitler in the war. He fully cooperated with the Nazis. Several thousand non-Italian Jews, as well as a few hundred Italian Jews, were sent to a concentration camp at Ferramonti-Tarsia in Calabria. Fortunately, they survived the war. Others were not so fortunate.

There is no doubt about Benito Mussolini's anti-Semitic policy and his "commitment" to Hitler with regard to the discrimination against and persecution of Jews. No one could have been as close to the Germans as was Mussolini without having absorbed the Nazist ideology. He realized that it would be necessary to prepare and inform the general public about Fascist discrimination against Jews. He implemented anti-Semitism through the Italian educational system from the primary grades to the university. Newspapers and magazines, at all cultural levels, were Mussolini's "voice." Through the media he achieved the systematic introduction of his anti-Semitic campaign.

News services in Italy were censored and reports about German atrocities were considered propaganda by the Italians. Despite the racial laws during this period, Jewish refugees fled to Italy where they were protected by Italian officers and diplomats. They were not deported as was the case in other countries in Nazi Europe. Although Jews had been assimilated into Italian society, some non-Jewish Italians who served the Nazis were responsible for the deaths of Jews. However, anti-Nazi and anti-Fascist Italians resolved to help Jewish fugitives. Many were executed or deported to German concentration camps where they died of starvation, disease, or hard labor. Nevertheless, many Italians of all social positions were compassionate and had the courage to take risks to save them.

On July 25, 1943, King Victor Emmanuel III summoned Mussolini to his villa and arrested him. The Italian army was told to lay down their arms to the Allies on September 8, 1943. Imprisoned in the Abruzzi mountains, Mussolini was rescued by the Nazis and brought to Lake Garda (Province of Brescia) in northern Italy where an Italian Social Republic was established at Salò. This provisional government lasted from September 1943 to April 1945 and became known as the Republic of Salò.

Mussolini issued a political manifesto declaring Jews to be enemy aliens. He then passed the last anti-Jewish law calling for the dissolution of the Union of Italian Jewish Communities and all Jewish charitable institutions, as well as the confiscation of their property. Betraying their neighbors and hunting fugitives, the Fascists sent many Jews to internment camps.

Nazi troops began to subject Italian Jews to deportation. On October 16, 1943, the SS surrounded the Jewish quarter in Rome along the streets of Porta d'Ottavia and the Teatro Marcello. They began searching for Jewish families in Rome; men and women, young and old were captured.

Never did the Jews in Rome, who felt secure because of the Vatican's proximity, expect the German military commander to send an SS force into their Roman quarter. The Pope was surprised to learn that the Nazis plundered the synagogue's library and sent its precious manuscripts to Munich. He had been assured by the German ambassador that the Jews would not be harmed by Herbert Kappler, the SS chief of

German security in Rome. Soon after, the SS police also confiscated the Jewish community's administrative offices.

During the October 16th raid, 1,259 Jews were transported to a temporary detention center in the Italian Military College, within 600 feet of the Vatican. No one in Rome believed what was happening. The Jews continued to hope in vain. They were loaded in trucks, brought to Rome's Tiburtina Station, and crowded into empty freight cars. Conditions were horrible; sanitary facilities did not exist; there was little food and no water. After almost a week of captivity, the train reached Auschwitz. All were gassed except 149 men and 47 women who were sent to the work camp where numbers were tatooed into their arms. They worked at the coal mines of Jawiszowice. Few survived.

Pope Pius XII has been depicted as indifferent to the fate of the Jews during World War II—a criticism that perhaps reached its climax in 1963 in Rolf Hochhuth's play *Der Stellvertreter* (translated as *The Deputy*) and continues to be the focus of books about Vatican diplomacy and the Holocaust. The testimony of survivors contradicts this historical misrepresentation.

Princess Enza Pignatelli Aragona,[1] a dedicated Christian known for her charity among the poor in Rome, visited the Vatican frequently. When the Nazi raid began in the early hours of October 16, 1943, the princess was awakened from a sound sleep by the telephone. The caller was a Christian friend who lived in the Jewish quarter near the Tiber.

Her friend was alarmed: German police were collecting the Jews in the area and loading them into trucks for transportation to an unknown destination. All were being taken away without regard to age, sex, or health. Pope Pius XII should be informed immediately.

Princess Pignatelli at first was opposed to what she was asked to do. She could not get to the Vatican even if the Pope were to admit her to an audience. The city transportation system did not operate at that early hour and she had no car. The moment of hesitation passed. She telephoned the German embassy to the Vatican. An embassy aide, her friend Gustave Wollenweber, was awakened. Could Wollenweber bring his car around and take her to the Vatican at once? Ironically he complied. It was early morning. In a few minutes the German embassy car was at her door and they were en route to the Vatican. A German diplomat of an anti-Semitic government was accompanying an Italian princess to the Vatican to protest the arrest of Jews!

Imagine how the Vatican official in charge of papal audiences blinked his eyes at the audacity of his excited visitor who wanted to see the Pope immediately, without an appointment and without indicating her business. Faced with a woman's persistence, he passed the word to Pius XII who received her without delay. He listened with pain and surprise as she poured out the story of the raid against the Jews. "But the Germans promised not to touch the Jews!" he exclaimed.

Pope Pius XII knew that only a fortnight earlier the Jewish leaders had handed over to the SS, the Nazi police, fifty kilograms of gold as a price of security from molestation. He picked up his telephone. The wheels were beginning to turn. Determined to do what he could, he protested.

It was alleged that Pius XII never protested to the Germans the October 16th deportation of the Roman Jews. But documentation proves that there was an official, personal protest through the papal Secretary of State, Cardinal Luigi Maglione. He delivered it on Pope Pius XII's order to the German Ambassador, Ernst von Weizsäcker, on that same fateful morning. This protest was eventually published in the Vatican's official *Actes* for that date, October 16, 1943.

With all the emphasis at his command, Cardinal Maglione expressed to the German envoy the Pope's profound distress over the fact that, "under his very eyes," poor and innocent people should have to suffer simply because of their stemming from a particular race and for no other reason.

Weizsäcker listened attentively to Cardinal Maglione's protest. He was ready with his answer. Did Pius XII really insist that Berlin be informed of the papal indignation? He cautioned the papal secretary of state: "I think of the consequences that a protest of the Holy See may precipitate. The order for the action comes from the highest level. Will Your Eminence leave me free not to take account of this official conversation?"

Weizsäcker then assured Cardinal Maglione that he would do everything possible at the local level to cope with the threat to the Jews of Rome. But he did not want to take responsibility, he said, for forwarding a papal protest to his superiors in Berlin. On this assurance Cardinal Maglione did not press for a protest to Berlin. From experience he possibly was convinced that in matters dealing with the Jews, an intervention with Berlin would do no good and instead might produce the opposite effect. He was reassured by Weizsäcker's promise to diminish the threat locally.

In the Nazi plans, 8,000 Roman Jews were marked for elimination. But the operation was suspended after that first day. Why?

From different parts of the world, people insisted that Pius XII publicly condemn the Nazis. But to the very end the Pope was convinced that, should he denounce Hitler, there would be retaliation. Because of his fortitude and courage many more lives were saved.

Fifty years ago, when 47,000 Jews in Italy were forced to hide from the Nazis-Fascists, most people were totally unaware that the Holocaust was taking place. While they discussed the war, there was little mention of the terrible genocide. The Allies did not rush to stem the tide of the Holocaust because few believed what was happening.

In his letter to the editor of the *Wall Street Journal* (October 27, 1995), William Herskovic explained that he was deported from Drancy, France, in September 1942 with his wife and two baby girls. The latter were murdered upon their arrival at Auschwitz. He spent three months in Peiskretcham, one of Auschwitz's satellite concentration camps.

In December 1942, Herskovic escaped with two other young men to Breslau, Germany. There the local rabbi did not want to hear what he had experienced and survived. When Herskovic finally arrived home in Belgium, neither Ulmann, the chief rabbi, nor others to whom he appealed believed his report that the Nazis were slaughtering men, women, and children in the concentration camps.

During the Allied bombing, 2,000 female prisoners were evacuated on forced marches from Ravensbruck to Mauthausen concentration camp. Only 740 survived. On their "death marches" inside Germany, concentration camp survivors crossed paths with the rapidly advancing Allied armies. Only in 1945 did the world even begin to understand the magnitude of the Holocaust.

Benito Mussolini was executed by Italian partisans on April 28, 1945. Italian officers and men joined the partisans. Others were captured by the Nazis and sent to prison camps. Eighteen divisions of the German army remained in Italy. One week later German retaliation began in northern Italy.

Isaac Dostis, a Greek Jew now living in Leonia, New Jersey, lost some thirty relatives in the Nazi concentration camp at Auschwitz.

Eight family members, who were hiding in the homes of sympathetic Christians, were saved. If caught, both Jews and Christians would have been sent to concentration camps or murdered on the spot. "If you were lucky," Dostis stated, "the Nazis would shoot you. If you were not, they would hang you and leave you hanging as a warning to others."

Few victims survived the concentration camps during the Holocaust. In Italy, when the Allies liberated both the Bolzano-Gries camp in northern Italy and the San Sabba camp in Trieste on April 29–30, 1945, Jews and other prisoners were transferred to the International Red Cross.

Nissenbaum sisters (the girls at either end) at a convent in Florence. They were hidden together with the daughters of Abraham Ehrenberg. After the war Ehrenberg saw to it that the Nissenbaum girls were sent to Israel.

2. Jews-Nazis-Fascists

In the Introduction to *Atlas of the Holocaust,* Martin Gilbert does not fail to record that "in addition to the 6 million Jewish men, women, and children who were murdered, at least an equal number of non-Jews was also killed, not in the heat of battle, not by military siege, aerial bombardment or the harsh conditions of modern war, but by deliberate, planned murder."[2]

Adolf Hitler became head of the Nazi Party in 1921, and under his leadership the party became a powerful political force in German elections by the early 1930s. He was appointed chancellor when the Nazi Party assumed power in Germany in 1933. He established a dictatorship.

German democracy ended. A reign of terror began. It was a period of fear, distrust, and suspicion. Basic rights—freedom of speech, press, and assembly—were restricted. The Nazis controlled all social institutions: civil service, the educational system, churches, the judiciary, industry, business, and other professions.

The Nazis had launched a campaign of terror against all Jews. Hundreds of synagogues throughout Germany were set on fire, Jewish shops looted, and ninety-one Jews killed in the streets on November 9, 1938, *Kristallnacht,* the "Night of the Broken Glass." Immediately following, more than 35,000 were sent to concentration camps where many died.

Adolf Hitler ordered his armies to enter Czechoslovakia in March 1939. Tens of thousands of Jews were trapped; some were refugees from Germany and Austria who had fled to Bohemia and Moravia. Others fled to Poland. On September 1, 1939, the German army invaded Poland and more than 60,000 Polish soldiers were killed, of whom 6,000 were Jews. Among the 400,000 Polish soldiers captured, there were 61,000 Jews. All were denied the basic rights of prisoners of war and treated as inmates of concentration camps with less rations, and forced to do especially heavy work. Non-Jews and Jews suffered cruelty and were killed with barbaric, brutal methods. Some were machine-gunned; others locked in buildings and then set on fire. Thousands were deported from France in sealed freight-cars; others were sent to forced labor camps. The Nazi inhumanity was indescribable.

Throughout eastern Europe, Jewish families were forced to give up their homes and relocate into ghettos. These were restricted areas set up by the Nazis in the poorer, more dilapidated sections of towns and cities. Ghettos were fenced in, typically with barbed wire or brick walls. It was like a prison, with armed guards at gates. Entry and exit were by permit or pass only. Conditions were horrible. Many families were crowded into a few rooms with no heat, food, or privacy. It was difficult to keep clean. People perished from malnutrition, starvation, exposure, and epidemics. There were, however, individuals and groups in every occupied nation who risked their lives to hide those targeted by the Nazis.

Anti-Semitism in Europe incited citizens of German-occupied countries to collaborate with the Nazis in their genocidal policies.

In 1940, some Jews were serving in the French Foreign Legion, hoping to fight against Nazi Germany. They were rounded up and sent to concentration camps in French North Africa. Another group of skilled workers was sent to Upper Silesian coalfields.

Reference to a papal protest appeared in the Swiss newspaper *La Tribune de Genève* on September 8, 1942: "Although the Vichy government ordered that the Pope's protest must be ignored, news spread rapidly, thanks to the courageous attitude of the Catholic clergy....The British government has in its hands instructions from Vichy to the French press: 'Under no circumstances should mention be made about the Vatican protest defending French Jews to Marshal Pétain'."[3]

In 1941, Germany invaded Yugoslavia and Greece; 145,000 Jews were driven from their homes. Jews were active in the Yugoslav Resistance. Whenever it was possible to escape, they fought in partisan groups. As Jews escaped into the woods, they ambushed German trucks and killed the Nazis who were persecuting them.

In the Soviet Union no Jew was to be spared. Killing was to be done in the towns and villages, no resources wasted in deportation to camps or murder sites. In 1942, three new death camps were prepared:

Belzec, Treblinka, and Sobibor. Most Jews were to be killed within a few hours of arrival.

In 1943 the Allies met in Moscow and issued a declaration on German atrocities that did not mention Jews. They deplored those atrocities, but did not want Jews to emigrate.

The Nazis intended to kill all the Jews of Europe. Although the United States and Great Britain were aware of the persecution of Jews, they were possibly influenced by anti-Semitism and feared a massive influx of refugees. No attempts to stop or slow the genocide were made until pressure forced the United States to undertake limited rescue efforts in 1944. As the Allies approached, the tide of war turned and victory for the Nazis was no longer certain.

The Nazis adhered to the principle of collective responsibility. Punishment applied not only to the "transgressors," but also to their families—infants, children, adults. There were public executions. Assistance to the Jews was classified as help to the enemy, punishable by torture and deportation to concentration camps. Emulating the Nazis, orders were issued by the Fascists with total disregard for human suffering. Failure to comply carried the death sentence.

Help from Christians took on different forms: giving Jews false documents, escorting them to safety, offering food or lodgings. Any amount of aid to the Jews gave them courage and hope. Most Jews in the professions looked and dressed like Christians. They were professionals, intellectuals, wealthy businessmen, well-educated individuals. Some Jews passed as Christians. At times, the Jewish men and women dressed in clerical garb supplied to them by nuns and monks. The Italians saw their Jews as Italians. When Jews obtained false documents, they had to learn about their new identities: name, date, and place of birth, as well as fictitious relatives (friends acted as relatives) and familiarity with the Catholic religion. For example, many Jews learned the *Ave Maria* and the *Pater Noster*.

Truly Christian rescuers were aware that, according to the Church's teachings, all Jews are God's children and should be protected. Sometimes efforts were made to instruct young children in the Catholic faith in order to diminish the danger of discovery should they be questioned by the Nazis.

The rescuing of Jews by righteous Christians was influenced by the characteristics, friendships, motivation, and conditions associated with each case history. Indeed, some Italians lost their lives because they had rescued Jews; others were sent to concentration camps.

While some rescuers were motivated by money, many unselfish rescuers sacrificed their lives for principles and ideals and saved human beings. The majority courageously provided protection at great risk to themselves and their families.

Jews who were able to pay for their sustenance made it a point of honor to pay their rescuers. Some people resented the Jews and, after receiving remuneration, either killed them or denounced them for additional payment by the Nazis. In the absence of moral commitment, Jews were trapped. However, many righteous rescuers were sympathetic and ready to face the danger of being caught. They accepted the tragic consequences as true heroes.

Sensitive and sometimes knowledgeable about the Nazi crimes, Catholic rescuers were motivated by their religious convictions. They looked at Jews as human beings who were suffering unjustly. They atoned for the anti-Semitism by saving as many as possible. The upbringing of Catholics was such that they should have considered cruelty toward the Jews as sin. Italians who responded to the appeal of humanity had high moral standards and values and acted out of compassion. Religious motivation among Italians did play a part in saving many. It gave them the initial impetus they needed and the strength to continue on this dangerous path. Undoubtedly, some saw themselves as instruments in God's plan to save lives.

Rescuers' moral convictions and independence were instrumental in saving lives. According to Nechama Tec, decisions to help were influenced by "social class, political beliefs, degree of anti-Semitism, extent of religious commitment, the prospects of monetary reward and friendship."[4]

Regardless of the country from which the refugees came, it was a natural duty for rescuers in Italy to protect the Jews. Nechama Tec describes six basic characteristics and conditions that may be applied to all rescuers: individuality, independence in pursuing personal values, insistence that they did nothing heroic or extraordinary, commitment, the unplanned and gradual rescue, and perceptions of the needy.[5]

Even some anti-Semites who were socially prominent, devout Catholics and politically active were appalled by Hitler's inhumanity. As patriots, saving Jews was part of opposing the Nazis.

Most Jews had some financial resources and had not been impoverished by years of ghettoization. More important is the fact that assimilation in their communities enabled Jews to pass as non-Jews. The Italian Jews' risk of detection was lessened because of their physical appearance, clothes, language, friendships, and contacts. A non-Italian Jew could be betrayed by his appearance, behavior, and attitudes. To stay alive he needed courage and self-assurance. He had to avoid being recognized. Jews had no rights. Noncompliance led to severe punishments, outright executions, or concentration-camp deportation.

Everywhere the Nazis retaliated as more natives joined the partisans. In a small town near Mir in Poland, twelve nuns, suspected of feeding partisans, were executed. The loss of battles created a need for victories against vulnerable civilians.

Oswald Rufeisen was saved by the nuns in Mir and lived with them from August 1942 to December 1943. His life as a partisan and the good deeds he performed have been recorded. He helped everyone. Known as Father Daniel, he lives on Mount Carmel in a monastery overlooking the Mediterranean. A World War II hero, he was an Israeli who wore the Nazi uniform; a Polish Jew who, as an officer with a German police unit, organized a ghetto breakout; a fugitive from the Nazis who found refuge with Polish nuns and became a Catholic monk. Father Rufeisen, a Catholic convert, is a fighter for Jewish survival and devotes his life to establishing bridges between Judaism and Christianity.[6]

Approximately 85 percent of Italy's Jews survived the Holocaust. Italians were considered racially inferior by the Nazis whose contempt for their ally was transformed into profound distrust and hatred. Italians thought the Jews would be exempt because they were loyal, prosperous, and assimilated citizens. They did not believe rumors of deportation and extermination. When the first roundups began in September 1943, most Jews went into hiding. The danger period was shorter for them in Italy than for those in other occupied countries. Poland was occupied for more than five years. The Netherlands, Belgium, and most of France were occupied for well over four years. Mass deportations of more than 380,000 Jews did not begin in Hungary until April 27, 1944.

"The Jews in Italy before the Holocaust," writes Susan Zuccotti, "strongly resembled most American, Canadian, and Western European Jews today. Mildly observant and respectful of their heritage, they were nevertheless fully integrated, represented in all political parties and factions, and thoroughly steeped in the customs and culture of their day. Proportionately few in number, they were concentrated in the largest urban centers and almost unknown in rural areas. They lived, finally, in a society with little prejudice and no formal barriers to their achievement.

"And yet the Holocaust occurred in Italy. Its roots lay in the racial laws imposed upon a reluctant populace by their Fascist dictator. It peaked only during the German occupation—a time that brought the worst elements of the society to the surface and intimidated all others. It was opposed by courageous individuals who saved thousands. But still the Holocaust occurred, endorsed by the government and the press, enforced by thousands of Italian fanatics, and sustained by a terrorized, preoccupied, or simply indifferent majority. The Holocaust in Italy was a twisted legacy—a blend of courage and cowardice, nobility and degradation, self-sacrifice and opportunism. In contrast to other countries, perhaps, the worthy behavior outweighed the unworthy, but the horror was nonetheless real."[7]

Like other Italians, Jews in Italy were inclined to ignore the racial laws. They were ignoring unjust regulations, but they were also risking punishment. They evaded the law, did not report for internment, secured false documents, and were as adept as their Christian compatriots at fooling the authorities. All were individualistic.

Survivors in Italy owed their lives to their own initiative and the help of one or several non-Jews. By September 1943, most Italians disapproved of the war and were disgusted with the Fascists and their German allies. Their commitment to rescue the Jews was usually a spontaneous decision. They were sympathetic Christians who could provide shelter, food, and documents needed by the Jews in hiding. Italians interpreted or ignored rules to help Italian Jews who differed from them only in their religion which was unostentatious, as was that of Italian Catholics.

When the Vatican spread the word that the doors of convents should be opened, nuns allowed outsiders, even men, into their secluded cloisters; priests ignored civil laws; bankers did not report Jewish bank accounts; innkeepers, landlords, and villagers did not report "unusual guests." Contempt for the authorities prevailed and helped save Jews.

Despite their reputation as warm and humane people, Italians are not known for their dedication to charity sometimes associated with altruism. Yet there are many examples of altruistic behavior. Throughout the war, Jews were rescued from Nazi and Fascist brutality by ordinary people, including Catholic priests and nuns.

Susan Zuccotti tells the sad story of Sisto and Alberta Gianaroli, peasants who risked the lives of their seven children by sheltering Jews, and that of Pio Troiani and Torquato Fraccon who, with their sons, were executed because of involvement in rescue work.[8]

But there were Italian police who helped with deportation. There were informers, cruel prison guards, politicians who decreed that Jews should be interned. Thousands of Italian men volunteered for groups like the Muti Legion or the Carità and Koch bands. They mercilessly raided churches and convents and tortured their own countrymen. There were semiautonomous bands, like the Italian SS and the *Brigate Nere*. They killed partisans and village hostages. After torture and interrogation, the Jews were turned over to the Nazis.

Fascist collaborators were desperate and violent. Fanatics destroyed a synagogue when one of their men was murdered by a partisan in Alessandria, near Turin. The anti-Semitic Italian press carried out orders without reflection, indifferent to the persecution that existed.

In the winter of 1939–1940, when Italy was still a neutral country, 150 refugees fled from Germany with visas permitting them to enter the United States. Unable to get transportation, they were trapped in Italy when war was declared in June 1940. They were immediately arrested, chained together, and taken to an old monastery above the town of Campagna, a mountain village near the Bay of Salerno. Under guard of the Italian police, the 2 Protestants, 8 Catholics, and 140 Jews—assisted by Don Francesco Sacco—were confined to cramped quarters for three years.

When Italy surrendered and the Allies landed at nearby Salerno, the Germans took possession of the town. The Allied bombardment cracked the monastery's roof and the refugees fled to the mountains where they lived for ten days on grapes and figs. To drive the Germans out, the Allies began shelling Campagna. The town's civilians, wounded by the shells or shot by the Germans, were without medical care.

In this emergency the refugees who were hiding in the mountains returned. Among the group were lawyers, artists, bank managers, writers, tailors, and four surgeons who, working with only two artery forceps, one needle holder, some tubes of catgut and a few improvised instruments, performed over forty major operations in two days. This story appeared in the November 1, 1943, issue of *Life* magazine.

Germany surrendered unconditionally on May 8, 1945. More than 11 million civilians had been murdered since the German invasion of Poland. Millions of non-Jewish civilians had been killed in reprisal actions and in mass executions in German-dominated Europe. Only the Jews were systematically searched out for death to ensure that none survived. But despite Nazi efforts, about 300,000 Jews survived the concentration camps and death marches.

3. Italian Military

Italian military had a policy of continuous postponements in the implementation of the racial laws, so much so that the Berlin government expressed its dissatisfaction. Officers and soldiers, in particular, made every effort to temporize in order to send Jews into hiding. According to Ambassador Roberto Ducci, the vast majority of the Italian populace had preserved its feelings for humanity, wherein one does not persecute people without reason. Most Italians had a sense of morality and respect for human dignity that prevented them from participating in a crime.

Although these Italians knew the risk, they took care of the Jews. En route as they left France and crossed the mountains with 1,100 people, the Italian military helped transport the children, women, the elderly, the sick. They embodied the sensitivity of the Italian people and provided arrangements for the Jewish refugees in the best hotels. Unfortunately, they were all trapped by the Germans.

Sidi Duiri Sharon and her brother, Simi Duiri, were in France. They stated that Italian soldiers protected them from the French police. The soldiers took a group of fifteen from the camp in Saint-Martin-Vesubie to Ondono, near Cuneo in northern Italy. There they were hidden in two abandoned shepherds' huts. It was Saturday and it was snowing. Several babies were suffering from the cold. To their amazement the next morning they saw a procession of people carrying jugs of milk, buckets of food, and some straw to sleep on. They said that in church the priest had told them there were some people on the mountainside and some small children who had nothing to eat, and that it was their duty to help them.

In 1942, Dan Millin's family lived in the German-occupied town of Karlovac, near Zagreb, Yugoslavia. An Italian officer, Colonel Luigi Supino, had a room in their house. When the Nazis came to take the

family away, the Colonel threatened to shoot them. That night he sent
two "carabinieri" to guard the house. To save one of their cousins, he
dressed him in an Italian uniform. He then accompanied the entire family of ten into Slovenia, which was under Italian occupation. When
they received official ID papers they went to Vicenza, in a village
called Valli del Pasubio, and remained there for two years until Italy
capitulated.

Antonio Tursi, an Italian soldier, saved Milena Zarfati and Fatina
Sed who were deported as children from Rome to Fossoli. Later they
were sent to Auschwitz and Ravensbruck. In these concentration
camps the two young girls, ages thirteen and fourteen, witnessed the
horrors of death and experimentation. The twenty-four-year-old soldier
decided to escape from Ravensbruck when the Russians arrived and
the Germans were fleeing toward Poland with their prisoners. Before
leaving, Antonio Tursi quietly asked if there were any Italian women
who wanted to escape with him. Gina, who later became his wife,
responded. Milena and Fatina joined them. Together they roamed
Europe as a family. The terrorized children, whose families had been
killed by the Nazis, no longer wanted to live and had to be watched
constantly. Gina and Antonio provided food, nourishment, and love.
Antonio assured them that, should they not find relatives in Rome, he
would adopt them.

Fifty years later, inspired one evening by a TV program, Antonio
began his search to find them by calling the Jewish communities in
Milan and Rome. His difficulties increased when he confused the name
"Sed" with "Settimo." Finally Antonio located Milena, who then was
in touch with Fatina. Soon after they joined him and Gina for a joyful
reunion in Rome.

While Nazi military was destroying entire villages and murdering
Jews, Italian soldiers gathered Jewish refugees—total strangers—in
military trucks, cars, and tanks and moved them to protected areas.
Italian officials did nothing to interfere with this work of mercy and
compassion. The link between Jews and Italians who protected them
was their common humanity. As word spread, Jews fled from German
territory into Italy, frustrating the Germans who appealed to Mussolini.

Italian soldiers refused to deport Jews in Greece, Yugoslavia, and
Croatia. Instead they issued Italian naturalization papers and used
every possible pretext to protect them. They were then transported to

Athens. Unfortunately, after the Armistice between the Allies and Italy, many were captured by the Nazis.

In 1941, Ivo Herzer, a sixteen-year-old Yugoslav Jew, and his parents were helped by Italian soldiers. They were part of a group of fifteen refugees from Croatia who tried to reach the Italian occupation zone. They eluded the Nazis and approached Italian soldiers who accompanied them to Fiume. Not only did an Italian sergeant protect them on the train, but he also presented them to the authorities and requested food and drink.

The family lived in the town of Cirquenizza and became friendly with the Italians. A year later they were taken to a camp in Porto Re, on the coast. The camp commandant assured them that, as long as the Italian flag was there, they would be cared for. In 1943 they were allowed to build a hut in the camp, where Passover services were held. The Italian army also furnished a school building and provided textbooks. Ivo Herzer was studying Latin, Italian, and history as trains throughout Europe were taking thousands of children to their death. When they were moved to the Island of Arbe, only one soldier escorted 200 Jews as they went swimming every day. Most of them survived the Holocaust. Ivo Herzer lived in Virginia.[9]

In France the Italians defied both the Germans and the French by insisting that the Jews were under Italian jurisdiction. Jewish refugees enjoyed enforced residence in villages in the interior. This was almost like freedom. Although the Germans demanded immediate deportation, the Italians procrastinated and allowed the Jews to accompany the army as it withdrew.

Angelo Donati, an Italian Jew from Modena, hired fifty trucks and organized a massive rescue operation. When the Armistice between the Allies and Italy was announced, all hopes for their rescue were destroyed. The Jews were sent to the French holding camp at Drancy and trains carried them to Auschwitz. Some escaped and were accompanied by Italian soldiers who fled over the rugged passes into Italy. These soldiers helped them carry luggage and babies to the province of Cuneo southwest of Turin. Later this group of refugees, trapped by the Germans, was taken to Auschwitz.

Priests and nuns had special resources: convents and monasteries were spacious and Jews could be more easily hidden; food had to be provided for their own large membership and it could be obtained and shared without arousing too much suspicion; they could take risks because they had no dependents. However, they were not immune from suspicion and arrest. Those sent to prison were treated with brutality and contempt. Many were murdered in reprisal killings for helping anti-Fascists and Jews.

Eli Zborowski visited the Catholic family that had sheltered his family thirty-five years earlier in a Polish town where many Jews lived. When the woman was asked why she protected them, she said simply: "We are all Catholics here. How could anyone refuse to hide Jews when our Lord told us that we should help those in need?" Her courage came from within and was supported by her own commitment. It was true love in action extended to her neighbors—the persecuted Jews.[10]

When Jorgen Kieler, a twenty-three-year-old medical student working with the Resistance in Copenhagen, learned that the Germans were preparing to round up their Jewish neighbors, he and his friends helped organize thirteen fishing boats that carried more than 800 Jews to Sweden. Jorgen Kieler had his skull fractured during an interrogation. He also spent time in two concentration camps. Eventually he became director of the Danish Cancer Research Institute. On May 4, 1993, the Jewish Foundation for Christian Rescuers honored him, his sister, and the other Danes who saw to it that the majority of the group escaped the Germans.[11]

Giorgio Perlasca worked for an Italian importing firm in Budapest, Hungary. When Mussolini fell in July 1943, all Italians were requested to return home. Perlasca refused and was interned; however, on October 13, 1944, he talked his way out of the hotel where he was being held. He went to see Angel Sanz-Briz, the Spanish envoy who had been issuing protective passes to Jews, and applied for a job.

Perlasca was put in charge of the "safe houses" sheltering Jews from deportation and from the Arrow Cross militia. When Sanz-Briz left Budapest, Giorgio found a note saying that he could obtain a visa to Switzerland through the Spanish embassy in Vienna. Instead, without an official letter appointing him chargé d'affaires of Spain, he continued to issue protective passes by changing his first name to the Spanish Jorge. He saved approximately 5,000 Hungarian Jews. Only the apostolic nuncio knew what he was doing and encouraged him to continue his assumed role as a Spanish diplomat.

Between November 1944 and January 1945, Perlasca worked with Raoul Wallenberg from Sweden, Friedrich Born from the

International Red Cross, and Monsignor Angelo Rotta from the Vatican, obviously under direct order from the Pope.

In April 1945, Dr. Hugo Dukesz, one of the Jews saved by Giorgio Perlasca, expressed the affection and gratitude of those who survived: "There are not enough words to praise the tenderness with which you fed us and with which you cared for the old and the sick among us. You encouraged us when we were close to despair. Your name will never be omitted from our prayers. May the Almighty grant you your reward."[12]

Perlasca returned to Padua, Italy, and died in August 1992. He had fought in Africa and in Spain. He was honored by Israel and given honorary citizenship of Jerusalem. In Budapest, the Parliament not only gave him the "gold star"; a bust in his memory was also placed at Number 35 Szent Istvon Park where he used to hide the Jews; and the Jewish community placed a plaque on the wall of its synagogue.

In 1986 a group of Hungarian Jews made an appeal in European newspapers to locate Perlasca because they wanted to express their gratitude to the man who had saved them: "a tall, blond, handsome young man who was known as the Spanish Ambassador." Nino Bolognese, President of the Civitanova Marche Rotary Club, whose purpose is to honor heroes of the past, brought attention to Giorgio Perlasca who was living in Padua.

After more than forty years of silence, in 1993 Italy finally recognized one of its extraordinary heroes with the dedication of a "Giorgio Perlasca Day" in Padua. He was "a just man among nations," whose courage in saving lives exemplifies the most noble human values. His memory will be perpetuated through plaques, busts, and books. Above all, in the hearts of all those he saved, he will never be forgotten. "The youth of today should emulate my father's moral courage," said Franco Perlasca during the ceremony. "He never spoke about the good he did, because for him doing good and saving lives was the most normal thing to do."

Georgio Perlasca once stated: "The world does not need heroes, men who want to be known in history; but it does need persons who by their humanity know how to be history."[13]

In the Foreword to Elie Wiesel's book *Night/Dawn/Day,* François Mauriac recalled the horror of trainloads of Jewish children torn from their mothers by the Nazis. His dream of the progress of the Enlightenment and the discoveries of science vanished.

At that time Mauriac did not know that those children were on their way to the gas chamber and the crematorium. With a sigh, he said to Wiesel, the young Israeli journalist: "How often I've thought about those children!"

Elie Wiesel replied: "I was one of them." Reared on the Talmud and dedicated to the Eternal, Wiesel had witnessed the death of his entire family. He was quoted by Mauriac as saying, "Never shall I forget those flames which consumed my faith forever."

François Mauriac stated: "And I, who believe that God is love, what answer could I give my young questioner? If the Eternal is the Eternal, the last word for each one of us belongs to Him. This is what I should have told this Jewish child. But I could only embrace him, weeping."

4. Jewish Leaders in Italy

In Rome, neither Pope Pius XII nor the Jewish leaders believed that the Germans would deport Roman Jews. They were surprised when SS Chief Heinrich Himmler informed the SS chief of the German security police in Rome, Herbert Kappler, that "all Jews, regardless of nationality, age, sex and personal conditions, must be transferred to Germany and liquidated...."

Dante Almansi was president of the Union of Italian Jewish Communities. In 1939, he obtained government permission for DELASEM, a Jewish service agency, to provide relief for foreign refugees in Italy. Now he and Ugo Foà were summoned by Kappler whose sole purpose for the meeting was to delude the Jews, so that they would not seek sanctuary in the hundreds of churches, monasteries, and convents in Rome.

The Jewish leaders were told: "Within thirty-six hours you must bring me fifty kilograms of gold." Word of the extortion spread. It was a very dramatic moment. There was an avalanche of contributions. The Pope offered to provide the necessary gold. Large numbers of Christians also contributed to show their solidarity. It seemed that all Rome had risen up in defense of the Jews. The gold demanded by Kappler was secured. The Vatican's offer was not needed.

According to some historians, Kappler invented the gold ransom as a smoke screen to hide his real aim. In his book *Benevolence and Betrayal*, Alexander Stille states: "Kappler knew that an earlier dispatch about deporting Jews from Rome had been leaked by a sympathetic German diplomat to sources in the Vatican....Whatever the case, if his intention had been to distract the Jews, rob them of the means to flee, and give them the illusion of being able to ward off the threat of deportation, Kappler could not have devised a better scheme."[14]

Reports about the Holocaust were regarded as exaggerated Allied propaganda. When news of the October 16th roundup spread throughout Rome, there was no public protest. Any formal, diplomatic action by the Vatican would have been useless, but the Catholic clergy, and the religious throughout Italy, hid Jews whenever possible. Help was given by religious institutions—Jesuits, Redemptorists, Salesians, Franciscans, Pallottines, Capuchins, Sisters of Our Lady of Sion, The Most Precious Blood, Our Lady of Perpetual Help, The Pontifical Institute of the Religious Teachers Filippini, and hundreds of other institutions.

When the chief rabbi of Jerusalem met with Monsignor Arthur Hughes, the papal delegate to Egypt and Palestine, on September 5, 1944, they spoke about the Vatican rescue efforts. Monsignor Hughes quoted the Holy Father's words: "We must do all in our power to save the people of Israel. But every step we take must be calculated with the greatest caution, because I could not bear the idea that our activity might have an effect opposite to the one intended and cause the death of still more Jews."[15]

Monsignor Hughes, a member of the White Fathers, informed the chief rabbi about the situation in Italy where many Jews were saved by the Church. When the Germans took control of the country, the Pope encouraged the superiors of all convents and monasteries to conceal Jews. Hughes explained that in Rome, for example, the White Fathers had a monastery which housed four priests; thirty-two Jews were hidden in that monastery for an entire year. The German intelligence service in Italy was undoubtedly aware that for a year food for thirty-six people was delivered to a place that was supposed to be inhabited by four. Yet the monastery was not searched.

Many Jews had been hidden in a convent of English nuns. One day, German officers arrived and demanded that the Jews be handed over to them. The mother superior refused, declaring that the convent was under the personal protection of the Holy Father and that no one could enter it without his authority. She was astonished when the Germans withdrew!

Monsignor Hughes told the rabbi about an Irish convent building that had only one door. When the Nazis crossed the threshold, a German priest saved the situation by confusing the soldiers as he led them from room to room, and thus got them out of the house without incident. Dozens of Jews, concealed on the upper floor, were seized with fear.

Testimony of Clara Coen-Capon dated April 25, 1979, describing the loving care she received in Cave from November 1943 until she left the Sisters who saved her life and that of her one-year-old daughter, Laura. In October 1945, she gave them a photograph of herself and her three-year-old daughter.

Arrival of German soldiers in Rome.

After the Via Rasella bombings, a German soldier controls the windows facing the road.

During the raid, some victims were lined up on Via Quattro Fontane, in front of Palazzo Barberini; others on the corner of Via Rasella and Via del Boccaccio.

Hughes added that the Germans had a list of the priests who had organized help for the Jews. All those priests were hidden in the Vatican precincts and did not emerge until Rome was taken by the Allies. The Germans retaliated in northern Italy by executing several priests who had helped save Jews.

During the war Pope Pius XII remained in the Vatican; a great many Jews were concealed inside the Vatican itself. Castelgandolfo, for centuries the summer home of the popes, housed numerous refugees hiding from the Nazis.

"The atrocities committed by the Germans are beyond imagination," Monsignor Hughes explained. "I was able to grasp the meaning of the information given to me by the British Minister about the death chambers in Poland when I visited the torture chamber in Rome into which Jews were cast purely because they were Jews. Many non-Jews were also thrown in there because they were anti-Nazi. The terrible thing is that defeat did not make the Germans put a stop to their atrocities, even when they knew that this would cost them dearly. That is why the Holy Father has demanded the greatest caution in rescue operations."[16]

Dr. Eva Fogelman—a psychotherapist, social psychologist, and filmmaker—is also a founding director of the Jewish Foundation for Christian Rescuers. In 1994, she received the "Christopher Award" for her book *Conscience and Courage: Rescuers of Jews during the Holocaust.* In this book she clearly stated that she did not intend "to minimize the fact that six million Jews lost their lives by highlighting the rescuers during those crucial years."[17]

The Jewish community in Rome honored Italian rescuers in October 1994. Joining them were Jewish survivors who, represented by Rabbi Elio Toaff, expressed their gratitude: "We are reunited here today to remember because we do not want to forget the good that was done by many Italian citizens who saw the persecuted Jews not as people to abandon. They saw them as their brothers. Theirs was an experience which should be the basis of each of our lives, the ability to see in our neighbors the image of God himself.

"In fact, when the Germans came and people began to realize the Jews were being taken to the death camps, at that point the Italian people rebelled. When it came down to the issue of saving lives, a Jew's life was important to save. All of you here bear witness. You saved the Jews from deportation and death.

"So I say thank you for what you have done. But our thanks is not what really counts. What counts is the feeling you have, that you have done your duty all the way."

The Jewish community presented a special, ornate document to individuals, religious orders, and other organizations. It is hand-painted and beautifully designed with religious symbols and the following inscription in Hebrew and Italian: "Whoever saves one life, it is as though he had saved the entire world" (Sanhedrin, IV, 5). The document, recalling how the rescuers risked their own lives by offering hospitality, acknowledges the help given in order to save Jews from the Nazi-Fascist atrocities.

Rome, 1939: View of a Jewish business in its final stage of liquidation.

B. The Holocaust

1. Main Events

*T*he systematic, bureaucratic annihilation of millions of Jews and non-Jews by the Nazi regime and their collaborators during the Holocaust of World War II is outlined briefly in a pamphlet published by the Holocaust Museum in Washington, D.C.

In 1933, approximately 9 million Jews lived in the twenty-one countries of Europe that the Germans occupied during the war. By 1945, two out of every three European Jews had been killed: Jews, Roma (Gypsies), and at least 250,000 mentally or physically disabled persons were victims of Nazi genocide.

Millions of other innocent people were persecuted and murdered. More than 3 million Soviet prisoners of war were killed. Poles, as well as other Slavs, were targeted for slave labor, and tens of thousands perished. Thousands of political and religious dissidents were persecuted for their beliefs, and many died as a result of maltreatment.

From 1933, Hilter had dictatorial powers. He organized special security forces: the Special State Police (the Gestapo), the Storm Troopers (SA), and the Security Police (SS). New laws forced Jews to quit their civil service jobs, university and law court positions, and other areas of public life. Jewish businesses were boycotted.

In 1935, laws proclaimed at Nuremberg stripped Jews of their citizenship. By 1937, daily life became difficult. Jews could not attend public schools, go to theaters, cinemas, or vacation resorts, or reside, or even walk, in certain sections of German cities. During a centrally organized riot, *Kristallnacht* (the "Night of the Broken Glass"), the Nazis seized Jewish businesses and properties outright or forced Jews to sell them at bargain prices. Synagogues, stores, and homes were destroyed, men were arrested, others were murdered.

Approximately 35,000 men were deported to Dachau and various other concentration camps and several hundred Jewish women were sent to local jails. At the end of 1938, the arrests included several thousand German and Austrian Gypsies. Involuntary sterilization programs were introduced. Political opponents, trade unionists, and homosexuals were imprisoned in concentration camps; Jehovah's Witnesses were banned and many were sent to prisons and concentration camps.

About half of the Jewish population in Germany fled Nazi persecution. They emigrated mainly to Palestine, the United States, Latin America, China, and eastern and western Europe (where many would be caught again by the Nazis). Others were unable to obtain visas, sponsors in host countries, or funds for emigration.

Germany invaded Poland and World War II began on September 1, 1939. With the defeat of the Polish army, the Nazis began their campaign to destroy Polish culture and enslave the Polish people. Thousands of Poles—professors, artists, writers, politicians, and many Catholic priests—were massacred. Others, including Jews, were imprisoned in concentration camps. About 50,000 Polish children were taken to Germany for adoption; some were rejected and sent to camps where many died of starvation, lethal injection, and disease.

In 1942 children were often the target of special roundups for deportation to the concentration camps. Parents were powerless to defend their children. Upon arrival, babies and younger children were immediately killed. Those aged thirteen and older were frequently spared and used for forced labor. Others were used for medical experiments by German physicians. They were crowded into barracks fitted with wooden bunk beds stacked three on top of each other. Several people had to fit per level on the plank beds with no mattresses or blankets. Many died because of the brutal living conditions. The sick and those too exhausted to work were periodically identified and selected for gassing.

With the aid of non-Jewish friends and neighbors, some children managed to escape deportation. They were hidden in closets, attics, or barns for months or even years. Escape was more difficult for boys who were circumcised and could be identified as Jews. Many found refuge outside the ghettos and had to assume new identities in order to survive. Some Jewish children managed to pass as Catholics and were hidden in Catholic schools, orphanages, and convents across Europe.

In 1940, the Germans invaded Denmark, Norway, Holland, Belgium, Luxembourg, and France. The following year they invaded the Soviet Union. The Axis powers led by Germany were Italy, Romania, and Hungary. They were opposed by the Allied powers— Great Britain, Free France, the United States, and the Soviet Union. At Babi Yar, near Kiev, there were executions of some 33,000 persons, mostly Jews. Besides handicapped and psychiatric patients, German terror extended to more than 3 million Soviet prisoners of war.

Ghettos, transit camps, concentration camps, and forced labor camps were created for victims of racial and ethnic hatred. Approximately 3 million Polish Jews were forced to live in newly established ghettos where starvation, overcrowding, exposure to cold, and contagious diseases killed tens of thousands. Between 1942 and 1944, the Nazis deported ghetto residents to "extermination camps" in Poland. Sites close to railroads were selected: Belzec, Sobibor, Treblinka, Chelmno, Majdanek, and Auschwitz-Birkenau.

Mass murder was a daily routine; prisoners of all nationalities died in the gas chambers. In 1944 within a period of two months, almost a half million Hungarian Jews were deported to Auschwitz in forty-eight trains. Prisoners were forced to undress and hand over all valuables. They were driven naked into the gas chambers, which were disguised as shower rooms, and asphyxiated.

The Nazi legacy of murder, pillage, and exploitation affected every country of occupied Europe. There were millions of indifferent bystanders; but in some countries there was organized resistance. In Denmark nearly the entire Jewish community was smuggled to Sweden; in Italy 85 percent of Italian Jews were saved.

With the advance of the American troops, the King of Italy and his entourage, including Badoglio and other ministers, fled from Rome. The honor of Italy now depended on the military which was without proper leadership.

The Romans refused to be drafted for the army of the Republic of Salò. They demonstrated such solidarity in protecting Jews and anti-Fascists that the word circulated was, "Half of Rome is hidden in the homes of the other half."

Soldiers and officers, Allied prisoners who fled the concentration camps, families of patriots who were in danger of reprisals, German and Austrian deserters, partisans—all were wanted by the Germans and had to hide. For nine months the Romans, risking their lives, divided food, shared homes, medicines, clothing. The human solidarity embraced all of every race, of every religious faith, of every political ideology. These were cold months, without food; months of bombings and mass killings, of horror and death; months of courage and heroism of people whose names are unknown. They were part of the Resistance in Italy.

The Allies bombed railroad stations and military depots (Casilino, Prenestino, Tuscolano, Tiburtino) on August 13, 1943. Twenty-six days later in Frascati (where Kesselring, commander of the German forces, had his headquarters in the Castelli Romani) explosions were heard and seen in Rome. The B-17s of the 12th Air Force based in Africa (under the command of General Dwight Eisenhower) caused the death of one-fifth of the population in Frascati because the Italian government delayed official declaration of the September 1943 Armistice, signed five days earlier.

The Nazis took control of Rome from the belfries of churches and rooftops. They killed mercilessly. The Roman populace and the Italian military tried to retaliate. The Italians fought courageously at Porta San Paolo, in the piazzas, and along the streets. The battle ended September 10th at Stazione Termini. Troops of armed Germans took possession of many villas on the Aventine.

Italians who refused to give up their arms were immediately shot. Kesselring's ordinance appeared on billboards forbidding sabotage, strikes, private correspondence, use of the telephone, distribution of food. Everything was to be regulated by German law. Italian administrative offices were to function as usual. The Ministry of the Interior had to provide 60,000 workers. Because the quota was not met, an additional 30,000 had to be found by October 5th. There were very few volunteers. Others were captured on the streets and the total reached only 7,177. Kesselring was furious.

Italians tore down notices on billboards and refused to work for the Nazis. On November 5th, four bombs fell a few feet away from the cupola of St. Peter's Basilica, Vatican City, and damaged some buildings. The Fascists accused the Allies, but the unmarked airplane belonged to the Republic of Salò. This attack was attributed to Roberto Farinacci who had accused Pius XII of working with the Allies against the Germans. On March 1, 1944, another airplane belonging to the

Allies accidentally dropped three bombs in the Vatican gardens, damaging more Vatican buildings. Rome was bombed about fifty times by the Allies in an effort to stop the Germans. When American airplanes dropped bombs on December 28th, many Romans were killed and wounded.

Meanwhile the population boycotted the request for a census, ordered by the Germans and the Fascists. Showing remarkable unity, only 2 percent responded. Firemen were not to help the Romans unless sent by the Germans; the SS intensified the arrests, torture, killings, and deportations. Under the guise of "open city" the Germans continued to use Rome for their military operations and abolished the air-raid sirens.

Spies were everywhere. Father Libero Raganella was approached by a so-called Greek princess who requested help to hide a person from the Germans. She insisted but he did not relent; he was suspicious of her dress and mannerisms. Later Father Raganella learned that she was a spy.

Many women religious, who protected Jews and refugees in convents, did not keep records for the simple reason that the SS were looking for such lists to justify imprisonment and deportation. The nuns did not always recall names but remembered certain characteristics. For example, one of the Sisters of San Giuseppe della Montagna described David, a young boy and his family who were sheltered by the Sisters for many months. They never revealed their family name. Only in buildings protected by the pontifical guards were guests more tranquil. However, if caught by the SS outside the convent walls, Jews were no longer protected.

Several religious orders did not have room for guests because of their own needs. Mother Domenica, a member of the Canossiane Sisters, related that Archbishop Castellano, Bishop of Addis Ababa, told the nuns of seven communities—a total of sixty—that they had to evacuate. He had received orders from the Holy Father in 1942 that, since the religious were not safe there, they were to return to their generalate in Rome.

Sister Maria Grigolato remembers the building so crowded that some Sisters had to sleep in the corridors on folding beds. One night they were surprised by the police who came to search the building in an effort to locate Minister Ivanoe Bonomi. They opened closets and drawers; they searched every nook and corner; they also combed the garden. They went so far as to pull off the covers of a Sister sleeping in the corridor to make sure the Italian minister was not hiding in the bed. When their superior, Cardinal Carlo Salotti, learned about this search, he was indignant and complained to the authorities that the Sisters' privacy had been violated.

Sigmund and Minna Jawetz lived in Vienna, Austria. On *Kristallnacht* in 1938, Sigmund was taken to Dachau where millions of Jews and non-Jews were murdered. A decorated hero of World War I, he was released after four months and told to leave the country. Their daughter Stella Schecter from Cranford, New Jersey, relates how she and her older brother were able to come to the United States, but her younger brother was sent to England. Somehow her parents were able to make their way to Milan. When Hitler put pressure on Mussolini, they were sent to the Ferramonti concentration camp. "Had it not been for the Italians," Stella Schecter wrote, "our family would not have been reunited."

In May 1945 Nazi Germany collapsed, the SS guards fled, and the camps ceased to exist as extermination, forced labor, or concentration camps.

2. Rescuers

Many Italians had the courage of their convictions: doctors admitted Jews as patients into institutions where they protected them; bureaucrats destroyed files and records and produced false documents; politicians sheltered refugees; police warned those targeted for arrest. Rescuers understood the mission of mercy as human beings, as Italians, and as Christians.

The stories are numerous. Enrichetta Levi, frightened by the gunshots she heard as Jews were captured by the Nazis on Rome's streets, begged her father and her husband to seek asylum in a cloistered convent. They packed a few belongings and arrived in the monastery before dawn.

When Sister Maria Rita saw the refugees, she expressed her willingness to help them. She hastened to the mother superior and inquired whether the convent could accommodate three more guests. Cognizant that they were endangering the lives of all the nuns, they did not hesitate to welcome the Jews. Several nuns were moved to another section of the monastery, and the Levi family occupied their rooms.

Sister Maria Rita then inquired about documents. They had none. "This," she explained, "is the first step. You must have a new identity. If the Germans come, you cannot say you are Jewish. You must pretend you are workers here." With other Jewish refugees hidden in the monastery, the Levis were among the survivors of the Holocaust.

Miriam Nacamulli's grandfather was Rabbi Viventi of the synagogue in Rome. She lived with her grandparents, parents, and aunt. Their young maid, Teresa, had married and lived in the small town of Riano Flaminio. Teresa was very attached to the Viventi family and visited often. One morning she discovered that the family was gone.

After searching throughout the neighborhood, Teresa found the Nacamulli family living in a damp cellar. She insisted that they come to live with her. Reluctantly they joined Teresa in the country and remained there until the end of June 1944.

The Nacamullis used false identification for fear of spies planted everywhere, anxious to receive a reward from the Fascists and Germans for reporting Jews. Their suspicions were verified when they learned later that both the Viventi family and Teresa's family were scheduled to be shot. Thanks to the American soldiers who arrived two days earlier, both families survived.

Mirella Calò Tagliacozzo lived on Via del Pellegrino in the section of Campo dei Fiori. She was the youngest daughter of Emma and Graziano Calò and had three sisters: Fatima, Giuliana, and Fiorella. Her father disposed of his shop where he sold parts for cars and hid in the countryside. He entrusted the rest of his family to their neighbor, Signora Novelli. She was the owner of a house for prostitutes that was adjacent to the shop.

Graziano Calò's family was hidden in the basement of this house for nine months. German soldiers frequented the prostitutes regularly. Therefore the family was in constant danger. Mirella recalls that, whenever the German soldiers were in the brothel, the children were not allowed to speak or cry. Huddled in a corner of the basement, Mirella and her three sisters would wait patiently for word that they could move from their corner. To this day that experience is still a nightmare. Indeed, Mirella expresses her indignation if children are told to keep quiet in her presence.

When Pope Pius XII encouraged convents to "open their doors," the Calò family joined about 400 other refugees in a convent of cloistered nuns in front of Campidoglio. There they were sheltered and lived a more normal life until the end of the war.

Mirella's father offered to pay Signora Novelli for having saved his family. She refused. "I accept nothing," she said. "It was I who received the gift of your family for nine months."

Not so fortunate was the family of Mirella's husband. His parents were deported. Her father-in-law died in Auschwitz; his wife, Tosca Di Segni Tagliacozzo, returned to Rome and wrote about her experiences in the concentration camp.

Enrico Modigliani, a member of Parliament, has this childhood memory. His father was an employee of the Fascist Union controlled by the government. Expelled because of the racial laws, in 1939 he became a salesman. Enrico's uncle, Franco, and his wife fled to the

United States. There Franco Modigliani became a well-known economist at MIT and, in 1985, he received the Nobel Prize.

On July 25, 1943, Mussolini was replaced by Badoglio who continued fighting alongside the Germans while negotiating a treaty with the Allies. Until September 8th, even though the racial laws were not abolished, there was a semblance of freedom in Italy. But on the 9th of September, the Germans assumed control of Italy.

Though but six years old, Enrico understood what was happening and why the family had to remain in their summer home in Velletri. Meanwhile in Rome, the Germans took the lists of Jews from the Fascist police and went to every Jewish household. They searched not only in the ghetto but throughout Rome and the environs. The Modigliani family had already departed.

A friend rushed by train to Velletri and compelled them to go with her to her summer home near Gensano. This haste to assist their Jewish friends and neighbors was the typical, spontaneous reaction of many Italians. There was complete solidarity between Jews and many Romans who helped families separate and change residence frequently.

The Modiglianis lived in a small villa. One evening some peasants visited them. Enrico was saying his Hebrew prayers before going to bed—the *Shemà Israel* (Deuteronomy VI, 4–9), the most characteristic prayer that accompanies a Jew from childhood until death. When the door of his bedroom opened and he noticed a stranger, he shifted from the *Shemà Israel* to the *Ave Maria*.

Another episode he recalled is playing a game with his family. His mother pushed the door so no one could enter; his father tied a cord around his waist while he held his five-month-old sister in his arms. Then his father would lower him and the baby from the window. The game was that Enrico had to untie the cord and run to the peasants who would protect them.

In the beginning of 1944, the Germans took a special census to control the population. It was dangerous to remain in the country, so the Modigliani family planned to go back to Rome. Partisans supplied them with documents and a new name. Enrico's family became "Macchia." Only six years old, he was the one to constantly remind family members that their name was "Macchia." They no longer used the Jewish family name "Modigliani."

On returning to Rome they lived in the abandoned house of

Jewish friends. Their neighbors thought that the "Macchia" family had escaped from the bombings in southern Italy.

Later they took refuge in a convent and lived there until June 5, 1944. Enrico recalls the most beautiful day of his life. One evening from the terrace of the palazzo on the top of a hill they could see infinite lines of Germans fleeing Rome by every possible means of transportation. The following day the Americans arrived. He has a mental picture of the dispirited-looking Germans in comparison with the young American soldiers who came to their rescue, smiling and helpful, distributing chewing gum and chocolates—the first Enrico had in his life.

British prisoners given refuge by the Vatican.

3. Rescue Italian Style

Italy's humane attitude toward Jews extended beyond its own people and beyond its national borders. Wherever the Italian army was the occupying power, as in parts of Yugoslavia and France, the Jews were protected from serious harm. Yugoslav Jews report that they were taken almost from the hands of the approaching Germans onto Italian army trains, dressed in Italian military uniforms, and brought to Italy, where they were concealed.

Over the centuries Jews had become well-integrated into Italian society. Even during the period when they were forced to live in ghettos, Jews continued to participate in business and other relationships with Gentiles.

In 1870, when the separate states of Italy became a single nation, the Jews were emancipated from the ghettos. As the various Italian states accepted each other after centuries of rivalry and war and foreign domination, so they accepted the Jews who were not perceived as "other," but rather as another part of the new national group.

Italy extended a hand to foreign Jews as well. When the chips were finally down, Italians affirmed that Jews were equal human beings with an equal right to live. Asked why he sheltered a Jew he had never seen before, an Italian trolley worker shrugged his shoulders and replied, "A man with his child, running in the streets like a hunted animal, where else would he go?" The wife of a janitor who had hidden a family of thirteen—a grandmother, her married children, and her grandchildren—answered, "They were innocent people." A surgeon's wife said, "We didn't do anything heroic. We did what everybody should have done." A dentist said, "It was nothing. It was simply human decency."

Dr. Rubin Pick emphasized the Italian mentality when discussing the safety open to the Jews of Italy: "I was a Polish national," he said, "studying medicine in Italy when the racial laws were passed in 1938. Under these laws, foreign Jews—including those who had become citizens after 1919—had to leave Italy. My father left for Palestine. I applied for permission to stay so I could finish my studies, and the authorities let me stay. I was living in Trieste and commuting to Padua. My sister was a student at the university in Trieste, so she too applied, and again they agreed. The Italian mentality was: How could you let a young girl be by herself, unprotected, in the city? So they told my mother that she could stay too. On hearing this, my brother said, 'You're letting my brother, my sister, my mother stay and making me go alone?' So they said, 'Okay, you can stay too.' "[1]

When Italy entered the war in 1940, Rubin and his family were sent to the Ferramonti-Tarsia concentration camp in southern Italy. It was a concentration camp Italian-style. If you had a good reason, you could apply for permission to leave. He applied because he still had some requirements to complete—the equivalent of an internship. They let him return to Trieste where he not only completed his internship but remained there free of danger until the Germans arrived in 1943.

Because Italian Jews did not have a history of persecution, many did not foresee the approaching danger. Dr. Rubin Pick, however, stated that two hours after the Germans entered Trieste, he was already outside the city with his mother and sister. For Italian Jews, danger was something new, and too often they didn't know what they should do.

Indeed, a great many of the Italian Jews who died during the Holocaust might have lived had they been more attuned to the Nazi threat. In Siena, for example, Rabbi Giuseppe Lattes emphasized that the fourteen Jews who were arrested and deported were all partners in mixed marriages of children of mixed marriages. Convinced that in Italy they would be treated as Gentiles, they thought they didn't need to accept offers of refuge.

Thousands of stories are documented about efforts to save Jews from the Holocaust. People do have a choice between good and evil; a caring individual can make a difference; resistance is both possible and effective. It is ironic that while the nation of Italy was serving Hitler, many Italians were protecting Jews and other refugees.

Whenever protests against Nazi atrocities were made by the Church, thousands of priests in concentration camps trembled. Bishop Jean Bernard of Luxembourg, an inmate of Dachau from February

1941 to August 1942, declared that the treatment of prisoners worsened immediately.

In Rome, during the German occupation, the only hope was that a light was still shining behind the heavy curtains on a third-floor window of the Vatican. There, sitting at his desk, was a lonely figure bearing upon his fragile shoulders the weight of a suffering world. Pope Pius XII was now the leader, not by violence, but by the unswerving gentleness of the strong.

As a young priest in the Vatican, Monsignor John Patrick Carroll-Abbing was an active member of the Resistance. He lived in caves with refugees, daily risking his life in the battle zone to organize medical aid, to evacuate the sick and wounded, and to care for children made homeless by the war. His dream for these children became a reality. For thousands of children in the Boys' and Girls' Towns of Italy, he became father and guide.

Both an eyewitness and a participator, Monsignor Carroll-Abbing clearly states in his book, *But for the Grace of God:* "Strange, how little attention has been paid to the point of view of the people who were most directly involved. Nothing easier than for Pius XII, at a distance, to have made a clamorous protest against the German—and, of course, the Russian—war crimes, if he had been willing to ignore the inevitable consequences for millions of already tortured people."[2]

4. Moral Courage

A statement by the U.S. Catholic Bishops was issued toward the end of 1942: "Since the murderous assault on Poland, utterly devoid of every semblance of humanity, there has been a premeditated and systematic extermination of the people of this nation. The same satanic technique is being applied to many other peoples. We feel a deep sense of revulsion against the cruel indignities heaped upon Jews in conquered countries and upon defenseless peoples not of our faith....Deeply moved by the arrest and maltreatment of the Jews, we cannot stifle the cry of conscience. In the name of humanity and Christian principles, our voice is raised."[3]

In an effort to eradicate an uninformed popular misconception and answer the criticism that the Vatican had failed to speak out, it is important to recall the work undertaken by the Catholic Church.

Prophetically, in May 1932, Pope Pius XI's encyclical *Caritate Christi* condemned the egotism that, if it "insinuates itself into patriotism, exaggerating it into unjust nationalism, there is no excess of which it is incapable. Instead of the divine law of love and common brotherhood which embraces all races and people, uniting them under one common Father who is in Heaven, it is hatred, which propels all to ruin."

Hitler rose to power in 1933, despite organized Catholic opposition. Yet, Catholics comprised approximately one-third of the German population. On July 20, 1933, as papal Secretary of State, Eugenio Pacelli signed the Concordat with Germany guaranteeing the right to freedom of worship for Catholics and the right of the Church to regulate her own affairs in Germany. Five days later, the Nazi government promulgated a sterilization law that affected Jews and particularly offended the Catholic Church. Soon after, thousands of Catholic

52

priests, nuns, and lay leaders were arrested. The Catholic Youth League was dissolved. The leader of Catholic Action was murdered.

On March 14, 1937, Pope Pius XI issued an encyclical *Mit brennender Sorge* (*With Burning Anxiety*) charging the Nazi government with "evasion" and "violation" of the 1933 Concordat.

On September 20, 1938, the German ambassador to the Vatican sent a dispatch to the Führer in which he noted Pius XI's remarks to Belgian pilgrims: "Mark well that in the Catholic Mass, Abraham is our Patriarch and forefather. Anti-Semitism is incompatible with the lofty thought which that fact expresses. It is a movement with which we Christians can have nothing to do. No, I say to you, it is impossible for a Christian to take part in anti-Semitism. It is inadmissible! Through Christ and in Christ we are the spiritual progeny of Abraham. Spiritually, we are all Semites."

Seven months after becoming Pope, in October 1939, Pius XII secretly agreed to act as an intermediary between a new anti-Nazi German government and Great Britain. Historian William L. Shirer, who served as a foreign correspondent in Berlin for CBS Radio from 1934 to 1941, describes how Dr. Josef Müeller, a leading Munich lawyer, journeyed to the Vatican to establish contact with the British minister to the Holy See. This was known as the Zossen Conspiracy.[4] But the German generals lost courage and never arrested Hitler.

Pope Pius XII's first encyclical, *Summi Pontificatus,* stressed the fundamental unity of all mankind under the Fatherhood of God: "The human race is bound together by reciprocal ties, moral and juridical, into a great commonwealth directed to the good of all nations and ruled by special laws which protect its unity and promote its prosperity." He condemned "the idea which credits the State with unlimited authority...for it breaks the unity of supra-national society, robs the law of nations of its foundation and vigor, leads to violation of others' rights and impedes agreement and peaceful intercourse."

On June 29, 1941, Pius XII denounced the human suffering of "old people, women, children, the most innocent, the most peaceful, the most defenseless." He spoke of religious persecutions "which the very concern for those who suffer does not allow one to reveal in all their painful and moving detail."

Before anyone else of international stature paid the slightest attention to the Holocaust, Pius XII condemned the Nazis in his 1942 Christmas message. He spoke about the persecution against "those hundreds of thousands who, without any fault of their own, sometimes only by reason of their nationality or race, are marked down for death or progressive extinction."

The Germans understood his remarks. In fact Himmler's chief deputy, Reinhardt Heydrich, retaliated on January 22, 1943: "The Pope has repudiated the National Socialist New European Order. His speech is one long attack on everything we stand for. 'God,' he says, 'regards all peoples and races as worthy of the same consideration.' Here he is clearly speaking on behalf of the Jews. He is virtually accusing the German people of injustice toward the Jews and makes himself the mouthpiece of the Jewish war criminals."

The New York Times editorialized that "this Christmas more than ever, the Pope is a lonely voice crying out of the silence of a continent."

In February 1943, the Dutch bishops wrote a pastoral letter that was read in all Catholic churches: "We would fail in our duty if we did not publicly raise our voice against injustice....Our sympathy goes out in a very special manner to the Jews and to our brethren in the Catholic Faith who are of Jewish descent. In this we are following the path indicated by our Holy Father, the Pope."

In an address to the College of Cardinals distributed clandestinely in Poland, June 2, 1943, His Holiness noted that "every word on our part, addressed on this subject to competent authorities, every public allusion, has to be seriously weighed and measured by us, in the interest of the suffering themselves, so as not to render their lot still graver and more unbearable."

Pope Pius XII asked Don Pirro A. Scavizzi, a hospital train chaplain involved in rescue efforts, to bring large sums of money, documents, and letters to the priests in Poland. He carried a message from the Pope that was sewed into the lining of his coat: "The Pope suffers agony on your behalf. Many times We have thought of scorching Nazism with the lightning of excommunication and of denouncing to the civilized world the criminality of the extermination of the Jews. We have heard of the very serious threat of retaliation, not on Our person but on the poor sons who are under Nazi domination. We have received through various channels urgent recommendations that the Holy See should not take a drastic stand. After many tears and many prayers, We have judged that Our protest not only would fail to help anyone, but would create even more fury against the Jews, multiplying acts of cruelty."

There were constant threats and great danger to the city of Rome, the Jews, the Pope, and its Catholic population and clergy. After the Roman Jews were shipped to Auschwitz, many other Jews were hidden by Catholics. When the Germans occupied Hungary and began the deportation of Jews, Vatican protests, which began March 23, 1944, were not heeded.

Finally, on June 25th, Pope Pius XII personally wired the Regent Admiral Miklos Horthy and asked him to use his power "to save many unfortunate people from further pain and sorrow." Horthy stopped deportations almost immediately. He was arrested and imprisoned by the Nazis on October 15th.

The British ambassador to the Holy See knew that his dispatches were being deciphered by the Fascists, so he omitted everything the Pope was doing for the Allies and the Jews, while underscoring everything which seemed amenable to Mussolini. Yet in his diary he wrote that never before in all history had a Pope engaged so delicately in a conspiracy to overthrow a tyrant by force.

Reviewing a book by David Wyman on the Holocaust, *The New York Times* noted: "In September 1942, at the time of the mass deportations from France, pressures by Eleanor Roosevelt and refugee-aid agencies finally resulted in State Department permission for 5,000 Jewish children trapped in France to enter the United States." However, "the offer was eviscerated by consistent stalling and even more severe tightening of immigration restrictions by the State Department's visa division."[5]

According to David Wyman, when Bulgaria was willing to let its 30,000 Jews go to Palestine in 1943, British Foreign Secretary Anthony Eden's argument was: "We should move very cautiously about offering to take all Jews out of a country like Bulgaria. If we do that, then the Jews of the world might be wanting us to make similar offers in Poland and Germany. Hitler might well take us up on any such offer."[6]

David Kaplan remarked in *The New York Tribune* that "Americans didn't want more Jews in the United States, the British didn't want them in England…nobody seemed to have an answer except to let Hitler keep on killing them." Kaplan observed: "The United States and its Allies during World War II could have stopped Adolf Hitler's final solution for the Jewish people of Europe, but chose not to do so."[7]

News of Hitler's extermination plan was circulated at a

Washington, D.C., press conference, November 24, 1942. This was the biggest mass murder story in history; yet the tragic news was barely mentioned by the media.

Critics continue to write about what Pope Pius XII should have done regarding Nazi atrocities during World War II. They imply that the Pope and the Catholic Church were, and are, anti-Semitic. *The New York Times* referred to Pope Pius XII's "shameful silence" during the Holocaust. His Holiness had not denounced the Allied bombing of Dresden and other civilian targets. He had not denounced Hiroshima. Nor did he denounce the Allies' postwar deportation of 2 million people back to nearly certain death in the Soviet Union.

The charge of "shameful silence" is unreasonable. Even if the Pope had been indifferent to the fate of the Jews, he knew the Nazis were also persecuting millions of Catholics. Why should he be silent about that, unless he thought that "speaking out" would be ineffectual or self-defeating? Also he never denounced the treatment of 2,000 Catholic priests at Dachau "for fear of provoking worse disasters." The Nazis had suppressed the encyclical Pope Pius XII had helped his predecessor prepare in peacetime. Would they be any more receptive in the middle of a war?

Outwardly aloof, Pope Pius XII was privately active. He did not talk; he acted. The Jewish world seemed to agree for, on October 12, 1945, the World Jewish Congress sent a gift of 2 million lire to the Vatican; Israel's second Prime Minister, Moshe Sharett, told the Pope his "first duty was to thank him and the Catholic Church for all they had done to rescue Jews."

As the war came to an end, Isaac Herzog, the chief rabbi of Jerusalem, said: "The people of Israel will never forget what His Holiness and his illustrious delegates, inspired by the eternal principles of religion which form the very foundations of true civilization, are doing for our unfortunate brothers and sisters in the most tragic hour of our history, which is living proof of divine Providence in this world."

In 1954, the Jewish historian Léon Poliakov wrote that the Church's tireless humanitarian efforts in the face of the Hitler terror, with the approval and under the stimulus of the Vatican, can never be forgotten.

At the Pope's death in 1958, leaders of the Catholic Church and diplomats from scores of nations called at the papal palace in Castelgandolfo to offer their condolences. Queen Elizabeth of

England, President Eisenhower, President Coty of France, President Heuss of Western Germany, King Baudouin of Belgium, and Queen Juliana of Holland were among those who sent messages of sympathy from all over the world to the Vatican. Golda Meir, Israel's representative to the United Nations, was the first of the delegates to react. She sent an eloquent message: "We share in the grief of humanity at the passing away of His Holiness, Pope Pius XII. In a generation afflicted by wars and discords he upheld the highest ideals of peace and compassion. When fearful martyrdom came to our people in the decade of Nazi terror, the voice of the Pope was raised for its victims. The life of our times was enriched by a voice speaking out about great moral truths above the tumult of daily conflict. We mourn a great servant of peace."

Leonard Bernstein, on learning of Pope Pius XII's death while conducting his orchestra in New York's Carnegie Hall, tapped his baton for a moment of silence to pay tribute to the Pope who had saved the lives of so many people without distinction of race, nationality, or religion.

Pius XII had tremendous communication with Jewish organizations and with individuals as may be seen in *Records and Documents of the Holy See Relating to the Second World War, 1965–1981* (Vols. VI, VIII, IX, and X—the four volumes that deal with his humanitarian activities). The Pope was as outspoken and helpful to the Jews as he could be without inviting further retaliation and punishment upon the very people he was trying to protect. His intervention was not limited to "Catholic" Jews as suggested by John F. Morley's book, *Vatican Diplomacy and the Jews during the Holocaust,*[8] as well as in the BBC's 1995 television program, which did not take into account the many demonstrations of gratitude to Pius XII from the Jewish community throughout the world.

The BBC documentary consists of a series of interviews following an introduction of Pius XII as "a spiritual leader of hundreds of millions, but his reputation is that he kept silence while the Nazis slaughtered the Jews. Pope Pius XII—a pragmatic hero or moral coward...." Such words choose to ignore the documentation provided by witnesses of Pope Pius XII's humanitarian efforts.

Under St. Peter's Square Colonnade refugees wait to be admitted to the dining hall.

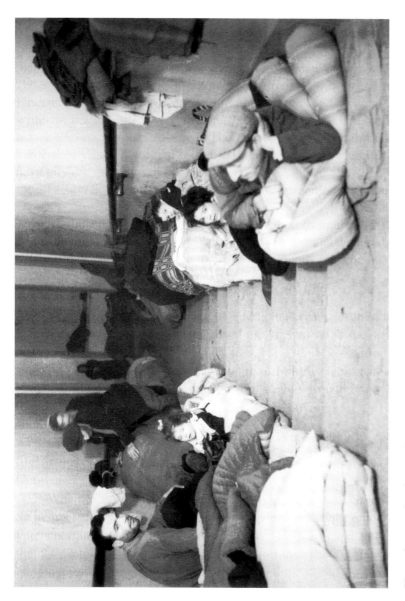

Homeless and refugees in makeshift dormitories at Castelgandolfo.

Food and medicines distributed by the Vatican to local residents.

Groups of refugees assisted by the Vatican.

Rome, 1943–1944: Class photograph of students and Marist Brothers at the San Leone School in Rome. Jewish children lived in hiding at this school.

Part II

A. Italian Jews

_____

1. Rome

Posterity has repeatedly asked why Pope Pius XII did not publicly denounce Hitler and the Nazis who persecuted the Jews. The fact is that His Holiness became a victim of public opinion in order to protect those who were victimized.

"Thousands of Roman Jews would have been captured by the Nazi troops on October 16, 1943, had it not been for the prudent politics of the Vatican," wrote Carlo Sestieri, a well-known Jew who was hidden in one of the Vatican buildings, his wife protected in a nearby convent. He suggested that "perhaps only the Jews who were persecuted understand why the Holy Father, Pope Pius XII, could not publicly denounce the Nazi-Fascist government....Without doubt, it helped avoid worse disasters."

With the unification of Italy in 1870, the Vatican lost control of the Papal States. Only in 1929 was the sovereignty of the Vatican State established when the Italian government and the Holy See signed the Lateran Treaty (Concordat).

Soon after the Fascist government passed its racial legislation of November 17, 1938, adopting Germany's policies against Jews, the Vatican focused its diplomatic activity on helping them. Pius XII attempted to change the racial laws regarding marriages between Jews and non-Jewish Italians, as well as those affecting the rights of baptized Jews.

Although the Jewish population had been assimilated in Italian society, Jews were excluded from civil service and restrictions were placed on Jewish ownership of industries and property.

Pope Pius XII decided to maintain the Vatican's diplomatic

network throughout the war. In a letter to the bishop of Berlin, he jus-tified his attitude of reserve and prudence in order to avoid possible greater evils.

Oral history interviews reveal the extent of Pope Pius XII's help. He was personally concerned about every human being. Although countless requests arrived daily at the Vatican, all received the Pope's attention. Young and old appealed for help in locating missing rela-tives. At the Pope's command, the Vatican established a special infor-mation office—a unique repository that contained records of prisoners of war from every part of the world. The employees included Vatican refugees whose task was to assure families of their loved ones' safety.

Beneath a painting of Pius XII with outstretched arms on the wall of the reference room is an excerpt from the Pontiff's 1943 Christmas message: "We have in this way felt the palpitations of thousands of hearts with the emotional tumult of their most intimate affections or in the intense yearnings and the nightmare of uncertainty in the exultant joy of recuperated assurance or in the deep pain and serene resignation to the fate of their loved ones."[1]

Not only prisoners of war throughout the world, but also many political prisoners appealed to Pope Pius XII. Among them was twen-ty-two-year-old Adriano Ossicini, the leader of an anti-Fascist group. In 1943, he was incarcerated in Regina Coeli prison. Although he was given a dangerous injection and tortured, the young man refused to give any information about his political activities and assistance to the Jews.

Ossicini was a medical student and director of the students belonging to a Catholic Action group. When Pius XII learned that he was imprisoned with other members, he immediately wrote a personal letter to Mussolini requesting the reasons for his arrest. The police commissioner responded that Ossicini had been involved with the anti-Fascist movement. The Pope then sent a second letter inquiring why he had been retained while the others were freed. The letters were of no avail. Pius XII was informed that Adriano Ossicini had refused to sign dismissal papers. Only the day before the fall of Fascism was the young man sent home. He became an internationally known psychia-trist, a university professor, and the vice president of the Senate of the Republic of Italy for two terms. His story is told in Cesare De Simone's book *Roma città prigioniera*.[2]

Pope Pius XII did address the problem of Jews lodging in religious houses. On October 1, 1943, he discussed it with his secretary of state. Immediately Monsignor Giovanni Battista Montini authorized a group of cloistered nuns to accept an entire family including the male member because he was elderly and needed the attention of his wife.

The historian Renzo De Felice published a list[3] of over 150 convents in Rome with the number of guests who were protected. Today, thousands who were helped recognize that they could not have survived without this assistance.

In his statement dated January 1995, Carlo Sestieri wrote: "With regard to my personal experiences during the Nazi occupation of Rome, October 1943 to June 1944, I can only confirm what I said verbally. During the period following the Armistice of September 8, 1943, my brother and I with a cousin Claudio Ziffer were given hospitality by the Jesuit Fathers in the Convent of the Gesù. It was a rather pleasant experience as I recall. We were more than fifty, not only Jews but also police, soldiers, and others who needed protection for political reasons.

"The hospitality was complete. We participated with meals and all comforts including hot showers of the then Teutonic seminary. We expected the arrival of Allied troops in a few days and we realized the situation could not last very long. We were asked to make other arrangements. After several weeks, thanks to the interest of Don Giuseppe De Luca, we found refuge in the Palazzo della Cancelleria, in a small apartment that belonged to the sacristan who also provided us with nourishment. We were fifteen, including Jews, soldiers, politicians, even a general from the Air Force.

"Naturally Monsignor Giulio Ciricione, the pastor of San Lorenzo in Damaso, was informed. He provided every possible comfort and placed his wonderful library at our disposal. Mine was not an isolated personal experience, since I am aware of numerous friends and relatives who received hospitality in convents, monasteries, and hospitals conducted by religious.

"Considering the risk involved all this was, without doubt, a marvelous and altruistic effort on the part of various responsible religious. In many cases it was shared by generous private friends who were laymen ready to risk their own lives.

"Actually I do not know precisely if all this may be attributed to the well-loved Pope Pius XII, if it was merely tolerated or, at least, that permission was granted verbally; certainly on the part of the Vatican authorities, there was nothing contrary."[4]

Through Mother Pascalina Lehnert, who was in charge of his household, Pope Pius XII sent truckloads of assistance to various convents and centers to provide food and clothing wherever the Jews in Rome were hidden. Mother Pascalina was given the nickname "MP," because the trucks came from the warehouse called "Magazzino Pontificio."

An interesting document has been provided by Senator Giulio Andreotti who, as a young student, had served as a messenger for the Vatican. Several decades later, Henry A. Kissinger stated, "No Italian leader has made a greater contribution to the postwar history of his country."[5]

In his letter of November 21, 1994, Andreotti wrote: "You asked me if, during the period of the German occupation, I did anything for the Jews who were being hunted in Italy and sent to the German concentration camps.

"At that time I was president of the Catholic University students whose purpose was to help those who were being persecuted. In particular we organized a small group to obtain false identification cards.

"The Benedictine Sisters of Priscilla printed them in their small archeological printing shop. Professor Gonella would complete them in the Vatican with the seals of several towns already liberated in southern Italy, and therefore not controlled by the Nazi-Fascists.

"Unfortunately, when the Jewish ghetto was suddenly bombed in October, we were unable to find safe quarters and protective documents for so large a group on such short notice.

"Encouraged by Pope Pius XII himself, we performed our mission which included trips to northern Italy to get mail for the prisoners of war hidden in the rectories. As president, I was received by him in private audience many times during that period."[6]

In a papal audience of April 17, 1944, His Holiness affirmed to Giulio Andreotti that, "despite threats by the Germans to deport him, he was not afraid and would remain at his post in the Vatican."[7]

With the arrest of Mussolini, Victor Emmanuel III appointed Pietro Badoglio as his prime minister. After the Armistice, both the king and Badoglio abandoned Rome and fled to safety in Brindisi. The only authority that remained in Rome from September 1943 to the liberation by the Allies in April 1944 was the Pope. The Romans proclaimed him *Defensor Urbis*. A street near the Vatican is named Pius XII, *Defensor Civitatis*. Throughout the Catholic world, Pope Pius XII is called the *Pastor Angelicus*.

Following a papal audience, Nicolas De Kallay, Hungarian prime minister, wrote: "Under these circumstances the Church has no way to intervene. Germany, having abandoned every human manner of acting, has followed a path that leads us to complete mistrust. Therefore, as long as such inhuman tendencies prevail in Germany, the Pope does not see any possibility for the Church to mediate among the nations at war."[8]

By what authority, if any, did religious and clergy break the rules of cloister and take in the Jews, refugees, and anti-Fascists who were being sought by the Nazis? The only possible answer is that they knew the Church, through the Pontiff and the bishops, encouraged and authorized it.

In the midst of Nazi bombings and terrorism, the superiors of religious orders were dispensed from the obligation of having cloistered areas in their convents. Countless Jews were lodged in these institutions and all canonical restrictions were suspended.

Among Vatican officials who received a medal from the Israeli government are Cardinal Vincenzo Fagiolo and Cardinal Pietro Palazzini. The latter recently stated in an interview that Pope Pius XII was a just Pope who guided the Church at the proper time ("È stato il Papa giusto nel momento giusto"). Cardinal Palazzini's book, *Il clero e l'occupazione di Roma*,[9] gives an accurate account of the Vatican's protection of Jews and other refugees. He worked with Monsignor Roberto Ronca in the seminary of St. John Lateran in Rome.

According to Article 13 of the treaty between the Holy See and Italy, the basilicas of St. Mary Major, St. Paul Outside-the-Walls, and St. John Lateran with their adjoining buildings were considered extraterritorial zones. Indeed, St. John Lateran was the center of Vatican hospitality. The danger was constant, especially since some refugees were well known: Meuccio Ruini, Marcello Soleri, Alcide De Gasperi, Giuseppe Saragat, Pietro Nenni, Ivanoe Bonomi, Alberto Bergamini, Alessandro Casati, Umberto Ricci, Luigi Turano, Delfino Leopoldo Parodi, Giorgio Del Vecchio, and others. Even after the Liberation, several families remained hidden there.[10]

Pietro Nenni, Socialist leader and deputy chairman of the Council of Ministers, was with his wife at St. Peter's Square on March 12, 1944. Their daughter was in a concentration camp. When Pope Pius

XII appeared on the balcony, the crowd fell on their knees. Returning to the Lateran Seminary, Nenni noted in his diary: "At the moment of the papal blessing I sensed that the crowd had forgotten its trials and immediate worries to communicate in a celestial vision of eternal blessedness."

Refugees were cared for at the seminary according to the spirit of the Church and the wishes of Pius XII. Each one was obliged to sign a declaration that, from the moment of admission into the extraterritorial zone of the pontifical Roman major seminary belonging to the Holy See, he did not have arms with him nor had he deposited any or hidden any in the area; that he would follow the norms that regulate the statute of the interned in neutral states; that he would submit to all the rules and controls that the Holy See and the State of Vatican City deem necessary to adopt respecting the neutrality of the host state.[11]

During the Nazi occupation of Rome fifty Italian soldiers who had been guarding Villa Wolkonski, the German embassy, sought refuge in the convent of the Daughters of Charity of St. Vincent de Paul on Via Carlo Emanuele I, No. 49. These Sisters cared for sixty orphan refugees. The Nazis requisitioned the convent and orphanage. They searched for the soldiers, ordering the Sisters to evacuate within twenty-four hours. As two Italian soldiers attempted to flee, they were killed and their bodies thrown into the convent garden pond.

Sister Nicolina Anedda, later known for her charitable work in the pontifical assistance program, turned to Monsignor Ronca for hospitality at the basilica of St. John Lateran. The orphans were housed there for ten months. These Sisters joined the Sisters of Maria Bambina, part of the seminary staff, in the preparation of meals for all the refugees, including Italian soldiers who had served the Nazis. They even offered a wing of their own convent to be used by the orphans.

Regarding this reciprocal charity, Cardinal Palazzini stated: "Amidst the clash of arms, a voice could be heard—the voice of Pius XII. The assistance given to so many people could not have been possible without his moral support, which was much more than quiet consent."[12]

Church members and religious organizations, as well as many Italian diplomats and military officers, were determined to resist any demand encroaching on their sovereignty. They did not like German interference. Neither did Italian journalists. They were aware that the

Church was protecting Jews in convents and monasteries, but this they did not reveal.

Through the Vatican, Roman Jews received assistance to emigrate. Those who lost their jobs because of the racial laws could find employment in the Vatican (e.g., in the Vatican Library). Students interested in law who could not attend Italian universities were accepted at the Pontificium Institutum Utriusque Iuris. They believed that the Pope, who was a symbol to all Roman Jews, would not allow them to be arrested. Nor did they believe that Mussolini would allow them to be deported. After all, everyone knew that they had been loyal Italian citizens. They patiently waited for the Allies.

The Führer was quoted by one of his transcribers as saying: "If there were an uprising in Germany, I would respond immediately with the arrest and death of all the leaders of the Catholic Church and I would condemn all those interned in concentration camps."[13]

Filippo Tommaso Marinetti, the founder of Futurism, was born in Alexandria, Egypt. He published an article, "Fondazione e Manifesto del Futurismo," on February 20, 1909. In it he recognized the need for a radical literary renewal.[14] He was not only a writer but an organizer, a polemist, a financier. In 1923 he married Benedetta Cappa, a Milanese artist and writer. With their three children—Vittoria, Ala, and Luce—they moved to Rome. In their home at Piazza Adriana 11, across from Castel Sant'Angelo, the Futuristic movement was firmly established with archives, paintings, and a library.

Marinetti was a friend of the Jews in Rome. Since he did not have Fascist Party documents, he was pursued by the Nazis and obliged to move with his family to an apartment in Venice. Later they escaped to Bellagio on Lake Como where the founder of Futurism died in 1944.

When interviewed, Marinetti's daughter Ala explained that, because of her father's generosity in allowing their Jewish friends from Egypt, Mr. and Mrs. Grassi, to live secretly in their home in Rome until the end of the war, the records of the Futurist movement were saved from destruction by the Nazis.

Senator Giuseppe Bevione, who founded l'Assicurazione INA during Mussolini's government, was given the death penalty for political reasons. Pope Pius XII's chamberlain, Monsignor Adone Terzariol, saved him and his family by placing them in communication with "zio" Arturo who planned his escape. Vera Medici's father went with a Vatican truck to Regina Coeli prison to save her cousin, Senator

Bevione. He was taken to Porta Latina where he was hidden for a long time under the patronage of Pius XII.

In 1940, Umberto Pugliese, a Jewish general of the "Genio Navale," was dismissed from the Marines. Gianni Caproni, the founder of Caproni Airplanes, used his influence to help General Pugliese resume his former position as general, notwithstanding the racial laws that were enforced. In fact, when the English attacked the naval units in Taranto, Pugliese was called upon to direct operations to restore the port.

After September 8, 1943, General Pugliese was no longer safe. The Caproni family hid their friend in an attic of their home, Lungotevere Arnaldo da Brescia 15, Rome. The attic was barred by a large closet and was inaccessible. Food and news were sent to him by Romeo, his faithful chauffeur, through a lift on the second floor.

During this period, the children's German teacher, Lilly Baum, was also hidden in the attic until 1945 when the Americans arrived. Professor Lilly remained with the Caproni family until she married Austrian Ambassador Schorr. They emigrated to America. Maria Fede Caproni joined Lilly Baum Schorr in 1986 to celebrate Gianni Caproni's 100th birthday in the gallery of airplane pioneers, Smithsonian Museum, Washington, D.C.

Also protected by the Caproni family were two young Jewish teachers—Fontana and Inge Weiss—who lived in their summer home in Venegono Superiore until May 1945. Inge later married an Austrian, Baron Schrenck.

Gianni Caproni sent Eugenio Fargion, general director of Caproni Airplanes, to Switzerland where he remained hidden from September 1943 to May 1945. After the war he returned to Milan to collaborate with Caproni and became director of the Arrigoni. Like so many other Jews indebted to the Caproni family, he recalled with gratitude the help received.

Racial laws were not implemented at the Church of San Lorenzo where the Jews were treated with respect, friendship, and mutual assistance. Father Libero Raganella recalled a family with three boys who went to the seminary school; their sister studied with the nuns. Although they were not obliged to attend, they insisted on being in the religion classes. When reprisals occurred and people were arrested, Father Raganella broke into a cloister to hide the family. He testified that the Church authorities appealed to all religious to hide those for whom the Germans were searching after the first roundup and to help all who needed assistance in hiding. In the Seminary of San Lorenzo alone, six high officers of the Italian army wore clerical clothes.

Signor Dell'Ariccia tells the story of Santino Di Vitto, a Fascist, who was arrested after the Liberation. He had helped the Jews in Abruzzi and protected many of them from the Nazis. The Jews found a lawyer to represent Di Vitto, and soon after he was freed from Regina Coeli prison in Rome.

Monsignor Quadraroli, a Vatican secretary, made false IDs for the two Di Veroli brothers and other members of the family who went to a convent on Via Cicerone. Olga Di Veroli stated: "In Rome, people opened not just the doors, but their hearts as well; they put on the table the little they had and shared it with everyone."

Mino Moscati explained that his father was the custodian of the temple, which had been declared a national monument. The very morning of the October 16th Nazi roundup, his parents knocked desperately at the door of the convent of nuns on Via dei Fienili. The nuns took in his mother and sisters; a baker downstairs took care of him, his brother, and father. After the Allies arrived, Mino's father immediately returned to the temple to rekindle the candle in front of the Sacred Ark.

When the raids began in Italy, convents and monasteries became places of asylum. Miraculously, besides saving many Jews, the Franciscan Fathers also saved some sacred books and the Torah by hiding them in the tabernacle of their church. Thanks to the efforts of the Vatican, some convents had an "off limits" sign in German forbidding entrance. It is unbelievable that, with a few tragic exceptions, a paper affixed to the door proved to be most effective. The Fascist police and the Nazis walked by knowing full well that fugitive Jews and anti-Fascists were living there day and night. An invisible hand was protecting them—the hand of Pius XII. Of course, neither the German commandant nor the German ambassador informed Berlin that this immunity to search really meant safety for Roman Jews.

During this period all the convents in Rome were packed with religious and political refugees, as well as prisoners of war who had escaped from German concentration camps and were now clandestinely fighting the Nazis.

In a letter to the editor of *La Repubblica*,[15] Ines Gistron wrote: "Monsignor O'Flaherty placed me and my Jewish friend in a *pensione* run by Canadian nuns at Monteverde (Rome). We were given false IDs.

We lived with elderly women and young ladies, completely separated from the nuns in the cloister. After the Nazis began searching for Jews, the *pensione* was so filled that the Holy Father ordered the cloistered areas to be opened in order to provide for more refugees. I gave my room to a woman with two children and went to live in a very small cell.

"It has been said that Pius XII did not speak out against the Nazi crimes. On the other hand, we know about his actions. Because of his prudence, did he not succeed in saving many lives, including mine?"

In the Vatican and throughout the city of Rome, every possible building that was the property of the Catholic Church—including seminaries, residences, and boarding schools—was used to harbor refugees. For example, the Pontificio Collegio dei Sacerdoti for Italian emigration, now a residence for priests and missionaries known as the Casa del Clero, had many guests. Among those received from November 4, 1943, to March 6, 1944, most of the fifty-two residents were Jewish. (*See* Appendix, Document I, p. 214, for names.)

The Pontificio Seminario Romano Maggiore assisted hundreds of Jewish refugees, partisans, military and naval personnel. Some were priests or members of the nobility; others were professors and students, government officials, as well as the ministers of finance, interior, education, senators, ambassadors. (*See* Appendix, Document II, pp. 215–217, for names and information on each person.)

In 1961, Giulio Einaudi Editore published *Storia degli ebrei italiani sotto il fascismo* by the historian Renzo De Felice. In it are the names and addresses of the religious houses in Rome where Jews received hospitality. (*See* Appendix, Document III, pp. 218–221, where the entire list, including the number of guests, is reproduced.)

2. Milan

Outside Rome, many Jews did not know about the October 16, 1943, roundup, or about raids in Milan, Turin, and Trieste. In Florence, Genoa, Venice, and other cities throughout Italy organized arrests began during the following months.

Don Paolo Liggeri worked with Cardinal Ildefonso Schuster in Milan and saved many refugees. Another priest, Don Vittorio Luzzati, directed a network that included all of Lombardy and helped Jews reach Switzerland. When the Institute he directed was raided, he was arrested and deported to Mauthausen. He then spent a year in a labor camp at Dachau. He survived but many other priests did not.

In Turin, Monsignor Vincenzo Barale was arrested and imprisoned when a Jewish refugee he had helped was forced to name him. Also in Turin, thirty-nine-year-old Father Giuseppe Girotti, a Dominican who sheltered many Jews, was betrayed by a spy, deported to Dachau, and murdered.

In the northern part of Italy, ninety-two Jewish orphans at Villa Emma were saved by Lelio Vittorio Valobra, a Christian lawyer from Genoa who was vice president of the Union of Italian Jewish Communities. He was also national director of DELASEM (Delegation for Assistance to Jewish Emigrants). Most of the Villa Emma orphans were German, Polish, Rumanian, and Austrian refugees who had survived the terrible massacres in German-occupied areas and were hiding in this Italian-occupied zone around Ljubljana.

The two DELASEM representatives involved in saving many orphans—Eugenio Bolaffio, in Gorizia, and Mario Finzi, in Emilia with jurisdiction in Nonantola—disappeared in the death camps, but all the children survived. Some were hidden in the local seminary and others lived with families in the village of Nonantola, ten kilometers from Modena. The Nazis and Fascists combed the local institutions in vain, thanks to Don Arrigo Beccari and Don Ennio Tardini, who taught in the seminary and worked with DELASEM. After years of activity in rescue operations, they were arrested and imprisoned by Italian Fascists.

The entire population in Nonantola befriended these Jewish children. Josep Ithai, who smuggled the children to Switzerland, said: "What the Italian people did for the Jews is one of the most beautiful things in the time of the Holocaust, one of the moments that consoled the Jewish people. Italians helped all Jews from Yugoslavia, Greece, and France and saved thousands of them from deportation."

Ariel Leo Koffler recalled that life at Villa Emma was joyful and happy for they lived as normal a life as possible: "We studied and worked on the land. We had good relations with the townsfolk of Nonantola until the German army occupied Italy on September 8th." Koffler headed south, walking 350 kilometers to a small town called Fora Filiorum Petri in the province of Chieti, where he was hidden in a cave by the DiGirolamo family until the danger was over.

Fifty years later, Don Beccari related how he and Don Tardini forged identity papers for the children. It was Signor Lazzari, a local government employee, who gave them blank identification cards that he would steal from his office. They then filled in the false names. Once the papers were prepared, they sent the children to a priest in Como, who was able to smuggle them past the border guards into Switzerland.

The Italian clergy did not fully realize the risks they were taking. They really did not know what the Germans would do to people opposing them. They did not know about the concentration camps until later.

Many others helped. Davidina Cerioli stated that after giving the problem of where to hide the Mulho family some thought, her husband and brother-in-law decided to take them to a friend's little house in the country. They traveled by night through snow-covered fields and stayed several months. When some village people began saying the Ceriolis were hiding refugees, they returned and built a well-hidden bunker in their factory that saved the Mulho family.

Dino Mulho and his family lived in one room for fourteen months behind a wall in a large storage area. This hiding place was easily hooked up with water and drainage. The smoke from the little stove would go up over the courtyard of the convent next door and was not very noticeable. The new wall they built was covered with boxes.

Someone looking at it would assume that the boxes were stacked row after row all the way back, and would not realize that the storage area had been divided by the wall.

Giancarlo Zoli learned from his experience that when there is a grave need, people rise to the occasion. His assignment was to collect and guide the foreign Jews to the various safe houses, including convents, where they were hidden, often dressed up as nuns or friars. His role was to distribute the money coming from the archbishop, as well as false identity documents and food vouchers. He was always able to find a safe hiding place for the Jewish people whom he called "older brothers."

Ida Lenti had three refugee children. The mayor of Arezzo wanted to put them in a boarding school, but they held on to her and did not want to go. "They wanted to stay with me," she explained, "so the Fascists put us in the hospital ambulance to begin our trip to my mother in my home town in Veneto. On the way we were transferred to a German truck which took us to Florence, and then to Bologna where we stopped for a few days. Finally we got home to my mother—me, three kids, and twelve suitcases.

"My mother and I had to wash clothing for the German soldiers to make enough money to survive. It was more difficult for us having these children. But with the money we earned, I was able to send them to school and provide them with all their necessities. We had to sacrifice, and we also had to receive government welfare.

"Nobody betrayed us. Had the Germans caught us, they would have sent us all straight to Germany, for sure. But nobody found out they were Jewish children, because I never told anybody."[16]

Among the nuns arrested was Mother Donata who cared for hundreds of Jews at the Istituto Palazzolo in Milan. No one can estimate the good she did helping refugees emigrate to Switzerland via a network of convents, peasants who provided food, and guides who helped them reach the border.

In the spring of 1995, Marina Lowi Zinn of New Jersey was reunited with her rescuers in Gandino, a small town in the province of Bergamo, Italy. Over the years, she had corresponded with surviving members of the Ongaro, Rudelli, and Servalli families. Marina was born in Milan after her parents and older brother emigrated from Germany. Five years later, in 1939, her father Lipa Lowi went to

Belgium and did not return to Milan. Only recently did she learn that he had been deported and died in Auschwitz.

Marina remembers that because of the racial laws she, with her mother and brother, joined an uncle in Gandino. When the Nazis invaded northern Italy they were able to hide with others in Professor Rudelli's country house; later they had a room with the Ongaro family. But rumors spread that the Nazis were looking for them, so one night they walked eighteen miles from Gandino to Gazzaniga. Marina and her brother Sighi were well received by the Sisters of Maria Bambina and given a new name, "Carnazzi." Her mother used her maiden name, Maria Loverini. She could not stay with them because her pronounced German accent would endanger her. She lived with the Ongaro family and visited them secretly. Only the mother superior and the local priest knew that they were Jewish. The children learned to pray in Latin. Sighi requested to receive Holy Communion, but Marina wanted to wait for their father's return. They remained with the Sisters for one year.

When the Nazis became aware that refugees were hidden in the convent, the Jewish children were evacuated and Marina was sent to the Ongaro house in Gandino. In vain, her mother searched for her husband in Milan. One day she returned with a soldier. Marina, who thought it was her father, was disappointed to find it was her uncle. He was a member of a British brigade and the first Allied soldier to enter the town. Now the children would be protected in Milan. She and her brother enrolled in a Jewish school where, to their surprise, they met other children who had been hiding with them in the Gazzaniga convent!

Massimo Ottolenghi, an attorney, recalled the generosity of so many Italians. He also described how great tragedies occurred among mixed families. In Turin two Jews committed suicide in order to make things better for their "mixed blood" children and their Aryan wives. Often even the non-Jewish spouses and their children were deported and sent to the gas chambers.

Ottolenghi spoke about Dr. Mussa, chief physician at the hospital of Cirié, who took sick people and others into the hospital knowing that they were Jewish or that they were partisans; some were pregnant women who went into hiding to give birth. There was also a marshal of the carabinieri at the Ceres station who put himself at Ottolenghi's disposal and organized a system by which he could alert all the people he ought to have arrested.

Through his mother and the vicar of Ceres, Ottolenghi would send nuns to warn people at what time the marshal would stop and arrest them. Of course, there was no one around when the marshal arrived with two carabinieri.

In the area of Lanzo, Ottolenghi established another base for operations. This was a successful liaison with Monsignor Ulla, a Salesian priest. Starting from San Maurizio all the way to Cirié, and then going up to the Nava Valley, the entire Valley of Chialamberto, including every subdivision and village, had groups of Jews. Two of the local inns were full and their patrons were exclusively Jewish. The owners protected them from the Nazis and Fascists.

Ottolenghi stated that, when faced with the tragedy on a human level, the Italians left no stone unturned. Unfortunately there were exceptions. Fellow attorneys in Turin sold out their own high school teacher and his wife and children for 2,000 lire each. But the majority of the population had responded with compassion.[17]

The Nazis offered rewards for information leading to the arrests of Jews. Some Jews were betrayed by Italian informers—individual citizens motivated by anti-Semitism and pro-Nazism. Yet, the Italian record of assistance to Jews is remarkable.

3. Ferrara

The Fascist government controlled the media and education. They adopted the German school system which contributed in large measure to the building of the Nazi state. Fascists believed in the cult of discipline and obedience as well as the rejection of individuality.

In Italy many Jews were anti-Fascists. Jewish civilians did not submit passively but fought their oppressors. They joined the Italian underground to fight the Nazis and the Fascists. Having been totally assimilated and linked to the Italian community by ties of friendship and family, they were not singled out from their comrades because of their religion.

Italo Balbo, the Fascist governor of Libya (Africa), and his family always protected the Jews. His children, Paolo and Giuliana Balbo, have wonderful memories of their friendship with Matilde Bassani, their private tutor. She was a Jewish partisan and was arrested in 1943 for political activities and for giving assistance to families of political prisoners. She fled from the SS in Ferrara to Rome where she lived in an apartment belonging to the Balbo family. After the fall of Mussolini, the Balbos continued to protect her and other refugees.

Matilde Bassani traveled wherever she was needed and, after the liberation of Rome, continued to assist the Resistance movement. She was acclaimed by the Americans and the Allied military command for her invaluable help in infiltrating enemy lines and endangering her life to help the partisans. On January 22, 1945, Brigadier General William J. Donovan issued a certificate of appreciation for helping the Office of Strategic Services of the United States Government. She was also honored for her patriotism by the United Nations with a certificate signed by H. R. Alexander, Supreme Allied Commander of the Central Mediterranean Forces. Countless Jews joined Matilde Bassani and participated fully in the Italian Resistance.

The following episode, in Roberto Arbib's memoirs, reprinted in Renzo De Felice's book, *Ebrei in un paese arabo*,[18] gives an excellent portrayal of Governor Italo Balbo and clearly demonstrates that he was not anti-Semitic.

Roberto Arbib relates that, at a Fascist reunion of more than 2,000 Blackshirts in Libya (October 1937), Balbo spoke frankly: "And now, let's discuss the Jews. There were wild, hostile cries, 'Death to the Jews! Away with the Jews from our country!' Balbo raised his arms and angrily ordered absolute silence."

Arbib continues: "Eight of us Jews were ready to leave the Teatro Miramare in Tripoli, when Italo Balbo calmly said: 'Regarding the Jews, I intend to acknowledge, as I have always done, the industry, discipline and loyalty of the Libyan Jewish community to the regime and I apologize for having obliged them to open their stores on the Sabbath. I thought I was acting in their interests. The hostile exclamations of this assembly have irritated me because I do not make any distinction between Catholic Italians and Jewish Italians. We are all Italians and I wish to add that, since my adolescence, I have had only three truly sincere friends, and do you want to know who they are? Well, the three of them are Jews.'

"Balbo then called on Architect Di Segni to stand. 'Raise your arm,' he commanded. The man raised his arm. 'Now, raise the other,' he ordered. Di Segni replied, 'Your Excellency, it's missing.' Balbo made his point: 'Look, comrades, this Jew lost his arm during the Great War, fighting like a good Italian!' During Balbo's government, Libyan Jews were relatively undisturbed."

Italo Balbo was a member of Mussolini's Council and did not hesitate to express his dissent with the Fascist regime's policies. He disagreed with the racial laws and, as governor of Libya, tried to lessen the bitterness of the legislation. He had learned his politics in Ferrara, where Jews had reached positions of prominence and power. There they were engaged in business, the professions, and education.

Chaim Pajes, M.D., studied in Padua. No sooner did he receive his degree when he was immediately arrested. He lived through serving time in nine prisons. He described the horrors in an interview, but added: "The people treated me with kindness and humanity. I can also say that in the Italian concentration camps there was no mistreatment. The hunger was enormous, but we had the chance to govern ourselves. We could study, and we had schools for children, adult schools, even courses for medical postgraduates, because we had with us university professors from Vienna, Berlin, etc.; and we had our own newspaper of events. Then, warned by Mario Tagliaferri, a public security agent, I escaped from the concentration camp. After September 8th, when the Germans came searching for Jews in the area, the Italians helped us again. They gave us food, hiding places. I can say, you see, it might be an exaggeration, but for me the most beautiful country and the best people in the world I found here, in Italy."[19]

Bruno Segre was a Jewish attorney, the son of a Catholic mother. He created a committee for assistance to the Jewish fugitives and refugees hidden by peasants and living in tragic conditions. With the help of the clergy, some were sheltered in convents toward Carmagnola, province of Turin, and others lived on their individual initiative or by suggestions from the committee.

Attorney Segre remarked: "It was a time of great confusion, everyone got along as he could; the peasants behaved magnificently. The population of the Cuneo region, traditionally gentle, hospitable, did some wonderful things on behalf of the Jews."[20]

According to Dr. Emilio Foà, Jews felt a deep solidarity with the Italians in Italy. His father was interned as an anti-Fascist. In April of 1944, he and his family were sent to Birkenau, three kilometers from Auschwitz. His father and uncle were put to death immediately. He was the only survivor of a group of Jews deported from Mantua.

Giuliana Tedeschi and her husband lived tranquilly with their two daughters: a two-year-old and a three-month-old baby. One evening, while the children were sleeping, the SS invaded their apartment. During the discussion about their false IDs, Annetta Barale, the family's devoted housekeeper, was able to spirit the children out of the apartment. She succeeded in hiding them in the home of friends. Later she took them to the Sisters of the Cenacolo in Turin where they remained until the end of the war.

The Tedeschis were arrested and sent to the concentration camp in Fossoli, then to prison at Birkenau. Mr. Tedeschi was murdered. Thirty-year-old Giuliana lived in a block that faced the crematorium and was chosen for experimental surgery having to do with female sexuality.

Instead she was sent to the labor detail and worked in German factories for three years, desperate with fear for herself and her daughters. When Giuliana was finally released and located them with

Annetta at the Turin convent, her five-year-old daughter said: "When I first saw you, you seemed to me to be a beautiful lady, but now you're my mama."[21] The little one did not recognize her mother and clung to the skirts of her nanny, Annetta.

When liberated in 1945, Carlo Schönheit, a young cantor from Ferrara's synagogue, recited the *Kaddish* at the camp's crematorium in Buchenwald where he and his father had been deported. Although destined for deportation to Auschwitz, his sister Gina and his mother were spared because they were Catholic. The entire family survived to tell their story.

There were many brave young people in Italy. Twenty-four-year-old Lorenzo Spada was a local butcher and a partisan in the town of Demonte near Cuneo. After personally guiding a Jewish family of five across the border to Switzerland, he was tortured by the *Brigate Nere* and hanged in the square of his village.

During an interview for the RAI-TV documentary *Il coraggio e la pietà,* the author and chemist Primo Levi, whose works are well-known in the United States and Great Britain, stated: "In 1939, the racial laws were looked upon more as a great folly than as a tragedy, as a silly imitation of the German laws. Jews in Italy were and still are very few; they are and were very assimilated, indistinguishable from the rest of the population, either in terms of accent, or dress, or behavior."

Primo Levi was one of the survivors who wrote about his experiences in the death camp. Although a chemist by profession, he had been a member of the anti-Fascist Resistance in northern Italy. He was arrested and deported to Auschwitz in 1944. His book, *If This Is a Man?*, starts with the departure from the concentration camp in Fossoli (Modena).

Levi's writings are a testament to the indomitability of the human spirit. *The Drowned and the Saved*, a summation of his written work, is a reflective meditation on the horrors of the extermination camps. He reminds us that the first news about Nazi gas chambers began to spread only in 1942: "They were vague pieces of information, yet in agreement with each other; they delineated a massacre of such vast proportions, of such extreme cruelty and such intricate motivation that the public was inclined to reject them because of their very enormity."[22]

By the end of his life Primo Levi was convinced that the lessons of the Holocaust would be lost among the routine atrocities of history. He died in Turin, Italy, in 1987.

4. Assisi

Assisi is the birthplace of Saint Francis, the patron saint of Italy. During World War II, it was teeming with the so-called Nazi-Fascists who sympathized with the Salò Republic and were collaborating with the Fascist secret police. Thousands of non-Jewish refugees were pouring in from the south, fleeing the bombing as the Allies advanced north. In the tradition of sanctuary, clergy and religious sheltered those fleeing from the Third Reich. Harboring Jews was a personal choice for Catholic rescuers, whose humanitarian response was derived from values cultivated in childhood by deeply religious parents.

Bishop Giuseppe Placido Nicolini ceded many buildings to the German medical command for the establishment of hospitals. Assisi was declared a "hospital city." The German commandant appealed to Marshal Kesselring to save the town. There was no response. When the Allies were approaching, a Jewish refugee working undercover for the Nazis forged a letter from Kesselring which declared Assisi an "open city." No refugees were captured in Assisi.

Pope Pius XII's message to Catholic bishops and archbishops was loud and clear. They were to provide a sanctuary to hide thousands of Jews in convents, monasteries, and seminaries. The plan was implemented throughout Italy. They procured false identification for Jews, arranged kosher meals, and hid Jewish men, women, and children in cloisters. They even set up classes for Jewish children to study their own religious heritage. The altruistic response of the clergy was demonstrated in Assisi by Bishop Nicolini and Don Aldo Brunacci.

In 1943, Don Brunacci's assignment was to resettle thousands of refugees. He stated that, one day, after the regular monthly meeting of the clergy at the seminary, Bishop Nicolini called him aside. He showed him a letter from the Vatican secretary of state which explained that the situation of the Jews was becoming increasingly perilous. The

Church was calling upon the bishops to protect them. Instructions in this letter were to be held in the strictest confidence.

Meanwhile many Jews in Assisi remained hidden in monasteries and convents dressed as monks and nuns. Special seminars on catechism and liturgy prepared them to behave as Christians in order not to arouse suspicion. The network for escape for some Jews was through Cardinal Elia Dalla Costa, the Archbishop of Florence, who entrusted them to Cardinal Pietro Boetto. In Genoa, passage was arranged on neutral ships where they joined other Jews and political refugees.

Among those who helped rescue Jews was Father Rufino Niccacci, who was arrested and imprisoned in Perugia. He survived the German occupation. The state of Israel awarded him a gold medal and bestowed its highest honor of "The Righteous Gentile." Niccacci's story is told by the war correspondent Alexander Ramati in *The Assisi Underground.*[23]

Years later in the town of Montenero on the outskirts of Assisi, Father Niccacci built access roads and planted 10,000 trees along the avenues where he established a small settlement for destitute Christian and Jewish families. He built an Ecumenical House, to which Christians and Jews would come to discuss problems of rapprochement between Christianity and Judaism, a decade before Pope John XXIII.

Fifty years after the Nazis occupied Italy, Don Aldo Brunacci stated: "We not only placed the Jews in convents but also in private houses, and in hotels. I had one family in my house. There were moments of terror like when the police came to my house to take me for questioning on May 15, 1944. I quickly shut the door to the study and left with the police so they did not find them. This family then went to seek help from the bishop who said: 'As you can see, my house is full of refugees, but I still have my bed and my study. From now on I can sleep in my study on the couch, and you can take my bedroom'."[24] Personal documents belonging to the Jews, as well as their sacred books and religious objects, were hidden in the cellar of the bishop's residence until the Liberation.

The printing of documents was a risky job. Giorgio Krops, a young Jew from Trieste, was the contact between Don Brunacci and Luigi Brizi whose small print shop supplied false identification cards. They gave Jews typical family names from the area in southern Italy already liberated by the Allies. The Nazi police could not cross-check the names.

The biggest problem was to reproduce the German seals. In fact, after several failed attempts to do so in nearby cities, they were able to do the job in San Quirico Monastery in Assisi, thanks to some very skilled young Jews and two high-ranking Italian Army officers who had taken refuge there. Friends in the city government office were able to provide blank identification cards that just needed to be filled out and stamped. Once the Jews had these cards they were safe and could legally obtain food vouchers. Don Brunacci was arrested in 1944, but his life was spared through the Vatican's intervention.

Concealing Jews in Umbria was, as in Florence, the work of the local clergy. Don Federico Vincenti, supported by Archbishop Mario Vianello, sheltered over 100 Jews in Perugia. Don Beniamino Schivo, while endangering his own life, saved the lives of countless Jews in the area of Città del Castello. The Korn family was among them. Ursula Korn Selig and her mother fled from Breslau, Germany, in 1939. They went to Alassio on the Italian Riviera where her aunt and uncle had a hotel. Soon after, the Fascists appropriated the building and they were interned in Collazzone, a small village in Umbria. Her father and uncle were sent to an internment camp in Salerno.

Since 1950, Ursula has been living in New York and recalls going to a Salesian convent school in the village as a young girl. During the Nazi occupation she was protected by wearing a nun's habit. She also recalls hiding behind locked doors in a seminary and the many sufferings endured, especially an eight-hour march by night to the mountains while surrounded by Nazi gunfire. At all times the Korns were protected by Don Schivo. In 1986 he was honored as "Righteous Among Nations" at the Yad Vashem Holocaust Memorial in Jerusalem.

5. Genoa

In his Prologue to *Uncertain Refuge*, Professor Mario Toscano explains that demonstrations of solidarity in Genoa were not lacking: "DELASEM, with the fundamental assistance of Catholics in religious orders, was able to bring help to large numbers of the persecuted."[25]

According to Bernardo Grasso, Cardinal Borgoncini Duca was most helpful with documents needed by DELASEM. No priest rejected the Jews.

Cardinal Pietro Boetto was sympathetic toward the plight of Jewish refugees stranded in Genoa and gave them money to flee to safety. He also assigned his personal secretary, Don Francesco Repetto, to assume the burden of helping those who had lost their homes and to collect information about prisoners of war.

The president of the Italian Jewish community, Raffaele Cantoni, asked Repetto to head the assistance work throughout northern Italy. He gave him data about the people he was to be in touch with in other cities: in Milan, Avvocato Sala, President of Catholic Action and of the Society of St. Vincent de Paul, and Dottoressa Wittgens of Brera; in Turin, Cardinal Fossati and his secretary Monsignor Barale; and the parish priest of San Dalmazzo in Cuneo.

When Massimo Teglio's sister, husband, and two children were deported, he dedicated himself to saving others. This mission was performed through the archdiocese of Genoa. He worked with Lelio Vittorio Valobra who sent him to Don Francesco Repetto, secretary to the archbishop, for information about his family.

Elisa Della Pergola, whose father died in Auschwitz, was saved because Teglio took care of her family. He performed extraordinarily courageous acts. Asked if he relied mainly on the Catholic organizations, his answer was: "Without question. They had the greatest possibilities for refuge in religious institutions and in convents and monasteries."[26]

One day Anna and Maria Giordana, eleven and thirteen years of age, went to the mountains to gather mushrooms. Behind a bush was a little girl, frightened by the strangers. The child was shivering from the mountain air. They felt very sorry for her. After talking awhile, they located her parents and others who were hiding in the mountains. The girls ran home to tell their grandparents who gave them food and blankets to bring to the refugees. This friendship continued and in the cold winter months the Giordana girls brought their little friend Maria to their home to sleep.[27]

Professor Daniel Carpi, of Tel Aviv University, speaking from an Israeli perspective, stated: "The Italians showed that even in a period of darkness, a period in which the sun of civilization grew dark over the greater part of the countries of Europe, at that moment the position of the majority of Italians was positive."

Saved by Irma Andriol from Sozzano, Blanka Stern said: "The Italians were not just good people, they were human, they had courage....We had no rights; they restored our sense of humanity; in fact, our feeling of being part of the entire human race."[28]

Numbered among the many courageous individuals who saved the lives of Jews in Italy is Dr. Elio Del Giudice. Nada Volhaim related that he saved her. On the other hand, there were many rescuers who lost their lives. While Marcello Hoffman escaped from Nonantola to Switzerland, his friend Alessandro Bersani was denounced for helping him.

Abraham Cohen remembers that the Olivetti family gave him moral and financial help and the Catholic Church helped him find lodgings. Everything was arranged for him and his wife. One December day in very bad weather a priest accompanied him from Ivrea to Azeglio on a bicycle. Two days later the same priest arrived with Signora Cohen.

Don Raimondo Viale, the parish priest of Borgo San Dalmazzo, found hiding places for many Jewish refugees, distributed funds, and accompanied them to Genoa. There, through Don Repetto, they were given hospitality in seminaries, monasteries, and convents. With the help of the British ambassador to the Vatican, funds deposited in London and transferred to Rome were used to help care for them. Priests as well as laymen served as couriers to deliver these funds.

When Don Repetto was asked to take up the work of DELASEM, which was considered illegal under Nazi rule, he immediately answered: "The Jews are innocent; they are in great danger; we must help them at whatever cost to ourselves."

So that the DELASEM files with names and addresses of Jews in Genoa would not fall into the hands of the Nazis, Don Repetto placed the papers inside the pipes of the organ at San Lorenzo and set about enlisting the aid of priests, monks, and nuns across northern Italy who would be willing to hide Jews. Everyone was impressed by his sensitivity, courage, and total commitment.

In 1984 Don Repetto addressed a Jewish group and recalled with emotion the sufferings of the refugees: "You seemed to us then, and you were, something sacred. As such we wanted to receive you and as such we were bound to treat you."

Riccardo Pacifici was one of Italy's most learned rabbis and devoted himself to the practical concerns of the Jewish community under the racial laws. When Jewish children were prohibited from attending public school, Rabbi Pacifici organized a school in the temple offices saying: "Better to close a temple than shut down a school."

Pacifici was chief rabbi of Genoa when Mussolini was deposed by the Fascist Council and the Italian king. The Germans crossed the border in September 1943 and restored Mussolini to power as head of the Republic of Salò.

Prior to this time there had been no deportations from Italy of either Italian or foreign Jews. But with the Germans in Italy, it was likely that Jews who were not in hiding would be captured and deported.

To protect the rabbi, his wife, and their two sons, Archbishop Boetto offered hiding places. Rabbi Pacifici accepted for his family but refused for himself, saying that as long as there were Jews who needed him, he would not desert his post.

On November 2, 1943, the Germans threatened to kill the children of the Jewish custodian of the synagogue if he didn't summon the rabbi. Pacifici was captured, imprisoned, and tortured—despite the pleas of Archbishop Boetto and his offer of gold in exchange for the rabbi's release. Even under torture, the rabbi never revealed what the Nazis wanted: the names and addresses of other Jews. Rabbi Pacifici was delivered to Auschwitz on Saturday, December 11th, and was seen entering the gas chamber on December 12th.

Wanda, Riccardo Pacifici's thirty-six-year-old wife, had already been taken to the convent of the Franciscan Sisters on Piazza del Carmine in Florence. On her sixth night in the convent, the Germans broke in, found the fifty Jewish women hidden there, and deported them to Auschwitz. She, too, died in the gas chamber.

Only the children were left, hidden in Settignano (Florence) in Santa Marta's convent school for boys. Emanuele was twelve, Raffaele five. For eleven months the nuns concealed the children's identity. Since Pacifici was a Jewish name they called the boys by a different name—Pallini—and made excuses for them when they did not partic-ipate in church services. The nuns respected the Jewish religion. While the other children were told to kiss the crucifix before going to bed, Sister Cornelia would cover it for Emanuele and Raffaele. Quietly she would remind them to say their Hebrew prayers.

In 1944, the Allied armies liberated Florence. The nuns entrusted the two Pacifici boys to Eliau Lubinski—one of the soldiers of the British Eighth Army's Jewish brigade. He took them to their paternal grandparents who had survived the war and were living in Rome. The boys lived with Aunt Giuditta and Uncle Fernando.

Today, Emanuele Pacifici, a businessman, is an unofficial archivist of the history and culture of the Jews in Italy, and especially of events connected with the Holocaust. He has amassed thousands of documents and slides, and he lectures widely on the subject.

Pacifici singles out railroad workers for special praise. They invoked endless red tape to delay carrying out deportation orders, diverted trains, put equipment out of commission and, in one case, threatened to shoot the Germans escorting a train if they didn't allow the railroad workers to open the train and give water to the deportees.

Emanuele Pacifici is also president of "The Friends of Yad-Vashem" in Italy. On May 17, 1995, the organization sponsored an award ceremony at Campidoglio (City Hall), to honor Sister Marta Folcia who had taken care of him at Santa Marta's School in Settignano. She received the "Gold Medal of the Just among the Nations"—a singular honor given by the state of Israel to those who contributed and risked their lives to save Jews from the Nazi gas cham-bers. Her story is told in Pacifici's autobiography, *Non ti voltare*, with a Preface by Rabbi Elio Toaff.[29]

The book includes a report to Cardinal Elia Dalla Costa by Sister Esther Busnelli, Superior of the convent of Santa Marta, describing how the Germans searched the building on November 26–27, 1943:

"The Cardinal begged us to hide about fifty Jews. He thought they would be safe in the convent of the Franciscan Missionaries on Piazza del Carmine. Everyone thought danger had been averted. The Jews slept peacefully. It was 3 A.M. Suddenly about thirty German SS and Italian police entered forcefully through the garden and trapped all of them. They were placed in trucks and sent to Verona."

After describing the brutality and cruelty of the Nazis and Fascists when they stormed into the convent, Sister Esther Busnelli writes in her report to the cardinal: "We gave each one a most affectionate embrace; it was a scene to make the stones cry, but those hearts hardened by hatred seemed to feel no pain....Just and Merciful God, have pity on your chosen people."

Emanuele Pacifici's life was again miraculously saved on October 9, 1982. As he was leaving the synagogue in Rome, he was seriously hurt by Palestinian terrorists whose bombs injured 120 Jews. At the hospital Emanuele was taken to the mortuary and declared dead. When Rabbi Toaff blessed him, he revived!

6. Florence

Only from the fourteenth century do we have documentation on the presence of Jews in Florence. Cosimo I, in 1571, became grand duke of Tuscany and created a Jewish "ghetto" in what is now the historical center of Florence. The community selected a council composed of eighteen members. Rulings with regard to all legal matters, contracts, quarrels, marriages, and divorces were recognized by the civil authorities. Jews had their own religious, social, and cultural activities. They were well-respected and received the same benefits as non-Jews, including legal and constitutional equality.

The Florentine Jews participated enthusiastically in the Italian Risorgimento and the wars of independence. They entered all the arts and professions, contributing to the cultural and economic development of Italy. The ghetto was entirely destroyed at the end of the nineteenth century.

In 1842, the Jewish community proposed the building of a new synagogue, and a fundraising campaign began with a donation of 5,000 ducats by the Montebarocci family. Thirty years later its construction started when Cavaliere David Levi, former president of the Jewish University, left his estate to build "a monumental temple worthy of Florence."

The design of the Florence synagogue was inspired by Constantinople's Byzantine Church of Saint Sophia. It has interior walls and ceilings covered with arabesque. There are inlaid marble floors, rich mosaics, and carvings in wood and bronze. At the back of the apse is the Ark with black marble columns and mosaics.

The synagogue was seriously damaged in August 1944 by the Germans. Despite its great artistic value, several mines exploded in its interior, destroying the columns and part of the women's gallery. Its treasure was carried away by the Germans to the north of Italy.

Fortunately it has been recovered and, again, the synagogue has been carefully restored to its original splendor.

In 1938, Hitler went to Florence with Mussolini. The windows of every public building were draped with banners of the Nazi swastika flag, except the residence of Cardinal Elia Dalla Costa who kept windows closed to show his disapproval.

Cardinal Dalla Costa asked the religious institutions in Florence to open their doors to Jewish refugees. More than twenty institutions responded and hundreds of Jews were sheltered. In Lucca, Father Aldo Mei, a twenty-two-year-old priest, was killed by the Nazis for hiding Jews and partisans.

Within the Catholic hierarchy, individuals tried to persuade Pope Pius XII to condemn the Nazi atrocities and to threaten any participating Catholics with excommunication. But the Pope maintained his silence.

Despite this official silence, everyone in the Church worked to rescue Jews, and the list of "righteous Gentiles" in Italy contains the names of countless bishops, priests, and nuns. The Archbishop of Florence, Cardinal Dalla Costa, is remembered by both Jewish survivors and the Catholic clergy for his efforts during the Resistance.

Father Cipriano Ricotti, a Dominican monk, recalls that during the war he became involved with Jews. He was called by Cardinal Dalla Costa and asked if he would be willing to dedicate himself to the Jews who had come in from Yugoslavia and France. They came without documents and with no knowledge of the language, and it would have been easy for them to be picked up and persecuted. Therefore, together with other people, he provided hiding places for them in convents. If they had some money, he would find private homes whose owners would rent space to them.

There was, however, another need. How could they secure ration cards to authorize the purchase of food if these people didn't have documents? Through a young man he knew, he was able to obtain the city seal of an Italian town that was occupied by the Americans. With this seal, he succeeded in having false documents made up. Since the town was in Allied hands, the Fascists and Germans had no way to check whether the papers had actually been issued there. They attached photographs to these false identity cards and took them to police headquarters in Florence. A Sicilian friend, who had access to the seal of Florence, then issued false ration cards.

Ricotti was not the only priest recruited by Archbishop Dalla Costa. Monsignor Leto Casini relates that when Italy signed the Armistice with the Allies, European Jews who had been hiding outside Italy came *en masse* across the borders, thinking they were going to meet the Allied troops. Instead, the Germans occupied the north to try to contain the Allied troops advancing from the south. These Jews were worse off than before. Some went for help to Cardinal Dalla Costa.

The cardinal, worried that the position of the episcopal residence in the center of the city would make his involvement in rescue efforts too dangerous, wanted a more obscure figure to handle the effort. "I was then the priest of a small parish outside Florence," Casini recalls. "We formed a committee to settle the refugees."

Dalla Costa helped form two rescue committees, Casini's and Ricotti's. Each consisted of five or six Jews and one priest. Dalla Costa kept them working independently and uninformed about each other, so that each would be safe were the other discovered. Nathan Cassuto, the chief rabbi of Florence, was a member of Casini's group. Both committees included an almost mythical figure, a Jewish accountant named Raffaele Cantoni, who had made a daring escape from a train taking him to Auschwitz, and who obtained the money that Casini and Ricotti needed for food, shelter, and documents for the foreign Jews.

In Miami, Florida, Dr. Rubin Pick, a psychiatrist, tells his story of fleeing to Florence from Trieste in 1943, and being advised by Rabbi Cassuto to go to the home of Archbishop Dalla Costa. The archbishop's secretary directed Pick to the home of a priest, where he and two other young Jewish physicians found refuge and remained until another priest, Don Giulio Gradassi, offered Pick a safer place at his parish in the nearby countryside. During this time, Pick's mother and sister were in the convent where Wanda Pacifici was hiding. One night while the women were out, the Germans raided the convent. After this narrow escape they too went to the parish house of Don Gradassi.

Elena and Lot Minervi fled to La Verna, a little village in Tuscany. Although the monks and the entire population knew they were there, they were not betrayed. Everyone kept the secret.

The Italians saved a sinking ship with over 500 Slovak refugees. Feri and Zlata Noiman explained how they were saved. They fled to the mountains and were protected by Italians who took them to the Ferramonti-Tarsia camp in Calabria. Finally, when the Nazis retreated, they were allowed to leave the camp.

The town of Pitigliano had a flourishing Jewish community in the nineteenth century. It was called "Little Jerusalem." Among its oldest families were the Bemporad, the Camerino, and the Sadun. They took pride in their school and library with over 4,000 volumes, many of which were incunabula and manuscripts of great value bequeathed by the Consiglio family.

After the racial laws, many Jews gradually left the town. In 1944, bombs partially destroyed its sixteenth-century synagogue which had been restored in 1931. The entire structure was later demolished. Its cultural heritage was divided between the Jewish communities in Rome and Livorno. Today the old synagogue has been rebuilt.

The Servi family was well known and admired in Pitigliano. Their best friends were Catholics who sustained them during the tragic period, opened their doors to protect them, gave them food and nourished them, took care of their possessions in their absence, and later returned them. Theirs was a fraternal friendship, a genuine charity, a human justice.

Elena Servi was eight years old in 1938 when her father told her she could no longer attend school. "Why?" she asked him. "What have I done wrong?" With tears in his eyes, he answered: "Nothing."

At that age Elena realized that she was excluded from society because of the "racial laws" in Italy. Italian Jews who had enjoyed equal rights with other citizens were expelled from the military, civil service, schools, and businesses. They were humiliated, despised, persecuted in the land they had helped to build and unite during the Risorgimento and World War I.

In Pitigliano, where the prosperous Jewish community had lived harmoniously for four centuries, life suddenly changed. Fascist leaders had arrived to interfere with their tranquillity and had enforced the "racial laws." Not only were Jews forbidden in public places, but they were also to have no rapport with the rest of the population. Elena recalled how her Catholic friends continued their relationship. They "adopted" her and, in direct defiance of the Fascists, she would be seen at the theater and at a dairy bar enjoying ice cream with them.

The tragedy escalated in Pitigliano with the German occupation of Italy following the Armistice of September 8, 1943. On a beautiful autumn day in November, her family finally abandoned their home and all their possessions. They traveled from place to place seeking hospitality, fearing deportation, terrorized that some stranger might come along the road and report them. Although they had done no harm, they were now obliged to hide. For four months the Servi family moved around in deep snow, ready to flee on a moment's notice. In March 1944, they located a grotto in a vast field and remained there until June 14th, when that part of Italy was freed by the Allies. They were able to return home and live as free people. Today Elena Servi thanks God and continues to express gratitude in a tangible way to all who courageously helped them and risked their lives to save them.

The family of Elena's husband lived in Latera (Viterbo), the only Jewish residents in this small town. Their enterprising German neighbor had married an Italian gentleman from Latera. She arranged for them to reach Rome in a German military truck that was transporting flour. They remained in Rome until the Liberation, hidden with Antonio Giamarini whose brother had joined the Salesian Fathers. Elena's future husband and his brother, with false identification, were admitted into the "Angelo Mai" Institute to continue their studies. Its rector was Brother Nicasio Freddiani, a friend of the family from the same town.

Elena Servi's aunt and uncle who lived in Florence found refuge in San Miniato (Pisa). In a letter to Elena, their son recalls: "The family protecting my parents was aware of the risk they were taking, should their identity be disclosed. They were living in the house of Signor Neri (an employee of my uncle), whose son was a priest. With their false IDs they appeared to be like so many other elderly people, refugees from the bombed cities."

When the local partisans attacked German soldiers, the Nazis ordered the entire population inside the Cathedral of San Miniato. The doors were closed and, in retaliation, as the Nazis retreated, they bombed this magnificent tenth-century cathedral crowded with innocent people. Miraculously Elena's aunt and uncle were not injured. However, there were many victims. The episode of the destruction of the cathedral was depicted in the film *La notte di San Lorenzo,* by the Taviani brothers. It was filmed in the town of San Martino.

The Tuscan region was the site of horrible massacres of countless innocent Italians—men, women, and children. Their story is told in part by survivors of Nazi terrorism. (*See* "Massacres in Tuscany," pp. 197–198.)

Nedo Fiano was eighteen years old in Florence when he was deported. Ten members of his family were sent first to Fossoli and then to Auschwitz. His mother was killed as soon as they arrived; his father, two months later.

In an interview, Nedo stated that the Jews had received absolutely no information about Auschwitz. They thought it would be like going to the camp at Fossoli where lives were not in danger. Before arriving at Auschwitz, they were able to freshen up at the local café in the station. Unaware of their destiny, they walked to the "Disinfection Room" to be murdered in a building surrounded by majestic-looking trees. Everything was orchestrated so that there would not be scenes of terror.

Jews and non-Jews in Italy were totally ignorant of the savagery, the destruction, the crematory ovens, the revolt in the Warsaw ghetto, and the extermination camps. (*See* Appendix VI, "Statistics on the Holocaust," pp. 231–238.)

Guards control access to Vatican City during the war.

7. Venice

"To those who did not return from extermination camps: 'May their memory be blessed.' Also to those who have given back life to the Community, making sure that Jewish traditions in Venice would not disappear." This is the dedication one reads in the book, *Gli Ebrei a Venezia, 1938–1945.*

This book, edited by Renata Segre in 1995, is a compilation of historical documents of one of the darkest periods of Venetian history. It portrays the Jewish community from the beginning of the Nazi-Fascist persecution to its rebirth in Venice: a period of racist ideology when Italian citizens of Jewish origin no longer participated in government, education, scientific research, or theatrical performances; a period when Jews were ostracized, humiliated, and considered "non-persons"; a period when Mussolini's anti-Semitic campaign succeeded in the deportation of Jews to Nazi concentration camps.

The arrests of Jews in Venice began December 5, 1943. Within one month, between December 13, 1943, and January 5, 1944, they were transferred to the concentration camp in Fossoli. Train Number 8 left Fossoli di Carpi on February 22nd and arrived at Auschwitz February 26th. Train Number 13 departed on June 26th from Fossoli, stopped at Verona for additional refugees, and arrived on June 30, 1943. Among those identified were twenty-one children who were born after 1931; 150 elderly who were born before 1885. Those over seventy were also sent to Auschwitz in August 1944. Among the Jews, the youngest, Umberto Nacamulli, was two years old.

The renewal of terror by Nazis and Fascists took place in the Clinica Prosdocimi in Marocco di Mogliano near Treviso. Prisoners were transferred to the Risiera di San Sabba, near Trieste. On August 17th, Italian and German soldiers stormed the Casa di Riposo

Israelitica in Venice and added the elderly Jews to those at the Risiera di San Sabba.

Between October 6th and 11th, Jews in hospitals were arrested: Ospedale Civile San Giovanni e Paolo, Ospedale Psichiatrico di San Clemente e di San Servolo. They constituted Convoys Number 39T, 41T, 42T and were transferred to Risiera di San Sabba, Trieste. It was here that Gruppenführer Odillo Globocnick, an intimate friend of Himmler, who had distinguished himself for the atrocities committed in Poland, prepared the only gas chambers in Italy. To add to this initiative, Haupsturmführer Franz Stangl, last commander of Treblinka, established headquarters in Treviso and in Venice.

With the help of several Italian police, and especially with the collaboration of Mauro Grini, a Jew from Trieste, the SS continued a reign of terror. Grini had been arrested with his family and was to be deported to Germany. He agreed to help the SS while his family remained hostage at Risiera di San Sabba.

The Sereni family separated on September 9, 1943. Paolo Sereni, his brother, and family went to hide with friends in Milan. His invalid mother, a Catholic, remained in Venice with his sister. The latter were considered "Aryans." Toward the end of March 1944, his mother insisted that they return to Venice where they lived incognito with friends.

Mauro Grini denounced the entire Sereni family. On September 21, 1944, the Serenis were imprisoned in Santa Maria Maggiore and were transferred to Risiera di San Sabba October 2nd. Only then did they learn about the existence of gas chambers. Ten days later, among those eliminated was Paolo Sereni's father. His mother never left San Sabba nor did the rest of his family survive the gas chambers. On January 11, 1945, Paolo, his sister, and brother were deported to Ravensbruck. He alone lived to tell the story.

Paolo Sereni returned to Italy toward the end of 1945. His testimony was recorded in Venice on November 3, 1975: "Able-bodied individuals were given the conventional name, *Nacht und Nebel* (N.N.) and were secretly deported to Germany and killed or imprisoned. According to Hitler's instructions, 'they were to disappear without leaving any trace.' No information was to be given about them, their location, or their destiny."

Gradually this "N.N." procedure was extended to thousands of civilians who were arrested and condemned to death with their families, as were the hostages, 10 to 100 for every German killed.

Sereni's testimony continued: "Jews were not prepared for the events of this period. Information was unclear. They did not realize what the Nazis had planned, perhaps because the information that circulated was so tragic and catastrophic that they could not conceive such wickedness. On the other hand, how could they flee? Where could they find a hiding place? How could they procure false documents? How could they reach Switzerland?"

Itala Meneghetti wrote of the terrible winter of 1945. Father Gentile, observing the charitable traditions of the Franciscan Order, approached Itala cautiously and asked her to assist Raul, a young refugee from Fiume. The Nazis were searching for him. The young man was suffering from hunger and bitter cold, hidden in a tiny area of Cannargio. He was a skeleton and was dying of tuberculosis. His parents were desperately in need of assistance to care for him. They lived in a warehouse at Sant'Aonal and would come late evenings as often as possible to bring whatever food they could find. They offered to give their last possession, a gold watch, to help him.

Raul explained to Itala and her friend Alice how their home had been sacked by the Nazis in October 1943, when he attended the Institute of Architecture. His friends were arrested and massacred along the Riva dell'Impero. He and his parents had no documents to protect themselves and no means of sustenance.

The women were shocked. Itala opened her purse and gave Raul an envelope. "This is from the National Committee of Liberation," she said. "Keep the gold watch." The scantily dressed young man was trembling from the cold. With tears in his eyes he said: "One of the consolations of life is the knowledge that there are sister-souls in the world."

Itala and Alice returned soon after with an electric burner, false identification cards, and Dr. Vittorio Kratter whose mother sent some sugar. Father Gentile found another room for Raul who survived, joined the Resistance, and vindicated his lost friends. With Father Gentile, who later died in a leprosarium in Tibet, there were others in Venice who must be remembered for their moral courage: Rosa Zenoni Politeo, Anna Pallucchini Tositti, Father Giulio, the Patriarch's secretary, Mrs. Kratter and her other son, a pharmacist, Emma Caniato, Albertina Scarpa, Maria Fava, Attorney Gaetano Duse, and his young associate, Virginia.

Also to be remembered are: Aldo Camerino, Marianna Bassan,

and her daughter Iris, Regina Polacco, Professor Giuseppe Sabbatini, a famous Latinist from Trieste. After eighteen months of separation, Dr. Samuele Bernath, a philanthropist saved by the Fantinato family in Fratte, was reunited with his wife Alda and their children, Giselda and Alessandro. Dr. Bernath continued to assist all those in need and, in particular, the partisan brigade "Damiano Chiesa."

In her *Diario: Ricordi di prigionia,* Letizia Morpurgo Fano wrote a letter to her children describing the departure from Trieste to a concentration camp in Venice on September 10, 1943, two days after the Armistice. It was their first train ride. In touching terms she reminds them that "every time they settled in a hotel, the Germans caught up with them and they had to run away. Residence in the Rialto Hotel on the Grand Canal was like a dreamworld. But this, too, did not last. Again we had to flee from the Germans. In the last hotel, La Bella Venezia, the doctor diagnosed your dad's illness as scarlet fever." The Fano family had to be separated. Their governess, Uccina Calò, took care of them in the home of their friend, Rina Vianello. The children were miraculously saved. When their parents went to the Jewish nursing home, the Nazis began searching for them. Mr. Fano, who had been director of the Palestinian Office, was to be arrested. Again they fled and found refuge in a small, dark room with Gabriella Rossini. In 1943, on Christmas Eve, three men knocked on the door at midnight. The men were merciless. With Gabriella and her husband, who were guilty of hiding them, Letizia and her husband, desperate and frightened, were forced to travel by gondola to the prison of Santa Maria Maggiore.

"We could no longer see you, my dear children. Your dad and I were separated. He was taken to a hospital. I remained in prison. In August 1944, I pretended I had acute appendicitis and was rushed to the same hospital, where I could see your dad occasionally from a window. We communicated with Hebrew sign language. The doctors tried to help us. Visitors were not allowed. Only our dear friend, Father Felici, standing near the door, would bless us, and then look at your dad and say, 'All is well.' We feared for his safety. He would take my newspaper in which I placed money for you. I always worried that, should he be caught, he would be deported. For the sick who were ambulatory, the deportation day arrived, October 11, 1944. They departed with admirable dignity. For your dad and me, the day of liberation came, April 27, 1945. Always be affectionately grateful to the Vianello family for your safety. Mama."

Tina Navarro Dina, who lives in Mestre, described the sufferings endured as a child when, with her extended family, she had to move frequently from one hovel to another without food and other necessities. In order to avoid being captured by the Germans who were deporting the Jews, they would separate and meet at various destinations. Finally her father succeeded in contacting the Levorato family in San Lorenzo, Venice. They were able to accommodate only three people, but they arranged for Tina and Pina to go to "Canal al Pianto," a Catholic boarding school. The Sisters were good and understanding. No one else in the school knew they were Jews.

Maddalena Danilo recalls the day the elderly and sick in the Casa di Riposo of the Jewish ghetto were marched out of the building for deportation, some in wheelbarrows with their legs dangling and their faces drawn, frightened by the cruelty of the armed Fascists and Nazis. She remembers how the Fascists forced her father to drink a full glass of castor oil. Later, when Cà Giustinian was bombed, her father was apprehended. Instead of shooting him on the spot, a German soldier decided to denounce him to the Nazi authorities officially. The execution did not take place.

In 1943, Paolo Revoltella, now a dentist in Italy, was seven years old when Jews in Venice had to go into hiding. His father, Ettore, was a childhood friend of Lello Grassini who tried desperately to help the Revoltella family. But his efforts were of no avail. The entire family was sent to Fossoli and then to Germany. The elderly grandparents died on the way. His mother and sister were sent to the gas chambers in Bergen-Belsen. Lello and his brother Angelo were deported to Birkenau. Angelo Grassini also died. Lello survived and was sent to a concentration camp in Poland. Later he was transferred to Eastern Prussia where he was freed by the Russians. He died from tuberculosis in 1945.

Mario Brandes of Cesena had never been interested in politics and was totally ignorant about local reunions of the Communist leaders. He was arrested by the Fascists in November 1943 and incarcerated for five months of interrogations by the SS about the meetings in the "Trattoria alle due Torri." Even after being tortured he was unable to reveal anything because he had never participated. He succeeded, however, in alerting the Jews in Cesena by telephone that they were in danger and thus saved many persons from deportation.

In April 1944, when the SS learned that Mario was a Jew, he was sent to the concentration camp in Fossoli (Carpi, Modena). He was placed with about 100 Roman Jews. On May 1st, there was an unusual roll call. Without warning, the soldiers fired shots in their midst, killing Pacifico Di Castro, a young Roman Jew.

One day, the Fascists sent Mario to Carpi to get a sack of grain. He asked: "What if I decide to run away?" Their response was: "You will not run away, because we will kill ten Jews if you do not return." Some time later, Mario did run away. He threw himself into the fields of grain during the night. From the tower the guards shot at him. Fortunately they thought some animal was roaming around. They did not kill him. An old man found him fallen in the fields, his feet bloody. He hid Mario in the granary and gave him some food.

Mario returned to Venice and joined the partisans. After the Liberation, he went home. In July 1948, arriving in Israel with a Rumanian passport, he served as a soldier and learned Hebrew. He returned to Venice in 1950. He married there and now has three children.

When the Germans arrived in September 1943, Gianni Milner was seventeen years old—a student in the Lyceum. His family was related to Giuseppe Jona, President of the Jewish community in Venice.

One day during a conversation, Gianni told Professor Jona that he had gone with his mother's friend, Marilù Negri, a member of the Red Cross, to help Italian prisoners who had been captured by the Germans in Dalmazia and were being sent to concentration camps. As prisoners were transferred from the ship to the train, they would throw messages out of the train windows and he and other boys would send them to their families.

Professor Jona listened attentively and then spoke to Gianni about tolerance and freedom. That night he committed suicide, after hiding the lists of the Jewish community members so that the Nazis and Fascists could not locate them.

Gianni's maternal uncle, an officer in the navy, came with Samuele Goldschmidt and his daughter Gilda Nadia from Trieste to hide them in the Milner house until they could be relocated. Gilda remained with the Dominican Sisters of Santi Apostoli until the end of the war; the Germans located her father in the Fatebenefratelli hospital. He was arrested for his participation in the Resistance movement and was freed in 1944.

In 1942, Bruno Finzi received his medical degree in the city of Perugia when he was twenty-four years old. He interned at the Ospedale Civile di Venezia. The following year he went to hide in Jesolo with his parents, but they were recognized and had to keep moving. For one month they remained with Father Piero Saccon, the pastor of Rolle di Cison, a church in Venice.

Meanwhile Count Brandolin, the anti-Fascist leader, prepared false identity papers and changed their surname to Ferrazzi—a family from Bari in southern Italy.

The peasants paid for Bruno's medical services with food. He also assisted the partisans in Combai and Miane. One day, the Germans gathered all the men below sixty, killed three of them because they were armed, and took the entire group to Treviso. They would be sent to German labor camps. Before departure they were examined by a doctor who was Bruno's former classmate. By pretending Bruno was sick, the doctor saved him from being deported. Ferrazzi continued his medical career among the partisans and was placed in charge of the local hospital.

Ferruccio D'Angeli's family had to be separated. Friends and relatives helped; without them they would have been captured. On November 29th, they went to the hotel near the Varese station. The staff was pleasant and gracious; they smiled at the children as they went to their rooms. Within a few minutes, the owners came: "We understand that you are Jews; you must leave immediately, the Germans control this area continuously." The family left for the Swiss border.

Upon arrival they found the Germans guarding the frontier with dogs; they were arresting and shooting Jews. The D'Angeli family soon learned that not 5,000 but 20,000 lire were needed per person to cross the border to Switzerland. They did not have sufficient funds and returned to Varese. There they survived sixteen months of flight and imprisonment.

Like so many Jews, the D'Angeli family did not know what they were fleeing from: deportation trains, extermination camps, cremation ovens.

Homeless and refugees in Montecassino.

VATICANO is clearly visible on the flank of a lorry assigned to the transportation of refugees.

Police check visitor's identification at St. Peter's Square.

Vatican City State motor vehicles used to distribute food
to refugees in Rome.

B. Memories

1. Religious Teachers Filippini

*R*eligious orders of men and women joined Pope Pius XII's human-itarian efforts to save the Jews during World War II. They responded without hesitation when word was circulated by the Vatican that the Holy Father wanted them to welcome into their convents countless Jews persecuted by the Germans. Among them were the Religious Teachers Filippini.[1]

These Sisters extended their hospitality to the Jews who lived with them in three convents in Rome: Via Caboto, Via delle Fornaci, and Via Botteghe Oscure. The latter was known as the Ginnasi Palace, an imposing structure donated by Pope Gregory XVI in 1836.

There were several entrances and a large courtyard. One of the wings was used for young boarders in the school. The students came from different regions of Italy and ranged from kindergarten to normal school.

Boarders were sent home to their families when war began, because the Sisters could not assume responsibility for their safety. By closing the boarding school, an entire wing was made available for living quarters. It was this wing—dormitories, dining room, laundry, bathrooms—that served to house the Jewish people who sought refuge. Approximately sixty guests had comfortable quarters. The building also provided a basement that resembled the catacombs, where everyone gathered during air raids.

The superior general at this time was Sister Teresa Saccucci, who had served as provincial superior in the United States. Her charity was extended to all; her hospitality was genuine. She risked her life as well as the lives of the Sisters for whom she was responsible, while responding to the call of the Vatican to assist the Jews who appealed for help. God blessed her efforts and those of all the Sisters; with their guests they were spared the concentration camps. (*See* Appendix, Document IV, pp. 222–223.)

The Religious Teachers Filippini also cared for many Jewish families at Via delle Fornaci, near the Vatican. Women and children occupied the rooms of the Sisters on the last floor in order to be better protected. Their husbands and other men were domiciled in the Vatican. The Sisters moved to the first floor. They also housed thirty Sisters of Saint Clare whose convent was destroyed, as well as the Sisters from Frascati and many orphans from Nettuno. Sister Carolina Sorge related that the Superior, Sister Anna Nuccitelli, miraculously provided for all their necessities.

Sister Maria Pucci, an eyewitness, was in another convent of the Religious Teachers Filippini, located on Via Caboto, not far from the Jewish ghetto of Portico d'Ottavia, Rome. She testified that there were twenty-five Jews hidden: the elderly, married couples, and children. Of the group, fifteen were barricaded in the auditorium with supplies and merchandise from their stores. They also brought the personal belongings they were able to salvage. In the area of the kindergarten there were two rooms, well fortified, where the others resided.

An Italian army captain and his lieutenant were accommodated in a room where the Sisters kept their linens, next to the chapel and the Sisters' dormitories. The Sisters knew that the Nazis and Fascists were searching for them. Italians professed to be Germany's allies; the Germans felt betrayed.

It was a terrible risk for Sister Augusta Basili, the superior, but she trusted in Divine Providence. Whenever German voices were heard or there was an air raid, the Jews would rush to the trap door and hide under the stage. The Sisters tried to console them, giving them loving care which to this day has not been forgotten. From time to time, the Sisters are reminded by Jewish merchants that their relatives survived the war because of the hospitality they had received. The Sisters recall that their Jewish guests sought comfort by joining them in prayer. Everyone's prayers were mixed with tears.

"I was teaching history in January 1944," Sister Maria Pucci reminisced, "when several children yelled, 'Sister, look what is in the air!'" Two airplanes, one German and one Italian (anti-Fascist) had collided. All the windows of the classroom were broken, and the children were pushing the glass away with their hands. Then they ran to me crying for help and I embraced them, consoling them as we ran to a shelter that the Vatican had prepared for us.

"Not long after there was another sad day for the Ostiense section of Rome. Many people died when the Germans bombed a train. There was a factory of oxygen tanks nearby. Instead of bombing the factory, the bombs hit the bridge where the train passed. The entire area was engulfed in flames.

"On March 3rd, bombing of greater intensity took place. Many homes were destroyed and people remained buried in the ruins. Eighteen people on the corner of Via Caboto died with the bombing of their homes. That morning many people were in the Church of Saint Benedict. The pastor, Don Giovanni Gregorini, exhorted the faithful to return home because the Germans were in the vicinity. No sooner did they leave when bombs hit the church. It was completely destroyed. Only the crucifix on the wall remained. Damage was done to the convent, but all the Jews and the two Sisters in charge—Sister Maria Segreti and Sister Genoveffa Mucci—were saved. Together they prayed and thanked God."

Seventy-year-old Attilio Di Veroli and his grandson, Michele, who had celebrated his fifteenth birthday in February, were among the Jews who remained with the Sisters. On March 23, 1944, they decided to return to their home on Via Portico d'Ottavia.

On that day thirty-three German SS police were killed during the partisan bombing attack on Via Rasella in Rome. They were recruits from the South Tyrol which had been part of Italy until 1943, when it was annexed to the Third Reich. As a reprisal, the Germans ordered ten Italians, who were in prison for political offenses, to be killed for each SS man who died.

To fill the quota, the Germans included seventy-seven Jewish victims from Roman prisons and five other prisoners, though they had not committed political crimes. The 335 men and boys were tied together and driven to the Ardeatine Caves along the Appian Way to the catacombs of San Callisto. The victims were sent into the Caves in groups of five. Following the orders of SS Colonel Herbert Kappler, German soldiers made the prisoners kneel on the growing pile of corpses. They shot them in the back of the head. The Caves were then sealed with explosives.

Attilio and his grandson had tried to hide, but were soon discovered and had been forced to join a truckload of prisoners. One of their relatives saved himself and described what had happened. The following day, Michele, Attilio's grandson, was the youngest victim among the 335 Italians who were victims of the Nazi atrocity in the Ardeatine massacre.

Sister Domenica Mitaritonna relates that the Sisters closed one section of the Via Caboto school so that no one, not even the children who attended, would see the Jewish families they were protecting. A mother, father, and four children abandoned their "Trattoria." Another family consisted of mother, father, seven girls, and one boy. The Sisters taught during the day and at night they would take turns to watch for the Germans.

One night a truck stopped near the convent. The Jews were alerted and ran to safety beneath the stage. As the German soldiers were preparing to enter, a man suffering from asthma was at the window of his apartment. He heard someone say, "This is an armory. Let's take it." Immediately the sick man shouted, "It's not an armory. No, indeed. It's a school, an elementary school." With that, the German soldiers departed.

After the Liberation, a Jewish child was given the name Ornella Lucia, to honor the Sisters' Foundress, Saint Lucy. Some Sisters also recalled how each night a young girl would be seen with outstretched arms as she sang the psalms. Sister Domenica awakened the others so that they might witness the intensity of the fifteen-year-old girl's prayer. It was a touching scene.

During this period everyone was suffering unbearable hardships. Food was scarce; bread was rationed; the Nazis were everywhere. The Religious Teachers Filippini had to evacuate their convents in Anzio, Nettuno, Terracina, and elsewhere. They were received with open arms when they arrived in Rome and were a source of encouragement for one another.

Sister Lucia Mangone witnessed Jews being pushed onto trucks for deportation while their wives and children cried. To save themselves these women gathered what they could and came to the convent of Arco dei Ginnasi. They abandoned their homes in the ghetto near the hospital of Fatebenefratelli, where the Jewish synagogue is located, and sought asylum with the Sisters to avoid being sent to a concentration camp.

Not long ago, Sister Lucia Marino met two Jewish women near

the Church of the Stigmata in Rome, who reminded her of the help she had given them during the war.

Several Religious Teachers Filippini had taught in the United States. They now belonged to the Italian Province and resided in the generalate which was located in Via Arco dei Ginnasi. Sister Assunta Crocenzi was one of them. She was an intelligent and attractive woman with a unique personality. For many years she had been a teacher and administrator in the United States. When she returned to Italy she served as general treasurer.

Sister Assunta's dynamism and courage served her well. Her faithful assistant, Sister Lucia, used to accompany the treasurer as she searched for supplies. She related that Sister Assunta not only provided food for more than 100 Jews living with the Sisters, but she also took care of their personal needs. One day, she wanted a supply of rice from northern Italy. She demanded an appointment with the German general in charge of the occupation of Rome. After a brief encounter, she received permission to leave the city. She was authorized to obtain all the rice she required in order to feed the Sisters and children under their care. She returned with a truckload.

During the Nazi occupation of Rome, in order to obtain food from the Germans, Sister Assunta succeeded in becoming friendly with some soldiers. One day she invited them to the convent at Arco dei Ginnasi for dinner. Instead of going to No. 20 entrance, they went to No.19 where the Jews were living. The Sister on guard duty refused to let them in that door. After much gesticulation, they finally understood they would not be allowed to enter and proceeded to the No. 20 entrance at Largo Santa Lucia.

In order to get supplies—potatoes, beans, and similar provisions—Sister Assunta would visit the convents from which Sisters had been obliged to flee. Along the way the vehicle would be checked by the police who did not realize the Sisters had food hidden under a mattress in the truck, as well as under their long habits.

The Sisters were terrified of being caught by the Nazis. When police would approach for inspection, they pretended to be asleep. The Sisters realized that they could be bombed by the Americans or shot by the Nazis. The men who drove these trucks were also risking their lives as they delivered food supplies to the convents. At the marketplace, Sister Assunta would number the cases of food and pray they would not be intercepted. It was a frightening experience whenever they would go to the market.

When he was about fourteen years old, Dr. Francesco Crocenzi, Sister Assunta's nephew, frequently visited her at the convent in Rome. She was fearless. He recalled having heard her order food by telephone. She used a special code. For example, she needed ten *prosciut ti*; the conversation was: "Sir, we wish to have ten *violins.*" Food was rationed and she could have been arrested for making such purchases. She also knew that telephone conversations were being checked by the Germans.

Sister Lelia Orlandi was stationed in Cave. She related that in November of 1942, during a heavy rainfall, the doorbell rang. Sister Lucia De Angelis greeted three Jews who begged for hospitality: Signora Capon, whose maiden name was Coen, was accompanied by her husband, Luciano, and their one-year-old daughter. They explained that they were in danger and that even the Sisters would be endangered by their presence.

Clara Coen-Capon and her daughter remained at the convent, and the Sisters arranged for Luciano, an engineer, to stay with the Franciscan Fathers at the nearby church. Clara wore the Sisters' habit in order to disguise herself. Her husband visited frequently. They became part of the community. The little girl called the older nuns "nonna" (grandma) and the younger ones "zia" (aunt).

The Sisters agreed that, should there be an inspection, they would say the girl was an orphan. This family remained in Cave until the end of the war. They gratefully attributed their safety to the Sisters. They returned often to thank them and were most affectionate.

On April 25, 1979, Clara Coen-Capon wrote the following: "During the racial persecutions in the early part of November 1943, I was the guest of the Religious Teachers Filippini in Cave, where the Superior, Sister Lucia, not having known us, but only out of the goodness of her heart, full of compassion for my little one-year-old daughter whom I held in my arms, offered me her habit so that I could remain disguised with them and save myself. She showed such motherly, loving solicitude toward us.

"A few days later my husband came with the morning newspaper which carried Mussolini's statement that the death penalty would be given to anyone who protected the Jews.

"My husband, who was a saintly, altruistic man, unwillingly

decided to take us away so as not to compromise the dear Sisters. After thirty-seven years, I still have before my eyes the vision of this loving Sister Lucia who, after listening to my husband and reflecting for a moment, exclaimed with great determination: 'We shall share your fate, remain here!'"

This was the story Sister Lucia told during a TV interview when she celebrated her 100th birthday. Shortly afterward, a Rumanian family who had seen the interview contacted Sister Lucia in order to thank her for what she had done to save their Jewish brethren. They brought gifts to express their gratitude—a beautiful handmade centerpiece from Rumania and a box of cookies.

At Monte Mario on the Via Trionfale, four young Jewish women took refuge in the convent. One was married, and her husband would come to visit her while the young Sisters kept guard. The women had habits in their rooms, should the need arise for them to hide from the Germans.

Sister Maria Vitrulli said that also in Gubbio there were Jews in the convent. The Germans came to search the building. When the Sisters assured them that there were no Jews, they left. She recalled that, because two officials were killed, the Germans collected forty Jews from the local area, made them dig their own graves, and then shot them in retaliation.

When the Americans came to Anzio, there were sixteen Sisters in the convent. Ten went to live with their families; six went to the generalate at Via Botteghe Oscure in Rome where they taught children whose schools were bombed. Sister Antonietta Bonavoglia was one of the teachers.

There, too, the daughter and the owner of the store "Anticoli" were housed with the Sisters. Other family groups of four to eight members were: Conigliani, Corrado, Di Castro, Di Segni, Di Veroli, Fatucci, Greco, Pavoncelli, Piperno, Sermoneta, Sonnino, Spagnoletti, Zarfati. Meals were served by Sister Adele Tedesco and Sister Alba Di Lauro.

A diary in the archives of the Religious Teachers Filippini shows the following entry, dated June 5, 1944: "Today began the exodus of the Jewish refugees. Over 60 women and children occupied the area designated for students, and also several rooms in the convent."[2] The June 8th notation speaks about the opening of a soup kitchen where the Sisters served meals.

When the Americans arrived, the Jews found a woman who had betrayed many of their friends and family members. She was a Jewish spy for the Germans. The following day, a group of Jews who had succeeded in avoiding the Holocaust captured the spy and took her to the ghetto, yelling "Pantèra nera! Pantèra nera!" They dragged her through the streets of the neighborhood. The Sisters were able to observe the scene from the convent windows at Via Gaetani.

The "Black Panther" was an eighteen-year-old girl, one of the most notorious of the Roman informers. Her name was Celeste Di Porto. She was nicknamed Stella (Star) by her family because of her great beauty. Her family had lost several relatives during the October roundup. Yet she became directly responsible for the arrests of fifty Jews. Twenty-six on her list were men and boys murdered during the Ardeatine Caves massacre of March 24, 1944.

Soon after the war a group of Jewish women visited the Religious Teachers Filippini at Via Arco dei Ginnasi. They came to express their gratitude and wanted to leave tangible proof of their appreciation. Their gift of love was a six-foot statue of Our Lady of Fatima. It was installed in the area where these refugees had lived with the Sisters. The statue has since occupied a place of honor in the very heart of Rome.

In 1994 when interviewed by RAI-TV for *A Debt to Honor,* a documentary on the Jews in Italy during the German occupation in Rome, Sister Giuseppina Coscia explained that the statue honoring Our Lady of Fatima, donated by these guests, is a daily reminder of their prayers and sufferings during World War II.

Sister Giuseppina attests that there were about sixty Jews at Arco dei Ginnasi. The group remained for almost two years. These women were given the religious garb and would wear it whenever there was danger of a Nazi raid. One day a young man visited one of the guests. As he left the convent, the Germans captured him and sent him to a concentration camp.

After the war, the Religious Teachers Filippini in the United States continued to help Pope Pius XII take care of the poor. A letter from the Vatican secretary of state, dated June 18, 1947, to Mother Ninetta refers to cases of supplies that had arrived within a few months from America: "29 cases on the ship, *City of Athens*; 60 cases on the *Exiria*; 90 cases on the *Waimea*." In the same letter the secretary of state requested soccer balls to help children adjust in the aftermath of the war.

Not too long ago, one of the Sisters applied for a teaching position. During the examination by members of a commission for a Concorso Magistrale, she sensed a certain atmosphere of indifference toward her. In an abrupt manner, one of the professors asked her to identify herself. When she said "Maestra Pia Filippini," he immediately inquired, "Arco dei Ginnasi?" She answered in the affirmative and the entire commission wanted to know why he asked the question.

The professor responded: "I shall always be grateful to the Religious Teachers Filippini for having saved the life of my Jewish wife. During the war she was hidden in their convent until the war ended."

Because of their efforts to alleviate the sufferings of World War II victims in Italy, the Religious Teachers Filippini in Morristown, New Jersey, received this acknowledgment from the Holy Father: "To Our Beloved Daughter Mother Ninetta Jonata—Your generous charity, beloved daughter, towards the suffering poor of Italy has been brought to Our attention. It has helped Us to widen the field of Our benefactions. With grateful affection, then, We impart to you and to your community Our Apostolic Blessing. From the Vatican, December 31, 1949, Pius pp. XII."

Again, March 26, 1951, in his own hand, Pope Pius XII wrote: "We desire to express to you, beloved daughter, Our lively appreciation of the truly charitable spirit which animated you and those associated with you in the generous donation of relief supplies which you have forwarded to the Vatican. It is always a source of consolation to Us to be reminded, through charitable acts such as yours, that Our children in America share Our great concern for the plight of those unfortunate souls who are living in circumstances of wretchedness and misery."

2. Redemptorist Fathers

Alphonsus De Liguori (1696–1787) was a prolific writer on moral, theological, and ascetical subjects. After practicing canon and civil law for several years, he joined the Oratorians and was ordained in 1726. Six years later he founded the Redemptorist Fathers, dedicated to mission work in rural areas among the poor. As bishop of Sant'Agata dei Goti, he inaugurated a program designed to reform the clergy, monasteries, and the entire diocese. During the last years of his life, he experienced visions and made predictions that were later fulfilled. Saint Alphonsus was canonized in 1839. Pope Pius IX declared him Doctor of the Church in 1871.

During World War II, the Church of San Gioacchino in Prati, staffed by the Redemptorist Fathers, was often the scene of Resistance activities. When it was no longer possible to protect Jews and anti-Fascists in the parish facilities, Pietro Lestini arranged for a group of about thirty to seal themselves in the attic of the cupola. They could only use a cord through the rose window to receive food and remove excrement with pails during the night.

This mysterious operation required both the organizers and the participants to swear to secrecy. When they occupied the cupola, the refugees were "walled in" because the Nazis had begun to requisition and search all convent property. Directed by Pietro Lestini, who was an engineer, with the help of candlelight the refugees succeeded in bringing bricks and mortar to the cupola under cover of darkness. By morning the construction was completed.

On October 24, 1943, the Redemptorist Fathers held a meeting with the entire community to discuss whether they should permit this rescue operation to continue in their parish. The majority voted in favor while one priest, Father Nobili, fearful of German reprisals, threatened

118

to alert the police. Father Antonio Dressino, the superior and pastor, raised his voice and severely reprimanded him.

Domenico Pizzato, the parish sacristan, was at risk daily as he sent food to the cupola. The food was provided by Sister Margherita Bernes, of the Daughters of Charity. She was treasurer of the convent and had worked for ten years among the people of Prati. Fearless, she succeeded in obtaining food from the local population who admired her. For seven months, even when bread was rationed, she managed to provide food for those hidden in the cupola of San Gioacchino.

The area of the cupola was cold and humid and especially suffocating in the summer. The floor was of sand and had been inhabited by spiders, flies, pigeons; shingles were loose so that drops of rain would penetrate. The refugees had little space to move around or to sleep. There were books, writing paper, newspapers, and pails for personal needs. They could not use the center area because it was not safe. Sketches on the walls depict the life they led.

The Jews, soldiers, and others who sought refuge were accommodated wherever there was space in the parish of San Gioacchino. Three Jews in the theater were to act as custodians in the event the Germans or Fascists would appear. They carried dust cloths at all times and would begin cleaning when there was noise in the area. Life for the refugees was difficult. A Redemptorist priest even censored their mail to eliminate any reference that might unwittingly reveal their whereabouts. But life in Prati was very difficult for everyone. Food was scarce. The Nazis and Fascists had infiltrated everywhere. Teenage Fascists terrorized the area.

Pietro Lestini's daughter Giuliana was a student at the University of Rome. Together they printed material encouraging others to support the Resistance and distributed leaflets throughout the area until the arrival of the Americans. In her book entitled *S.A.S.G. Sezione Aerea San Gioacchino* (Aerial Section San Gioacchino), Giuliana Lestini writes about her father "as having sentiments of solidarity and altruism that forced him to work clandestinely, to defend those persecuted because of race, religion, political ideas and love for a free and democratic country; it was a battle fought against every form of violence, aimed only at keeping as many as possible from torture, imprisonment, death."[3]

When he learned that some Nazi-Fascist soldiers were snooping around the Church of San Gioacchino, Pietro Lestini alerted Father

Dressino and Sister Margherita. Fearing the hidden ones would be discovered, they decided to remove the men one by one from the cupola.

Pietro Lestini had assumed full responsibility for the cupola project. With implicit faith in his judgment, Father Dressino instructed the
Redemptorist Fathers to say, if questioned by the police, that they were
totally ignorant of the project. He quoted His Holiness, Pope Pius XII,
who had advised them to use prudence in order to protect their religious community from German reprisals.

Meanwhile Lestini, Vice President of the Catholic Association of
San Gioacchino parish, provided clothing for all who came for help.
Food was made available by Sister Margherita who looked like a "fly-
ing nun" with her large "steamboat" headdress. On March 17, 1996,
Pietro Lestini, his daughter Giuliana, and Father Dressino were hon-
ored as "Just Among Nations" by the Israeli Ambassador, Yehuda
Millo.

The problem of hiding people increased when the Vatican sent
individuals who were in precarious situations—Jews, anti-Fascists,
political prisoners—to seek asylum. Every inch of space was used for
the permanent residents; others had to move on through the countryside where Giuliana and her grandmother helped them escape. Two
from Palermo were afraid to leave, so they remained to care for the
fields and animals, and others waited for the coast to be clear and danger averted. All needed encouragement for they were tired, sad, and
frightened. They knew that Nazis and Fascists had infiltrated Prati.
Under the direction of the Fascist official Peter Koch, a specialist in
torture, the Nazis and Fascists increased their search for deserters of
the Italian army and for Jews. Young men who tried to avoid military
duty were shot. Aiming especially to capture the partisan leaders, they
succeeded in locating Sandro Pertini and Giuseppe Saragat, both future
presidents of the Italian Republic, who were imprisoned.

The Nazis were enlisting young men for forced labor in
Germany. Signora Moscati, one of the residents with Sister Margherita,
begged Lestini to protect her fifteen-year-old son Leopoldo. Lestini
placed Poldo Moscati and his father in the little theater of the com-
pound. Then they were transferred to the cupola, but his father, who
suffered from claustrophobia, could not bear the confinement and left
before the wall was completely sealed. Months passed and finally
Poldo's mother arranged for him to go to the Collegio "Cristo Re,"

where he remained until the Liberation. The entire Moscati family was saved. Theirs was a happy reunion!

Lieutenant Clemente Confalone, who came from the Amalfi coast, was also with Poldo in the "cupola." Because of his meek religious spirit, some of the more worldly and cynical group of Romans— Francesco Papini, Aldo Antonini, and Giorgio De Simone—made him the butt of their jokes. However, Confalone succeeded in imposing on them the daily recitation of the rosary and spoke about divine goodness and the present evil among humanity. He later became a priest and pastor of his home parish in Maiori.

Giorgio De Simone was an architect, artist, and caricaturist. With Aldo Antonini, an artist, he covered the walls in the "cupola" with sketches and paintings depicting the character and appearance of their companions as they prayed, played cards, chatted, read books and newspapers. They made a calendar and map of the area on the walls. Franco Papini kept a diary in which he recorded Lestini's visits bringing the latest news, packages, letters from their families. He also described the difficulties in taking care of their personal needs.

Gigi and Aldo prepared designs and poems to express their gratitude to Sister Margherita, Father DeAngelis, and Father Roberto as well as the sacristan, Domenico Pizzato. Confalone wrote a letter of appreciation to the pastor, Father Dressino. The incomplete diary ends with the script of a theatrical performance they prepared in the "cupola."

After three months of enclosure, the group prepared for Christmas Mass. They appeared with clean clothes, hair and beards groomed, and joined people for the first time. The dinner took place in the convent dining room and was as close as possible to the traditional Christmas fare. It was followed by the performance of the "cupola" theater group.

Another extraordinary helper for Lestini's project was Mother Benedetta Saulo, an American citizen who was the superior of the Baptistine Sisters. She was noted for her dynamism as she went flying from country to country, bringing priceless assistance. These Sisters used their generalate to hide refugees who also occupied their novitiate at the Madonna del Riposo outside the city of Rome. No means of transportation was available for two kilometers; the Villa was hidden and protected by iron gates; there were other buildings on the grounds. After September 8th, Mother Benedetta Saulo gave Pietro Lestini one of the buildings for his refugees.

These Sisters also protected a group of the military fleeing from the German front of Cassino. The soldiers were on the way to join the partisans in Abruzzi. In Acilia they gave work and assistance to soldiers sent by Lestini. They collaborated in obtaining the Hotel Santa Chiara near Piazza della Minerva as a Baptistine convent in order to protect the refugees who needed temporary lodgings: Jewish women with children, wives of persecuted anti-Fascists, and other refugees from the south.

Don Francesco Morosini was a member of the St. Vincent DePaul Society and chaplain of the partisans from the Monte Mario section. He was betrayed by a certain Dante Bruna for a reward of 70,000 lire and imprisoned on January 4, 1943, in Cell 328 of the Regina Coeli prison. He was shot by the Germans on April 3rd at Forte Bravetta.

Father Morosini not only forgave his betrayer, but offered his life for the intentions of Pope Pius XII. Monsignor Luigi Traglia assisted him as he celebrated Mass. He was then led to the courtyard and the squadron assigned shot in the air while an official aimed at his head. Not even the Pope, who sent a special request to the German commandant to suspend the execution, could save him. His death was a warning to all religious who were protecting refugees and helping the partisans.

Fighting between anti-Fascists and Germans culminated with the incident of Via Rasella which led to the reprisal of the Ardeatine Caves. The situation in Rome became chaotic. The king and Badoglio had abandoned the city. Thousands of soldiers dropped their arms. Civilians joined forces with the remaining soldiers to fight the Nazis who were in control of Rome.

3. Fatebenefratelli

At Santo Spirito Hospital on the Isola Tiberina, Rome, the Fatebenefratelli saved the lives of many Jews and political refugees during the German occupation.

Cesare Lombroso founded the Fatebenefratelli in 1539 in Granada, Spain. He is now known as San Giovanni di Dio. Within a century these religious Brothers were administrators of 224 hospitals in several countries of the world. Everywhere hygienic principles and respect for the invalid were introduced and maintained throughout the centuries.

San Giovanni di Dio has been called "the creator of the modern hospital." With San Camillo de Lellis, he is the patron of the sick and of hospitals, as well as the patron of nurses and their associations.

In recent years, under the leadership of Fra Eustachio Kugle, the Fatebenefratelli continued to witness remarkable growth. One of the first hospitals he founded was in Ratisbona, Bavaria, a city on the shores of the Danube.

It was in Munich, the capital of Bavaria, that Adolf Hitler gave life to the National Socialist movement that took possession of all Germany.

When hostilities broke out with the invasion of Poland on September 1, 1939, the "Gestapo" in Bavaria suddenly entered the Fatebenefratelli convents, arrested all the religious, and submitted them to interminable interrogations and torture. The Brothers were classified as enemies of the Third Reich, political conspirators, and corruptors of youth.

The bombardments in Bavaria on August 17, 1943, caused much destruction. Fra Eustachio remained calm during this adversity, praying in the hospital chapel. Just a few feet away, 1,200 people were buried under the ruins. In the two Fatebenefratelli hospitals, everyone was convinced they were saved because of his prayers.

Fra Eustachio opened the doors of convents and hospitals to all those who needed assistance without regard to their religious or political beliefs. As their superior he instructed the Brothers: "In each person let us try to see, love, and serve the Lord Jesus, who considers done to him, whatever we do to one of our brothers."

Celebrating the Jewish Passover in the concentration camp at Ferramonti (1942).

Title page of subsidies and payments made to Jews who were freed from internment by the Commune of Lonigo (Vicenza) in February 1943.

4. Salesian Fathers

The founder of the Salesians, Saint John Bosco (1815–1888), was ordained a priest and began his work with neglected boys in Turin, Italy. When asked to give up his care of the boys, he resigned as chaplain and, with his mother, opened a refuge for them. He succeeded with the boys, using much love, encouraging them personally, and exercising a minimum of restraint and discipline.

John Bosco's work expanded and the need for dependable assistants led him to found the Society of St. Francis de Sales. By the time of his death in 1888, he had established sixty-four Salesian foundations in Europe and the Americas, and there were almost 800 priests. He had also founded, in 1872, the Daughters of Our Lady, Help of Christians, to care for poor and neglected girls. He was canonized in 1934.

In describing the work of the Salesians with the youth of Rome during the Nazi occupation (September 1943–June 1944), Don Ernesto Berta stated: "About 274 boys were cared for in our Roman institutions, with little or no tuition, while 292 persecuted individuals, among whom were many Jews, especially young people, were given room and board in our institutions in Rome and elsewhere in Lazio."[4]

For nine months the city of Rome was besieged. Some people did not leave their homes; others changed domicile every day. There were those disguised who lived in convents and wore religious garb; others who were in hospitals had unnecessary operations or casts. But Rome did not capitulate. Its inhabitants resisted to the very end.

The film *Roma città aperta* by Roberto Rossellini depicts the situation. With Anna Magnani and Aldo Fabrizi, one witnesses the countless deaths, deportations, bombardments. Not only the Vatican, but almost every church and convent came to the assistance of those in need of protection.

Andrea Riccardi in his book, *La Chiesa a Roma durante la*

Resistenza, writes: "Ecclesiastical hospitality represents one of the greatly significant phenomena...clergy and religious lived their commitment during the German occupation, risking not only their own lives, but also the institutions where hospitality was offered, and sometimes even the Vatican's position of neutrality."[5]

Although Rome was declared an "open city," over 7,000 people died during the German occupation and the Allied bombings; countless young Italians were sent to work camps, partisans were shot, and Jews were deported.

The catacombs of San Callisto on Via Appia Antica consist of thirty hectares of land belonging to the Holy See. Two Salesian communities were located on this property: San Callisto with a group of philosophy students and San Tarcisio for agrarian and elementary school students. Groups of refugees protected by the Salesians were living in the catacombs: Jews, Germans, Italians, Americans. Each group had different entrances to the catacombs. Since they were scheduled for meals at different hours, they did not meet one another. A series of bells served as an alarm system in case the Germans entered the catacombs despite its Vatican status.

Guns and ammunition were stored in the catacombs by Don Fernando Giorgi, an enterprising "partisan." Don Michele Valentini also belonged to the Resistance movement.

Only recently has knowledge been revealed about how the bodies of the Ardeatine victims were located. The Salesians kept no record. Don Francesco Motto, an Italian historian, has reconstucted the events in the review *Ricerche storiche salesiane.*[6]

Giuseppe Perrinella was a young Salesian seminarian in 1944. He recalled fifty years later how, together with five companions, he discovered the massacred victims. With him were Enrico Bolis, Giovanni Fagiolo, Carlo Ganci, Antonio Fabris, and Federico Dovis.

There had been a great deal of commotion on March 24, 1944; that day local traffic had been controlled by Nazi soldiers. Toward evening, they had heard an explosion. It was Giovanni Fagiolo's suggestion that they investigate the Ardeatine Caves where they had seen Germans for several days.

The group of seminarians followed a half-hidden red cord the Germans had used. Fortunately, the explosion had not completely closed the entrance to the Caves. They climbed a ladder near the entrance and looked through a small opening on the top of the cave.

Dozens of bodies lay on top of each other. Shocked by the terrible scene, they returned to the seminary and told Don Giorgi who was in close contact with the partisans.

Don Giorgi recalled the terrible incident: "When the young men reported about the bodies in the cave, I immediately informed the partisan command by clandestine radio. Don Valentini went to the Vatican and spoke with Monsignor Montini, the future Pope Paul VI, who said the Vicariate would contact the Germans. However, it was only in June, when the Americans liberated Rome, that I succeeded in bringing the first squadrons to the scene."[7]

Daniel Counihan was present at the Ardeatine Caves in 1944 when the bodies of the victims were dug up. One priest, Don Pappagallo, was among the dead. As a reporter Counihan questioned people who had knowledge of the massacre, including a man who had seen it from a hiding place.[8]

The sealing of the Caves with explosives in the late afternoon would indicate that the march to the Caves was already underway when a Vatican secretary wrote a memo reporting a telephone call at 10:15 A.M., on March 24th. The caller, who described the bombing, said: "Countermeasures are still not known; it is thought, however, that for every German killed ten Italians will be executed."

The action of the Communist-directed GAP (Gruppi Azione Patriottica) bombing of the German unit on Via Rasella was regarded as a direct challenge to the German high command in Berlin. According to the reprisal order, issued in Hitler's name, the reprisal had to be completed within twenty-four hours. The executions were carried out in secrecy.

Counihan has a vivid memory of reactions and details of his interviews. In an article dated October 23, 1981, he wrote that at the time no one he interviewed ever suggested the Pope knew the Nazis' intentions. Indeed, Rolf Hochhuth's *The Deputy,* Saul Friedländer's *Pius XII and the Third Reich,* and Robert Katz's *Death in Rome* have no basis for their implications that he did.

The record of the Pontiff's concern for the lives of unfortunate victims who fell into German and neo-Fascist hands during the occupation eloquently speaks of his sensitivity.

The Pope had intervened on behalf of many captured Resistance leaders, including Bruno Buozzi, Giacomo Matei, Leon Ginzburg, Giuseppe LoPresti, Enzo Malatesta, Gianfranco Mastei, General

Angelo Oddone, Mario Sbardella, Carlo Scalara, Stefano Siglienti, and Antonello Trombadori, the chief of the GAP in Rome.

He had also spoken on behalf of thirty-five of the Ardeatine victims prior to the tragic incident. The Pope's readiness to intervene for Resistance members would have impelled him to do so again, if he had been aware of the massacre before it took place.

The German embassy to the Vatican withdrew into discreet silence, and on March 29th, von Weizsäcker's office said that inquiries about persons jailed by the Germans should be addressed to the German police command, SS Lieutenant Colonel Herbert Kappler. At no time was a direct reference to the Ardeatine slaughter made.

Don Giorgi also worked with Monsignor Hugh O'Flaherty, the Irish Vatican priest who had created a clandestine chain to rescue, hide, and give new identity cards to Jews, former political prisoners, and soldiers who fled the Nazis. A small group of priests, who had distinguished themselves by helping Monsignor O'Flaherty, met with Pius XII on Easter Sunday in 1945. In a deeply moving tribute, the Pope thanked them for the assistance given to the Jews, who are "particularly dear to my heart."

The director of the Pius XI Institute of the Salesian Fathers was Don Francesco Antonioli. With a student enrollment of about 250, four-fifths of whom were boarders, the professional, trade, elementary, and middle schools were staffed by more than forty Salesians and over twenty lay teachers. Some of the protagonists—teachers, staff, and students—have written about their experiences at the Institute during this period.

In the surrounding area, over forty bombs fell one day, two of them in the courtyard just a few feet away from the school. Buildings were burning everywhere, and there were over 1,000 victims both civilian and military. In the villa, windows were broken and damage done, but everyone was safe.

The Salesians have a priceless document that lists the Jews who were saved, ages seven to twenty-two, with their true name, age, address, class attended, length of attendance, and sometimes their paternity and provenance. Parents who could afford tuition made monthly payments. The list mentions seventy young Jewish students with family names, such as: Anticoli, Astrologo, Vasco, Camerino, Cavalescu, Caviglia, Delorme, Di Castro, Di Nepi, Di Porto, Dresdner, Dereghello, Fuà, Funaro, Levi, Lowenwirth, Menasci, Mieli, Pajalich,

Piperno, Procaccia, Pugliese, Rossi, Scharbarci, Sinigaglia, Sonnino, Tagiacozzo, Templer, Terracina, Trevi, Varon, Volterra. Listed also are four Jews between ages thirty-seven and fifty-seven. Working among the "poor and abandoned youth," the Salesians followed their saintly founder's example. They combined Christian charity with human solidarity.

Former students recall their daily schedule which included sports, theatrical performances, prayers, and singing of parts of the Mass, e.g., the *Gloria* and *Sanctus*, as well as hymns to the Madonna and to Don Bosco. The directress of the Center for Jewish Culture in Rome, Bice Migliau, testified that Cesare Pugliese, her eighteen-year-old uncle, gave Hebrew lessons to Don Gamez. Sergio Anticoli recalls that, in March, he and his companions took refuge in the catacombs of San Callisto. Should the Germans arrive, the older students were given emergency means of escape.

Considering the scarcity of food in Rome, the students were well nourished. Don Alessandrini, the treasurer, succeeded in obtaining necessary provisions by keeping in contact with the Germans occupying the Salesian Institute "Mandrione."

At one time the SS and Fascists planned a surprise visit to round up the Jews and other refugees at the Salesian institution. The visit was suddenly cancelled. One reason was that they would have needed 300 men to surround it properly; the other was that they did not want additional problems. Rome was the city of the Catholic Church, and whatever happened there would concern the Pope himself.

Under the supervision of the Salesians there were hundreds of students attending Pius XI Institute, one-third of them Jews. It is difficult to believe that the Germans did not contemplate some disruption of the institution's tranquillity. Yet the SS did not interfere. Apparently they did not want a major clash with the Vatican.

On June 22, 1944, Rabbi André Zaoui, a captain in the French army, wrote to Pope Pius XII to say that he had visited the Pius XI Institute, and to thank him for saving so many Jews in Italy. His words resound the sentiments of all: "What a magnificent manifestation of fraternity, so great in its intimate simplicity. Israel will not forget you. Side by side you continue to accomplish your mission, practicing and teaching the law of love of God and neighbor."

And Israel did not forget the Pius XI Institute. Don Alessandrini, who helped care for so many young Jews, was officially recognized during the Holocaust ceremony that took place December 14, 1956, on Campidoglio in Rome.

The discourse on this occasion by Sergio Piperno, President of the Union of Italian Jewish Communities, summarizes the sentiments of the survivors of the Holocaust: "This manifestation would not be complete if today we would not renew our thanks to the Supreme Pontiff for his paternal solicitude during the entire Nazi occupation. He arranged for Jews to reside in the extraterritorial buildings of the Vatican, endeavored to have the harsh racial measures mitigated, sent entire Jewish families to convents where priests and nuns, notwith-standing the danger, assisted them." The audience echoed Piperno's praise of Pope Pius XII with cheers and a prolonged, standing ovation.

Both in cities and in rural areas throughout Italy, Italians defied Mussolini's orders and protected thousands of Jews until the armies of the Allies arrived. Italian civil authorities in some areas blocked orders to deport detained Jews, warned Jews of impending raids, and cooper-ated with individuals who were protecting Jews.

Joining them were the Salesians and other religious orders of Catholic priests and nuns who recognized the injustice of the persecu-tion of Jews. They rebelled against this infringement of the divine law of human fraternity and, following the example of Pope Pius XII, pro-tected their Jewish brethren from the horrors of the Nazi concentration camps.

Several years after the first concentration camp had been estab-lished at Dachau, near Munich, Germany (1933), other camps soon fol-lowed: Sachsenhausen (1936), Buchenwald (1937), Mauthausen (1938), Ravensbruck (1939).

Additional concentration camps were in Auschwitz-Birkenau, Belzec, Chelmno, Majdanek, Sobibor, Treblinka. Bergen-Belsen was a detention camp for POWs where thousands of victims died of starva-tion, exposure, and epidemics.

The only killing center with gas chamber and crematoria not on Polish soil was opened in October 1943 at San Sabba, Trieste. About 5,000 Jews, Italians, and Slovenian partisans were killed. San Sabba was liberated on May 2, 1945. (*See* Appendix VI, "Statistics on the Holocaust," pp. 231–238.)

5. Sisters of Sion

The Sisters of Our Lady of Sion were founded by Father Theodore Ratisbonne (1802–1884). He was born in Strasbourg of a well-assimilated German-Jewish family who converted to Catholicism. Ordained a priest in 1830, he consecrated his life to assist his Jewish brethren. Under his direction, Sophie Stouhlen and her companions undertook the education of young Jewish girls who asked to live as religious. They became known as the Sisters of Our Lady of Sion.

Theirs is a special mission: to promote understanding and justice for the Jewish community, and to keep alive in the Church the consciousness that in some mysterious way, Christianity is linked to Judaism from its origin to its final destiny. They witness to God's faithful love for the Jewish people and to his fidelity to the promises he revealed to the patriarchs and prophets of Israel for all humanity.

The apostolic life of the Sisters of Sion is characterized by a threefold commitment: to the Church, to the Jewish people, and to a world of justice, peace, and love.

Sister Luisa Girelli recalls that one morning they heard someone calling at the front gate on Via Garibaldi 28 in Rome. The mother superior went down and found several Jewish families begging to be let in, even if just for a few minutes, as they were afraid the Germans would capture them.

In an interview with Sy Rotter, producer of the Holocaust documentary *A Debt to Honor*,[9] Sister Luisa said: "Naturally we welcomed them in a spirit of fraternity. They were Jews and our religious order is founded on love for the Jewish people. One should help those in need, those who are being persecuted. Even if you are not a religious person, you would do it anyway. All you need is to be Christian, to have a little compassion, a little humanity."

Sister Dora, also a member of the Sisters of Sion, revealed that

131

over 200 Jews sought refuge at their convent on Via Garibaldi in 1943. Entire families came in small groups from the synagogue. The Sisters cooked for some Jews; others had a small kitchen where they took care of their own meals.

Sister Dora was twenty-one years old when she made her religious vows, December 14, 1943. Many Jews came to the chapel for this ceremony. Some of them sang with the Sisters' choir.

The Irish embassy was next door and Jews could escape easily should there be a raid. Word had spread that the Sisters' convent was considered Vatican property and they would be safe. There was a large enclosed area in the cellar where they were to hide when the bell at the gate would give the alarm signal.

One day Nazis and Fascists arrived to investigate. As they surrounded the garden, the mother superior went to them and requested proof that they had received permission to enter Vatican property. Neither the Nazis nor the Fascists had written authorization. They could not search the premises.

However, as they were leaving the garden, they captured one Jew. He was frightened when the alarm rang and jumped over the wall. Soon after, the Americans came and the young man was freed from prison.

Usually the Jews used the dining room for their Jewish services. Sister Filomena recalled that she not only prepared meals for this group but also had turns keeping guard. One night a Fascist wanted to enter. When she threatened to report him, he ran away.

It was difficult to find food for such a large group of refugees and for the Sisters who lived there. But since Sister Filomena had been Cardinal Pizzardo's maid before entering the convent, she decided to visit him to request more provisions. When he asked her what kind of food she needed, she bluntly said: "We need everything." The cardinal immediately contacted Mother Pascalina who, soon after, arrived with loads of food. She presented the Pope's card which read, "With the Pope's blessing for all."

Sister Dora and Sister Filomena are certain that their convent accepted Jewish refugees because the superior was notified by the Pope, through the secretary of the Congregation for Religious, to care for them.

Pope Pius XII visits bakery before distribution of bread to wartime victims.

Dining halls instituted by the Vatican for homeless and refugees.

Pope Pius XII in prayer after the Allied air raid of 1943 at San Lorenzo.

Pope Pius XII addressing the crowd after the bombing of Rome.

C. The Catholic Church

1. Vatican Policies

Neither the Nazis nor the Communists understood Vatican diplomacy. During World War II, when someone pointed out to Stalin the possibility of opposition and objection by the Vatican, the Russian leader asked: "How many divisions has the Vatican?"

In the newspaper *La Nazione* (Florence, February 5, 1996), Vladimir Naumov, Secretary of the Commission for the rehabilitation of people persecuted for political reasons, declared that about 200,000 priests were persecuted or killed under Stalin.

For several decades prior to the Fascist rule in 1922, Jews in Italy enjoyed a more liberal government. But anti-Semitism increased with Fascism. In March 1937, Pope Pius XI condemned racism in the papal encyclical *Mit brennender Sorge (With Burning Anxiety)*. When the racial laws were enacted in 1938, foreign Jews were arrested officially and sent to internment camps; Italian Jews were subjected to forced labor.

Hitler's hostility toward the Catholic Church was well known. The following appeared on May 31, 1937, in the Swiss newspaper *Basler Nationalzeitung*: "One thing is clear: the Third Reich does not desire a *modus vivendi* with the Catholic Church, but rather its destruction with lies and dishonor, in order to make room for a German Church in which the German race will be glorified."

One must not only examine the facts of Vatican policies, but also try to interpret the spirit of these policies. In vain did Pope Pius XI declare that the racial laws violated the Concordat. He wrote to Mussolini on November 4, 1938, and the following day he also sent a letter to Victor Emmanuel III. Three days later, the king transmitted the

Pope's letter to Mussolini. The Fascist leader did not answer, but he made it known that "the Vatican was demanding too much." If the Pope insisted, Mussolini was ready to fight the Church.

The Holy See presented an official note of protest for the violation of article 34 of the Concordat on November 13th. The controversy continued based on these arguments, not on the question of anti-Semitism. Speaking to a group of Belgians, the Holy Father said: "It is not possible for Christians to participate in anti-Semitism; anti-Semitism is inadmissible: spiritually we are all Semitic."

Eugenio Pacelli was elected Pope March 2, 1939. He began his pontificate with the problems of world peace, religious persecution, and racism. Representatives from the Nazi government did not attend his coronation ceremony. In fact, His Holiness was violently attacked by the official organ of the SS, *Das Schwarze Korps:* "We do not know if Pius XII, though young enough to see the new developments in Germany, is intelligent enough to sacrifice many old things of his institution. As nuncio and secretary of state, Eugenio Pacelli had little understanding of us; little hope is placed in him. We do not believe that as Pius XII he will follow a different path."

Mother Pascalina Lehnert was Pope Pius XII's faithful housekeeper. She recorded his words regarding Hitler in her memoirs: "Hitler is completely possessed; he destroys all that does not serve him; all that he says and writes has the mark of his egocentrism; this man is capable of stepping on corpses and eliminating everything that obstructs him. I cannot understand how so many in Germany, even among the best, do not comprehend this and do not learn from what he writes and says. Who among them has at least read his bloodcurdling book, *Mein Kampf?*"[1]

On July 28, 1938, Cardinal Eugenio Pacelli, addressing students of "Propaganda Fide," had stated that racism was not in the Italian tradition and condemned the fact that Italy had imitated Germany. *La Civiltà Cattolica* explained: "There is notable difference between German racism and that of the scholarly Fascist Italians. This confirms that Italian Fascism should not be confused with Nazism and German racism which is intrinsically and explicitly materialistic and anti-Christian."[2]

Two years later the Pope, concerned about the treatment of Jews who had converted, protested and objected to the Fascist government's racial laws.[3] He was determined to remain neutral rather than jeopardize those who were protecting the Jews in their homes and in convents.

When Pope Pius XII heard about the October 16th raid in Rome, he consulted his nephew, Prince Carlo Pacelli. He also asked Bishop Alois Hudal, rector of the German Catholic Church in Rome, to write a letter to General Rainer Stahel, German army commander of occupied Rome. Hudal's letter to Stahel was delivered the same day.

Bishop Hudal wrote a private warning of a possible public condemnation by the Pope when arrests were made by the SS: "In the interests of the good relations which have existed until now between the Vatican and the German High Command, I earnestly request that you order the immediate suspension of these arrests both in Rome and its vicinity. Otherwise I fear that the Pope will take a public stand against this action which would undoubtedly be used by the anti-German propagandists as a weapon against us."

That morning, the papal Secretary of State, Cardinal Luigi Maglione, on the Pope's order, summoned the German ambassador to protest the measures taken against people for the sole reason of their belonging to a particular race.

The Vatican's public comment on the events of October 16, 1943, appeared on October 25th in the Vatican newspaper *L'Osservatore Romano*. "As is well known, the Pontiff, after having vainly tried to prevent the outbreak of the war…has not desisted for one moment from employing all the means in his power to alleviate the suffering which, whatever form it may take, is the consequence of this cruel conflagration. With the augmentation of so much evil, the universal and paternal charity of the Supreme Pontiff has become, it might be said, ever more active; it knows neither boundaries nor nationality, neither religion nor race." But it was too late. Over 800 Roman Jews had been gassed and cremated two days earlier on October 23rd at Auschwitz.[4]

In principle the Germans respected Pius XII. Before the raid General Stahel placed "off limits" placards in German and in Italian on convents protected by the Holy See. The following was posted on some Vatican buildings: "Notice! This building is for religious purposes and belongs to the Vatican. House searching and looting are forbidden. The German Commandant, General Stahel."[5] But this protection did not last. Two months later, with the arrival of General Maeltzer, the situation changed.

In the early forties, regulations regarding cloistered areas in

Catholic convents and monasteries were very rigid. Religious orders would never have ignored their rules unless they had received proper authorization. At all times, friends and relatives were confined to a particular area designated for visitors. Not even one's parents would be permitted to enter the cloister. However, Pope Pius XII opened even these areas to provide hospitality for the persecuted Jews. Such hospitality could not have taken place if the Vatican had not spread the word for the Catholic Church to assist the Jews. According to a document published by Andrea Riccardi in *Vita e Pensiero* (Milan, 1975), the Vatican secretary of state wrote to all the superiors of religious orders on October 25, 1943, and encouraged them to help refugees.

In Rome, some convent buildings were designated "Zona Extraterritoriale Vaticana" and were protected by Vatican guards. Convents that did not have this protection had to be extremely careful and sometimes served only as temporary lodgings until a more permanent place could be found. Everything was secretive so as not to endanger the refugees and the religious who housed them. At times, only the superior knew who they were; records were generally not kept for fear of confiscation by the Nazis or Fascists. Many Salvatorian Fathers were not aware that their Superior General, Padre Pancrazio Pfeiffer, was the intermediary for various missions between Pius XII and the Germans.

A document dated October 23, 1943, found among the papers of the Vatican Secretariat of State, was written by the German Franciscan Father Aquilino Reichert, of St. Peter's Basilica. He asked that the following information be transmitted to the superiors of all convents: "The German military commandant, General Stahel, will probably respect the extraterritorial properties, the convents, etc., but certainly the SS, who have their own commanders, will not respect them. The attitude of the Vicariate, facilitating entrance for Jews, deserters, etc., does not seem prudent. The fact remains that ecclesiastical authorities are guided by their good heart and by principles of Christian charity that have permeated Italian customs. They must remember that with the SS, *one must be guided above all by prudence so as not to compromise the interests of the Church and the refugees by an act of badly understood charity.* The SS (who actually are about 300, but whose number will soon reach several thousand) will begin their raids in convents and in buildings of the Holy See; and this will cause grave damage and reprisals with respect to both parties." Reichert's personal advice for caution was not followed either by the Vicariate or the Pope.

The *Actes et documents…*(Vol. IX, p. 518, note 3) explain that the ecclesiastical properties were protected by an attestation of the German military authority. A copy of Bishop Hudal's report, informing the Secretariat of State about this protection, was written toward the middle of 1944. "The coordinating officer between the supreme command of the Führer and that of Italy, Colonel Baron von Veltheim, a Protestant, whom I know is an enemy of Nazism, has given me more than 550 declarations, signed by him with his seal, that convents, institutions, homes, etc., named by me were not to be inspected and visited by the military police. Today I can say that nothing has happened in any of the boarding schools, institutions, homes, etc., which have been provided with this declaration. Thousands of Jews, hidden in Rome, Assisi, Loreto, Padua, etc., were saved. I also sent these declarations to other countries."

Cardinal Paolo Dezza, S.J., summarized a very confidential report of an audience with Pope Pius XII. It appeared in the June 26, 1981, issue of the *Osservatore della Domenica:* "In December of 1942, I gave a retreat for the Holy Father in the Vatican. On that occasion I had a long audience in which Pius XII, speaking about the Nazi atrocities in Germany and in the other occupied countries, manifested his sorrow, his anguish. He said: 'They lament that the Pope does not speak. But the Pope cannot speak. If he were to speak, things would be worse.' And he reminded me that he had recently sent three letters in which he deplored the Nazi atrocities: one to the person he defined as 'the heroic Archbishop of Cracow,' the future Cardinal Sapieha, and the others to two bishops in Poland. 'They responded,' he said, 'thanking me, but telling me that they could not publish those letters because it would aggravate the situation.' And he cited the example of Pius X who, when confronted with a problem in Russia, said: 'You must keep silence in order to avoid worse evils.'

"And even on this occasion, the inaccuracy of those who say that he kept silence because he wanted to support the Nazis against the Russians and Communism appears very clear. I recall that he told me: 'Yes, the danger of Communism exists; however, at this moment the danger of Nazism is greater.' And he spoke to me about what the Nazis would do if they were victorious. I remember he used the phrase: 'They want to destroy the Church and crush her like a toad. For the

Pope there will be no place in the new Europe. They say that he should go to America. But I am not afraid and I shall remain here.' And he said this in a very firm and sure manner that one could clearly understand that if the Pope kept silence, it was not for fear or personal interest, but only just for fear of aggravating the situation of the oppressed. While speaking to me about the threats of invasion of the Vatican, he was absolutely tranquil, certain, trusting in Providence. Speaking to me about speaking out he was full of anguish. 'If I speak,' he felt, 'I shall harm them.'

"Therefore, even if historically one could discuss whether it would have been better to speak more or speak more strongly, what is beyond discussion is that if Pope Pius XII did not speak more strongly it was purely for this reason, not for fear or any other interest.

"The other part of the conversation that impressed me was that he spoke about all he had done and was doing to help the oppressed. I recall that he spoke about the first steps he attempted to make, in agreement with the German cardinals, but with no results; then about the conversations he had with Ribbentrop when he came to Rome, but with no results. At any rate he continued to do whatever he could. His one preoccupation was to avoid entering into political or military questions and to remain within the sphere of that which was the duty of the Holy See. In this regard, I recall that when the Germans occupied Rome in 1943 (I was rector of the Pontifical Gregorian University and it was I who accepted the refugees), Pius XII said to me: 'Father, avoid accepting the military because, since the Gregoriana is a pontifical house and belongs to the Holy See, we must be out of politics. But for the others, help them willingly: poor, persecuted Jews.' "

It is interesting to note that the Pope distinguished between military personnel and persecuted Jews. In fact, while the Jews were accepted at the Gregoriana, the military were given sanctuary at Palazzo Callisto.

Cardinal Dezza continued: "Pius XII wanted to be sure to say nothing that would arouse reactions and cause the situation to worsen. I would separate the two questions. Did he do well to be silent or would he have done better to speak? This is for me a question that can be discussed historically. Maybe Pius XI, another character, would have acted in a different way. However, it is evident that if Pius XII was silent or spoke little, it was for no other motive than that of fear to worsen the situation. Objectively one could discuss this matter; subjectively there is no doubt of the Pope's intentions: he truly tried to do what was best."

Pope Pius XII has been unjustly accused of cowardice and insensitivity in the face of the Holocaust—a silent partner in the massacre of millions of Jews. *The New York Times* columnists wrote about the "shameful silence" of Pope Pius XII. Specialists in Holocaust studies characterized the Pope as a symbol of moral irresponsibility. The Bronx Museum of Art displayed a painting called *Nazi Butchers*, featuring Pius XII in full papal regalia. Some Catholic writers beat their breasts loudly over the so-called cowardly silence of the Vatican, as if this proved their own liberality of mind. And an ABC News correspondent, covering Pope John Paul II's visit to Munich in November 1980, remarked that this city was the cradle of Hitler's Nazi movement, knowing the allusion would not be lost on a public that had been taught to view the papacy as a pawn of the Third Reich.[6]

While such slanders and insinuations continue to plague the Church, Pope Pius XII is beyond harm. Before he died, he had the consolation of receiving the gratitude of worldwide Jewry for his noble efforts on their behalf.

Pope Pius XII's focus was to save the lives of all refugees. Like a symphony leader he coordinated the Church's efforts and inspired his followers to assist war victims. Various groups operating from the Vatican managed to come together at his command. Through the gentle service of both religious and lay members of the Catholic Church, Pope Pius XII produced the necessary harmony to comfort suffering humanity.

2. The Holy See

Written documentation of the activities of militant Catholics and, in particular, of the good works performed by Pope Pius XII during the Second World War, has been, heretofore, scarce. Only those who worked closely with the Pope can enlighten us about his courage and tenacity. Cardinal Paolo Dezza, S.J., wrote on July 25, 1995: "Pius XII did a great deal to help the Jews persecuted by the Nazis and Fascists. He abstained from making public declarations in favor of both Catholics and Jews who were being persecuted by Hitler because, whenever he did speak, Hitler had his revenge by committing worse acts of violence against them. The clergy and bishops in Germany begged him to keep silence."[7]

In the March 1981 issue of the *Civiltà Cattolica,* Cardinal Dezza explains that in July 1944, after the arrival of the Allies, Chief Rabbi Israel Zolli celebrated a solemn ceremony in the synagogue, transmitted by radio, to publicly express the gratitude of the Jews to the Pontiff for the help given to the Jewish community during the Nazi persecution. He visited Pius XII on July 25th, with the president of the Jewish community, "to officially thank him for all he, personally and through the Catholics in Rome, had done in favor of the Jews, opening convents and monasteries, dispensing with papal cloister as stated in canon law, so that Jews could be received even in female monasteries and protected from the fury of the Nazis."[8]

When the Germans entered Rome, Zolli immediately went into hiding. He feared that the accurate Jewish community files might fall into German hands, and he therefore urged that they be destroyed. It is said, however, that President Ugo Foà ordered the head usher of the temple, Romeo Bondi, to deliver the address lists to the Fascist authorities upon demand.

A letter dispatched by Ugo Foà on July 4, 1944, registers the disagreements and differences of opinion between the two Jewish leaders. Zolli was convinced that the Church with its monasteries and convents would offer refuge to the Jews. Although there are no final figures on Jews sheltered by the Vatican, statistics show that seven out of eight Jews had been able to hide.

Cardinal Dezza tells the story of Rabbi Zolli who became a Catholic as soon as the war was over. While conducting services in the fall of 1944, he had a vision of Christ in a white cape that irradiated an inexpressible peace, while a voice resounded in his heart: "You are here for the last time."

On February 13, 1945, Rabbi Zolli was baptized a Christian and took the name of Eugenio to express his gratitude for what Pius XII had done for the Jews. Zolli did not consider conversion as breaking away from the past, but the development and completion of divine revelation—continuity between the Old and the New Testament.

In the Preface to Giorgio Angelozzi Gariboldi's book, *Pius XII, Hitler e Mussolini,* Giulio Andreotti wrote that, as a young man, he had the honor to serve the Vatican on various missions and was able to give testimony about Pope Pius XII's thoughts on Nazi-Fascism, about his directives to open the doors of the convents and monasteries to protect those who were being persecuted, and about his encouragement toward a new political order.[9] At the end of the war, indignant about the anticlerical campaign, Leo Longanesi told Pius XII to publicize the charitable works of the Church. The Pope answered, "Only God must be testimony to what one does for his neighbor."

The Augustinians of Sant'Anna near Porta Angelica were in direct contact with Pius XII because the rector of the Augustinian International College of Santa Monica was the papal sacristan at that time. The Germans knew that there were Jews living on the top floor of the college.

The Belgian rector was Bishop Canisius Van Lierde. He told Father David Sharp, an American, that Pius XII asked the Augustinians to shelter the Jews and care for them. Since there were other students in the college building who might be in danger should the Nazis defy international law, the Pope presented his proposal to both the superior general and to Bishop Van Lierde. The Pope's message was: "Christians must follow the works of mercy proclaimed in the Gospels; they must be charitable and protect those who need help." At the entrance of the third floor where Jews were housed is a large plaque with the names of those who lived at the college during the German occupation.

The Vatican sent Jewish men to the Augustinians of Santa Monica. Jewish women and children were sheltered next door at the Sisters of the Institute of Maria Santissima Bambina. These two buildings, facing Saint Peter's Basilica on Via Sant'Uffizi, were protected by Vatican Palatine Guards at their gates.

Sister Aurelia recalls that some women slept in the convent; others slept in the dormitories. The Sisters cooked for hundreds of refugees and served them in the dining room. Sister Aurelia not only taught kindergarten children, but her special charge was also to care for the two elderly Jewish wives of senators who were being sought by the Nazis and were in imminent danger. Fortunately, this was considered Vatican property and the Germans could not enter. Nor could anyone leave the premises and be safe. The area was surrounded by German SS ready to seize the Jews and anti-Fascists who might appear on the streets.

The Zionist Archives in Jerusalem contain a large number of documents concerning the activity of Archbishop Angelo Giuseppe Roncalli, Apostolic Delegate of the Holy See at Istanbul and the future Pope John XXIII. He spared no effort on behalf of the Jews of Central Europe and the Balkans.

In 1943, well before the establishment of the War Refugee Board in the United States, the Germans had repeated their order that the 25,000 Jews in Sofia be deported to Poland. Word of the impending disaster was flashed to Chaim Barlas, the representative in Istanbul of the Jewish Agency for Palestine. Barlas rushed to Archbishop Angelo Roncalli who listened sympathetically.[10]

Roncalli was a man of lofty spiritual stature, truly concerned about the people who were suffering. He was prepared heart and soul to assist in whatever way he could. Barlas stated that during the interviews, whenever there was news from Poland, Hungary, and Slovakia, the papal representative would clasp his hands in prayer, tears flowing from his eyes.

Archbishop Roncalli had developed a warm friendship with King Boris III and Queen Giovanna (daughter of the king of Italy) while serving as apostolic delegate to Bulgaria. He reacted with horror and indignation upon hearing about the deportations and began writing a message in the presence of Barlas.

Archbishop Roncalli sent thousands of immigration certificates, including Palestine immigration papers that he had obtained from the British, to Monsignor Angelo Rotta, the papal nuncio in Budapest. Roncalli declared that he was happy to do anything of a nonpolitical nature to assist him. As an emergency measure to guarantee safety, within months hundreds of Jews were "baptized" in the air-raid shelters of Budapest. Others escaped to Palestine, thanks to the immigration certificates forwarded by the archbishop. Because of the "safe-conduct" passes issued by Monsignor Rotta, many Jews survived the Holocaust in Budapest.

Of the 15,000 "safe-conducts" issued, Monsignor Rotta had given hundreds of these certificates to Sandor Ujvary, a volunteer worker for the Red Cross who roamed the line of marchers, with nuns carrying food and medicine for the Jews.

Protestant Bishop Laszlo Ravasz, persisting in his courageous attempts to halt the persecution, was outraged and protested over the brutal treatment of Jews. Bishop William Apor of Gyor was tireless in his efforts to hide and assist the Jews, as were hundreds of priests and nuns.

The U.S. War Refugee Board finally fulfilled its objectives by linking neutrals, the papal nuncio, and the International Red Cross in a powerful, unarmed alliance that the Nazis could not penetrate. A strong protest by them was personally delivered by Monsignor Rotta who had been barraged by urgent pleas from the Apostolic Delegation in Washington: "The Envoys of the neutral States represented in Budapest have been acquainted with the fact that the deportation of the Jews is about to be accomplished. They all know what this means, even though it be described as 'labor service'....The representatives of the neutral powers herewith request the Hungarian Government to forbid these cruelties, which ought never to have been started."

From June 9th to July 9th, 1944, more than 437,000 Hungarian Jews were deported to Auschwitz. On June 25th, Pius XII telegraphed a protest message to Admiral Horthy, the Regent in Budapest: "Supplications have been addressed to Us from different sources that we should exert all Our influence to shorten and mitigate the sufferings that have, for so long, been peacefully endured on account of their national or racial origin by a great number of unfortunate people belonging to this noble and chivalrous nation. In accordance with Our service of love, which embraces every human being, Our fatherly heart could not remain insensible to these urgent demands. For this reason We apply to Your Serene Highness, appealing to your noble feelings, in the full trust that Your Serene Highness will do everything in your power to save many unfortunate people from further pain and sorrow."

In *Summi Pontificatus*,[11] Pius XII implicitly condemned certain actions of the Reich: "Venerable Brothers, the hour when this Our first Encyclical reaches you is in many respects a real 'Hour of Darkness'[12] in which the spirit of violence and of discord brings indescribable suffering on mankind. Do We need to give assurance that Our paternal heart is close to all Our children in compassionate love, and especially to the afflicted, the oppressed, and the persecuted? The nations swept into the tragic whirlpool of war are perhaps as yet only at the 'beginnings of sorrows,'[13] but even now there reigns in thousands of families death and desolation, lamentation and misery. The blood of countless human beings, even noncombatants, raises a piteous dirge over a nation such as Our dear Poland, which, for its fidelity to the Church, for its services in the defense of Christian civilization, written in indelible characters in the annals of history, has a right to the generous and brotherly sympathy of the whole world, while it awaits, relying on the powerful intercession of Mary, Help of Christians, the hour of a resurrection in harmony with the principles of justice and true peace."[14]

The American chargé, Harold H. Tittman, Jr., who had returned after an interview with Pius XII shortly after Christmas, wrote on January 2, 1943: "With regard to his Christmas message, the Pope gave me the impression that he was sincere in believing that he had spoken therein clearly enough to satisfy all those who had been insisting in the past that he utter some word of condemnation of the Nazi atrocities, and he seemed surprised when I told him that I thought there were some who did not share his belief.

"He said he thought it was plain to everyone that he was referring to the Poles, Jews, and hostages when he declared that hundreds of thousands of persons had been killed or tortured through no fault of their own, sometimes only because of their race or nationality.

"He explained that when talking of atrocities he could not name the Nazis without at the same time mentioning the Bolsheviks and this he thought might not be wholly pleasing to the Allies."

Again, in 1943, Pius XII raised the problem of the extermination of the Jews in an address to the Sacred College of Cardinals.[15] He called attention to "the anxious entreaties of all those who, because of their nationality or their race, are being subjected to overwhelming trials and, sometimes, through no fault of their own, are doomed to extermination."

The Pontiff added: "Every word We address to the competent authority on this subject, and all Our public utterances, have to be carefully weighed and measured by Us in the interests of the victims themselves, lest, contrary to Our intentions, We make their situation worse and harder to bear. To put the matter at its lowest, the ameliorations apparently obtained do not match the scope of the Church's maternal solicitude on behalf of the particular groups that are suffering the most appalling fate. The Vicar of Christ, who asked no more than pity and a sincere return to elementary standards of justice and humanity, then found himself facing a door that no key could open."[16]

In his book on Pope Pius XII, Saul Friedländer states: "Any public statement by the Holy See of its attitude would henceforth create for it a further problem: the German Catholics, encouraged by their own bishops and for the most part firm adherents of National Socialism, would probably turn aside from Rome if Pius XII openly condemned the Hitlerite aggression. Fear of an eventual schism among the German Catholics could not but drive the Sovereign Pontiff to new concessions, just as would his wish to avoid reprisals by the regime against loyal Catholics and, lastly, his hope of bringing about a restoration of peace."[17]

Albrecht von Kessel, assistant to Ambassador Weiszäcker, affirmed after the war in *Der Papst und die Verfolgung der Juden*[18] that, from September 1943 to June 1944, Hitler continued to toy with the idea of occupying the Vatican and deporting the Pope to Greater Germany. If the Holy Father had protested, not only would he have been unsuccessful in halting the destruction but he might also have caused a great deal of additional damage to thousands of Jews hidden in the Vatican and in monasteries, as well as to the Church and to Catholics in German-occupied Europe.

In his *Diario*, Galeazzo Ciano noted on May 13, 1940: "The Pope is even ready to be deported to a concentration camp but will do nothing against his conscience. Informed of the mass murders, Pope Pius XII cried. He was profoundly shocked at Hitler's method of solving the Jewish problem. He cannot be accused of cowardice or indifference to human suffering."[19]

Rolf Hochhuth, in his play *Der Stellvertreter*, depicts Pius XII as an unprincipled politician, possessed of "aristocratic coolness" and eyes having an "icy glow," who stood by passively while millions of Jews were being murdered.

A very different picture was drawn by Sir Francis Osborne, a non-Catholic British diplomat, in close touch with the Pontiff for over ten years. As British minister to the Vatican from 1936 to 1947 and, therefore, an enforced guest in Vatican City from June 1940 to the autumn of 1944, he had the opportunity to know Pius XII.

In a letter to *The Times* of London, May 20, 1963, Osborne wrote: "First of all, I must emphatically declare that, so far from being a cool (which, I suppose, implies cold-blooded and inhumane) diplomatist, Pius XII was the most warmly humane, kindly, generous, sympathetic (and, incidentally, saintly) character that it has been my privilege to meet in the course of a long life. I know that his sensitive nature was acutely and incessantly alive to the tragic volume of human suffering caused by the War and, without the slightest doubt, he would have been ready and glad to give his life to redeem humanity from its consequences. And this quite irrespective of nationality or Faith. But what could he effectively do? Pius XII loved Germany in which he had spent nine happy years; but there is no evidence whatever that pro-German feelings warped his judgment."

Those who accuse the Pontiff of trusting Hitler or of underestimating the magnitude of the German peril would do well to read the following report by Osborne, the chargé d'affaires at the British Legation to the Holy See, written less than seven months after Hitler's rise to power: "I called on the Cardinal Secretary of State and took the opportunity afforded by a long conversation to ask him what he thought of recent events in Germany. His Eminence was extremely frank and made no effort to conceal his disgust at the proceedings of Herr Hitler's government. The Vatican usually professes to see both sides of any political question, but on this occasion there was no word of palliation or excuse.

"With regard to the German treatment of Austria, Cardinal Pacelli stated that the Germans were determined to pursue their present policy and would not be restrained by anything short of force. He deplored the action of the German government at home, their persecution of the Jews, their proceedings against political opponents, the reign of terror to which the whole nation was subjected."[20]

Osborne repeated what he had heard expressed in Italy and elsewhere that these events were but manifestations of the revolutionary spirit. Herr Hitler would soon settle down, temper the zeal of his supporters, and revert to more normal methods of government. Cardinal Pacelli replied with emphasis that he saw no ground for such easy optimism. It seemed to him that there was no indication of any modification of the internal policy of the German government.

Sir Francis Osborne recalled that, reflecting on the iniquity of Germany, Cardinal Pacelli explained apologetically how it was that he had signed a Concordat. He said that a pistol had been pointed at his head and he had had no alternative. The German government had offered him concessions.

"Cardinal Pacelli had to choose between an agreement on their lines and the virtual elimination of the Catholic Church in the Reich. Not only that, but he was given no more than a week to make up his mind. In a matter of such importance he would have liked more time, but it was a case of then or never. He wished me to know the facts so as to be able to appreciate the dilemma of the Vatican. The Church had no political ax to grind. They were outside the political arena. But the spiritual welfare of 20 million Catholic souls in Germany was at stake and that was the first and, indeed, the only consideration. If the German government violated the Concordat—and they were certain to do so—the Vatican would have a treaty on which to base a protest."

As Cardinal Secretary of State, Pacelli played a major part in the campaign against German racialism. As early as July 11, 1937, he had denounced the pagan cult of race in a public speech at Lisieux. Again this provoked a sharp reaction from the Reich Ministry of Ecclesiastical Affairs. In Italy, too, Il Duce keenly resented the Pope's attitude. Speaking to Nino d'Aroma in October 1944, Mussolini denounced Pius XII as a renegade Italian who had sided with the enemies of his country.

Guenter Lewy states that Hochhuth, in attacking Pius XII, "has personalized a problem which cannot adequately be understood in terms of personalities."[21]

The Nazis had warned the Vatican, the Curia, and the Pope himself against rash utterances and actions. The Pope did not want to risk the allegiance of the German Catholics. Would a papal decree of excommunication against Hitler have dissuaded the Führer from carrying out his plan to destroy the Jews? This is very doubtful. Pius XII was a diplomat who thought it his duty to avoid provocations that would lead to greater evils.

On November 28, 1973, Giorgio Angelozzi Gariboldi defended Elena Rossignani Pacelli[22] in a lawsuit against Carlo Ponti, who produced the film *Rappresaglia* based on the book *Death in Rome* by Robert Katz. With George Pan Cosmatos, Katz also wrote the screen version. The Italian courts found them guilty of calumny against Pius XII.

Under the pretext of reconstructing the tragic events during the German occupation of Rome that culminated on March 24, 1944, with the death of 335 innocent Italians at the Ardeatine Caves by the SS, these writers and producers have denigrated Pope Pius XII. Both the film and the book are historically inaccurate, without documentation, and without serious evaluation. In fact, the author's "poetic license" is simply contempt for the facts in order to permit a more sensational story. Ponti and Katz were ahead of their time, creating and twisting facts to increase commercial value.

The Pope is accused of having had knowledge of the massacre. In the book one reads: "No miracle was necessary to save the 335 men condemned to death in the Ardeatine Caves. There is a man who could have helped, in fact he should have at least delayed the German massacre, and should have been made accountable. This man is Pope Pius XII."[23] The accusation continues: "One must conclude that Pius XII chose to remain passive, even though he had full knowledge that his intervention would have perhaps stopped the reprisal. Having made this choice, he approved."[24]

When summoned to the lawsuit Tribunal, Father Robert Graham, S.J., a Vatican historian, suggested that testimony be requested of Eitel Friedrich Moellhausen, the German consul general living in Rome during the occupation period.

On August 6, 1981, Moellhausen wrote that, in German circles, no mention was ever made about Pius XII having had knowledge of the Nazis' plans before the devastating reprisals of the Ardeatine Caves were executed in Rome. He added that nothing would have changed Hitler's plans to avenge the killing on March 24, 1944, of thirty German soldiers on Via Rasella and that Weiszäcker, the German ambassador to the Vatican, trembled at the thought of future raids and reprisals against the Vatican where so many Jews were given refuge in convents and monasteries under its protection.

The Pope's "messenger" to the German headquarters in Rome was Pancrazio Pfeiffer, a Salvatorian priest. Contrary to the daily routine of obtaining release of prisoners and information for Vatican diplomats about the German occupation in Rome, Pfeiffer was unable to learn about the specifics of the reprisal until several days after the executions at the Ardeatine Caves. According to sworn testimony, Father Pfeiffer said that "Pope Pius XII was not aware of the Nazis' plans before the massacre."

Ponti, Katz, and Cosmatos were sentenced on November 27, 1975, by the appropriate courts in Rome. This was appealed, later reversed and, finally, the case ended February 7, 1981, in favor of Pope Pius XII.

Giorgio Angelozzi Gariboldi, in his book *Pius XII, Hitler e Mussolini,* states that Pius XII was tormented by the fact that thousands of innocent people were interned in concentration camps after the bishops' protest in Holland. The Pope prepared a document regarding Hitler's inhumanity against the Jews which he wanted to publish in *L'Osservatore Romano.*

However, according to Mother Pascalina, Pius XII burned the document. She recalls that he felt it would have triggered many more deaths and he should not assume responsibility for them. When Mother Pascalina reminded him that the document would be useful in the future, he answered: "But if the Nazis find these sheets which are stronger than the bishops' letter, what will happen to the Catholics and the Jews under German control?"[25]

Instead, Pope Pius XII asked Archbishop Amleto Cicognani, Apostolic Delegate in Washington, D.C., to have the Dutch protest printed and circulated by the American press.

With clear reference to the Third Reich, in a challenging discourse of Easter 1941, Pius XII denounced such violations, explaining that he could not keep quiet about the sufferings of prisoners who were being so oppressed. Nor could he refrain when international agreements regarding conquered peoples were being ignored.

Undoubtedly, a strong condemnation of the Holocaust by Pope Pius XII would have provoked Nazi reprisals against Catholics in German-occupied countries and in Germany itself. As head of the Catholic Church, the Pope was trying to protect his people. He also must have realized that a stronger public condemnation might cause the Nazis not only to occupy the Vatican, but also to invade churches and monasteries throughout Italy, bringing probable death to the clergy and their hidden refugees.

Throughout the autumn of 1995, both the French and the Italian press headlined the "rediscovery" of an unpublished document that threatened to turn into a Vatican scandal. It had been prepared in 1938 by the American Jesuit Father John LaFarge. Having read his book *Interracial Justice*, Pope Pius XI summoned him to the Vatican to prepare a draft for an encyclical that was to be an attack on totalitarian systems that foster racism and anti-Semitism.

With the assistance of Professor Gustave Gundlach, a German Jesuit, and French Jesuit activist Father Desbuquois, *Humani Generis Unitas* was submitted to their superior general, Father Wladimir Ledochowski, who would bring it to Pope Pius XI. The Pope finally received the draft in January 1939, too late; he was very ill and died the following month.

LaFarge's draft was found among his papers. This was not a Vatican document. It contained no annotations by Pope Pius XI; nor were there any by his successor. According to historian Robert Graham, S.J., "The draft was an obvious pre-Conciliar text in tone and theological concepts. Thank God it was never published."

World War II had engulfed Europe. Eugenio Pacelli was less inclined to take an open controversial position with regard to the Nazis. His expertise had been sharpened by nine years of diplomatic service in Germany. He knew that public protests would have worsened the situation for Jews and jeopardized Vatican efforts to save as many as possible. He therefore found it necessary to distance himself from his predecessor's position and prepared his own papal encyclical, *Summi Pontificatus (Of the Supreme Pontificate),* which treats of the Unity of Human Society.

3. Pope Pius XII

Eugenio Pacelli (1876–1958) was papal nuncio in Berlin from 1920 to 1929 and cardinal secretary of state from 1930 to 1939. He succeeded to the papal tiara March 2, 1939, and took the name of Pius XII.

Critics usually overlook the fact that the Vatican was a neutral state within occupied Europe. Whatever chance Pius XII had of aiding the victims of war would have been lost if this neutrality were violated. A direct condemnation of Hitler would certainly have resulted in a more frightful loss of life.

Jean Bernard, a priest from Luxembourg, was an inmate of Dachau. He relates in his postwar memoirs: "The detained priests trembled every time news reached us of some protest by a religious authority, but particularly by the Vatican. We all had the impression that our wardens made us atone heavily for the fury these protests evoked."

In his letter to Bishop von Preysing of Berlin, dated April 30, 1943, Pope Pius XII wrote: "As far as Episcopal declarations are concerned, We leave to local bishops the responsibility of deciding what to publish from Our communications. The dangers of reprisals and pressures—as well as perhaps of other measures due to the length and psychology of the war—counsel reserve. In spite of good reasons for Our own intervention, there are others equally good for avoiding greater evils by not interfering....It is superfluous to say that Our love and paternal solicitude for all non-Aryan Catholics, children of the Church like all others, are greater today when their exterior existence is collapsing, and they know such moral distress. Unhappily in the present state of affairs, We can bring them no help other than Our prayers."

In his first encyclical, *Summi Pontificatus,* Pope Pius XII attacked the concept of the all-powerful state—that the state was superior to

God, and therefore could demand man's obedience: "To consider the State as something ultimate to which everything else should be subordinated and directed, cannot fail to harm the true lasting prosperity of nations....The idea which credits the State with unlimited authority...leads to violation of other rights."[26]

He reaffirmed the rights of the family, the rights of parents to supervise their children's education, and the rights of conscience, stressing the fundamental unity of all mankind under the fatherhood of God.

There are many examples in the writings of Pius XII found in the *Actes* of the Holy See that he was not silent or insensitive to the suffering in Europe during World War II. In his Christmas address of 1940, he spoke of the disastrous effects of a conflict easily "forgetful of the rules of humanity, ignoring the customs and conventions of war."

At Easter in 1941, appealing to Germany and the Soviet Union, Pope Pius XII said: "Let your conscience and your honor guide you in the way you treat the populations of the occupied territories with justice, humanity and wisdom." Again, in May 1942, he condemned acts of violence and cruelty committed against civilians and the use of "military weapons still more murderous." In his Christmas broadcast of 1942, "to all men of courage and honor," he spoke about religious persecution.

The concept of unconditional surrender was promulgated by the Allies after their meeting in Casablanca in January 1943. Pope Pius advised the Allies on the fourth anniversary of the war: "True strength need not fear to be generous....Do not disturb, do not muddle the universal longing for peace by acts which, so far from encouraging confidence, will rekindle hatred and strengthen the resolve to resist."

Meanwhile, not only did Catholic priests, Sisters, and laity protect the Jewish families living with them, but they also joined Pius XII in prayer for their safety. When Rome was bombed, the Pope went to the Church of Saint Ignatius Loyola. He remained on his knees throughout the night, praying before the sacred image of the Madonna del Divino Amore. Both laity and religious joined him in prayer. The Pope had made a final plea to the German government to spare Rome. His prayers were answered. The city of Rome was saved! Joining the Pontiff as he prayed for peace were the clergy and faithful of Rome.

Among them were the Religious Teachers Filippini who for three centuries conducted schools in Rome sponsored by the Vatican. Their mission was "to educate young children to love God, the Church, and the Pope."[27]

On their way to Mass one day, a group of Religious Teachers Filippini were warned to return home immediately because the Germans were hiding in that area and their lives were in danger. Fortunately, the Allies were on their way to Rome to replace the Nazis and Fascists. Upon arrival, several American soldiers who had been taught by the Religious Teachers Filippini in the United States went to Arco dei Ginnasi to visit Sister Assunta Crocenzi. They presented her with a bouquet of flowers in gratitude for all she had done for them.

American soldiers also visited Monte Mario as they took over the city and the periphery of Rome. The Sisters were there to greet them. One soldier recognized Sister Florinda Martella who taught him in elementary school. The reunion was a happy one amidst the clapping of hands and embracing.

Pope Pius XII's humanitarian efforts did not end with the ceasing of hostilities that brought an end to World War II, but not to the sufferings of homeless survivors. Members of the Religious Teachers Filippini in the United States started a campaign to relieve the terrible destruction, hunger, sickness, and death caused by the brutal conflict. Cases of food, clothing, medicine, and other necessities were prepared and sent to the Vatican for the relief of destitute war victims. This lasted until June 3, 1966, when the last shipload arrived in Naples on the *Michelangelo*.[28]

Sixteen convents and schools of the Religious Teachers Filippini had been damaged, some beyond repair. In Naples alone, there were 120 bombardments. The Sisters related how their convent was seized by the Italian patriots as a place for battle against the German soldiers who were on an upper hill. Continuous shooting took place. They were forced to evacuate.

One Sister, hit in the arm and leg, remained in the convent. Others were forced at gunpoint to stay in an underground shelter. When the Sisters returned to Naples, everything was gone. The enemy had taken food, furniture, clothing, blankets—nothing remained. The terrace was covered with bodies of the dead. The wounded Sister was found sitting in the midst of all this destruction. Both convent and school, with a capacity for 1,000 students, were destroyed and had to be rebuilt.

German soldiers had occupied the Religious Teachers Filippini convent and school in Anzio as well as in Nettuno. Sisters and orphans were forced to flee to Rome where the motherhouse at Arco dei Ginnasi was already crowded with refugees.

After the Americans landed at Anzio they took over the buildings, previously occupied by the Germans, which were totally destroyed. Surviving children roamed about, suffering unspeakable misery— hunger, sickness, malnutrition, and death. Through all this, the Religious Teachers were indefatigable. To this day with their students they visit the graves of the 20,000 American soldiers who fought to protect future generations.

Frascati, Terracina, Rocca di Papa, and elsewhere in Italy the once beautiful, enchanting towns were leveled by heavy aerial bombardments. The dead were everywhere. Thousands of people who sought refuge were aided by the Religious Teachers Filippini in schools and convents throughout Italy.

News about the German occupation was devastating. But most people did not believe the atrocities perpetrated against the Jews that were reported around the world. They refused to believe what was happening. The information received was considered widespread rumor rather than hard fact. Indeed there was a wall of scepticism.

Finally, on December 17, 1942, from London, Washington, and Moscow, the Allies issued a joint declaration on the German persecution of the Jews. Diplomats appealed to the Vatican to endorse it.

In his Christmas broadcast, Pope Pius XII asked all men of good will "to make a vow to bring back society under the rule of God; it is a duty We owe to those who lie dead on the battlefields; to the mothers and widows and orphans who have lost their men; to the exiles torn from their homes by war; to the hundreds of thousands of innocent people put to death or doomed to slow extinction, sometimes merely because of their race or descent; to the many thousands of noncombatants who have lost life and everything else by those air raids which We have never ceased to denounce from the beginning."[29]

Mussolini and the Germans were displeased with the Pope's words. According to Chadwick, "Ribbentrop wondered whether the Pope was deserting his neutrality and ordered Diego von Bergen, his ambassador in Rome, to threaten physical retaliation. Von Bergen obeyed. The Pope stayed quite silent. Then, very calmly, he said that he did not care what happened to him; that if there were a struggle between Church and state, the state would lose. German security studied the broadcast and defined it as one long attack on everything we stand for.... 'God,' the Pope said, 'regards all peoples and races as worthy of the same consideration.' Here he is clearly speaking on behalf of the Jews. He is virtually accusing the German people of injustice towards the Jews."[30]

Father Robert Graham, Vatican historian, quoted Pope Pius XII telling his close advisers in 1942 that "a victory by the Axis could mean the end of Christianity in Europe."[31] The principal cause of concern was a German plan put into action in western Poland that was designed to obliterate Christian churches. This plan was to be implemented in an area that had 4.5 million inhabitants, mostly Polish and Catholic, in the German-occupied part of Poland called "Wartheland."

Religious life in "Wartheland" came under strict Nazi control in 1940. Churches could not exist in Poland. Only religious associations, societies or unions with no leader exercising responsibility, existed legally. Religious associations could not own property except for the space reserved for worship. Membership was limited to adults; movements such as youth groups were forbidden. Germans and Poles could not meet together in the same church. Catholics could have no relations with the Pope in Rome. When the Vatican complained, German authorities gave only "evasive answers."

Adolf Hitler had a "fanatical hostility" toward Christianity, and one of his main aims was to destroy it "as an identifiable force" by dismantling it and persecuting its members, wrote Father Graham. Hitler's hatred and persecution of the Catholic Church increased. In 1941 the government announced the formation of the "Roman Catholic Church of German nationality in the Reich District Wartheland." Pope Pius XII was warned by Catholic officials in the region that what was happening in "Wartheland" was planned for all of German-controlled territories. The plan was unrealistic and failed.

In 1946, *L'Osservatore Romano* noted that Arthur Greiser, the German official in charge of "Wartheland" during the Nazi occupation, was "a very fierce enemy of the Church and harshly persecuted it." Although Arthur Greiser was also responsible for hundreds of thousands of deaths, Pius XII appealed for clemency with Polish authorities when he was condemned to death. Greiser was hanged.

On May 11, 1963, in the midst of the controversy over Hochhuth's play, *The Deputy*, Douglas Woodruff, a well-known English journalist and editor of *The Tablet*, wrote a response to an article in *The Sunday Times* under the heading "Papal Policy and Mass Murder."

To the charges against Pope Pius XII for failing to intervene on behalf of Jewish victims of Hitler's extermination policy, Douglas Woodruff supported the Holy Father's position: "That the private representations were not able to achieve their object, or to secure more than occasional and small mitigations, does not mean that there was any other and better policy open to Pius XII which he failed to take."[32]

If Pope Pius XII could have saved the thousands of priests who were tortured and died in concentration camps, would he not have issued a protest to save them? Would a papal denunciation of Nazism, racism, and other atrocities of Hitler's Third Reich have been effective? Would a public confrontation or excommunication of Catholics who embraced Nazism in Germany have stopped Hitler's reprisals? The Pope's efforts were limited to diplomatic channels. His silence was a strategic approach to protecting more Jews and other refugees from Nazi terrorism.

When Cardinal Giovanni Battista Montini, the future Pope Paul VI, was archbishop of Milan, he responded to Woodruff's article. This article reached the newspaper on Friday, June 21, 1963, one hour after Montini had been elected to the Papacy.

Cardinal Montini's tribute to his predecessor, published June 29th by *The Tablet,* begins with an acknowledgment of Woodruff's contribution to historical truth: "It was a most welcome defense not only of Pope Pius XII, of venerated memory, and of the Holy See, but also of historical truth and sound logic, not to speak of common sense."

The article ends with these words: "Let some men say what they will, Pius XII's reputation as a true Vicar of Christ, as one who tried, so far as he could, fully and courageously to carry out the mission entrusted to him, will not be affected. But what is the gain to art and culture when the theatre lends itself to injustice of this sort?"

On June 7, 1979, kneeling in the Brzezinka concentration camp, Pope John Paul II said: "I kneel on this Golgotha of the contemporary world, on these tombs, many without names, similar to the tomb of the Unknown Soldier. I come to pray with you and to give testimony to the world about what constitutes, in our times, the greatness and wretchedness of man; his victory and his defeat."

Regarding World War II's concentration camps and systematic extermination, Pope John Paul II wrote in 1994: "First and foremost, the sons and daughters of the Jewish nation were condemned for no other reason than that they were Jewish. Even if only indirectly, whoever lived in Poland at that time came into contact with this reality.

"Therefore, this was also a personal experience of mine, an experience I carry with me even today. Auschwitz, perhaps the most meaningful symbol of the Holocaust of the Jewish people, shows to what lengths a system constructed on principles of racial hatred and greed for power can go. To this day, Auschwitz does not cease to admonish, reminding us that anti-Semitism is a great sin against humanity, that all racial hatred inevitably leads to the trampling of human dignity."[33]

Bruno Bartoloni's article in the *Corriere della Sera* (April 16, 1996) underscores the fraternal relationship between Pope John Paul II and Rabbi Elio Toaff. Commemorating the historic encounter that took place ten years ago in Rome's Jewish synagogue, Pope John Paul II spoke about the need to invite people to resolve present-day problems: "This meeting constitutes a sign of hope for the world that seeks authentic fraternal values rooted in a rich and profound spiritual heritage. The new spirit of friendship and reciprocal solicitude that characterizes the Catholic-Jewish relationship also constitutes the most important symbol that Jews and Catholics can offer a restless world— the primacy of love over hatred."[34]

4. Conclusion

Fifty years have passed. Many books have been written about the Holocaust and the 6 million Jewish victims. Yet, less attention has been given to the equal number of non-Jews who were killed by the Nazis.

Many people do not know about the countless rescuers in Italy during the German occupation. Some rescuers did not want thanks. In Venice, when it was time for recognition, Gigetto Cappello said: "Why give us a medal? Someone had to show a little humanity in the midst of this barbarism!" But the Jewish community insisted. Trees were planted in Israel in the "Forest of the Just" to honor Luigia and Giovanni Cappello, Maria and Antonio Simoneschi, Nori and Renato Goldoni, and many others.[35]

Italy and Denmark share the distinction of having saved the highest percentages of Jewish lives. While many Italian Jews found their own rescuers and lived with their own resources, they could not have survived without help from non-Jews who spontaneously assisted them.

Most Italians were not anti-Semitic; they were not concerned about those who did not share their beliefs. They bent the rules and saved lives.

Italian Jews were only 1 percent of the population in Italy. Their physical appearance, friendships, and general assimilation in Italian culture served them well. While sympathetic Christians provided shelter, food, and documents, most had financial resources that facilitated their survival.

Like non-Jewish Italians, the Jews in Italy ignored the racial laws and all unjust regulations; e.g., they would transfer property to Catholic friends to avoid its confiscation or they would secretly arrange matters with non-Jewish clients and continue their legal profession. Nor did everyone obey the law to report for internment. They knew how to obtain false documents. Like their Italian compatriots, many Jews were individualistic. They preferred to evade the law and take the risk.

In 1940, several thousand non-Italian Jews, and a few hundred Italian Jews, were sent to a concentration camp at Ferramonti-Tarsia. They survived the war.

Convents and monasteries sheltered Jews who sought refuge and allowed men, women, and children into their cloistered areas. "Instructions" from ecclesiastical superiors were given orally. Would anyone want to jeopardize Vatican neutrality and the Pope himself by filing such documents for the sake of posterity's incredulity?

Priests ignored the laws of their land; bankers did not report Jewish bank accounts as requested; landlords, innkeepers, and villagers refused to report newcomers as required by law. Many Italians had only contempt for their government. They were individualists. These "rescuers" aided total strangers.

Italians were altruistic. They expressed their altruism with courage and compassion. By sheltering Jews, they not only risked their lives, but also the lives of their children. These rescuers felt obliged to save human beings whose lives were in danger. They did their duty as Christians.

By autumn of 1943, most Italians were tired of the war. They had been victimized by both the Fascists and Nazis; their young men had died, soldiers had been abandoned, Trent and Trieste had been annexed. Apparently the war was a lost cause; they were disgusted with Mussolini and Hitler and joined the anti-Fascist Resistance.

In Italy there were rumors of death camps and execution of Jews. The Italians saw people being sent to labor camps; they did not believe they would be sent to gas chambers. Only when escapees' accounts of the gas chambers at Auschwitz reached the West were voices of protest heard. Protesting the deportation of Jews were the International Red Cross, the king of Sweden, the Allied leaders and, first of all, Pope Pius XII.

Paul Oskar Kristeller—Woodbridge professor emeritus of philosophy at Columbia University—had already published his scholarly work on the Florentine Platonist, Marsilio Ficino, when he was affected by Hilter's racial decrees in January 1933. Soon after, he left Germany and moved to Italy where his many Jewish and Italian friends helped him. Among them was Giovanni Gentile, director of the Scuola

Normale Superiore in Pisa and member of the Fascist Party, who admired Kristeller's scholarly accomplishments.

Prior to the summer of 1938, Mussolini had ignored Hitler's protests against Kristeller's presence in Pisa and the presence of other German Jews in Italy. Obviously his relations with Hitler increased because, through his war against Abyssinia, he had lost the support of England and France, and was now dependent on Nazi Germany.

Mussolini modeled his racial decree on Hitler's. All Italian Jews with government positions, including teachers and professors, and Jewish scholars not born in Italy had to leave the country within four months, that is, not later than January 1939.

"In Italy, there was not a single person from senator down to doorman who did not openly disapprove of the decree. When the Nazis occupied Italy, all the Jews feared deportation or execution....The Italians showed great humanity and generosity," wrote Professor Kristeller, who was among the lucky ones. On the basis of an invitation from Yale University for the spring session, he obtained a non-quota immigration visa and arrived in the United States in February 1939. When he obtained an appointment in the department of philosophy at Columbia University, Professor Giuseppe Prezzolini offered him hospitality in the Casa Italiana.

While he succeeded in escaping before the announced deadline, others who were not so successful were concealed and saved by Italians, especially by members of the Catholic Church. "Jews resided in episcopal palaces, monasteries, convents and in the Vatican itself," says Professor Kristeller. "Pope Pius XII, whose major duty was to protect the numerous Catholics, including baptized Jews, against the Nazi persecution, concealed the Jews and did not allow the Nazis to find and arrest them. Pope Eugenio Pacelli has been unfairly criticized for his silence on the Jewish persecution."[36]

Dorothy Rabinowitz, an editorial writer for the *Wall Street Journal,* wrote: "Oskar Schindler, flawed hero of Steven Spielberg's monumental film, *Schindler's List,* came to Poland a profiteer and ended up a rescuer of many hundreds of Jewish lives."

Undeniably there were other rescuers of whose exploits little has been written. The German invasion of Poland in 1939 sent a wave of Jewish refugees east into Lithuania where they desperately sought permits and visas to escape. The Dutch consul in Kaunas agreed to issue visas to Curaçao and Dutch Guiana, now known as Suriname. But the refugees needed permission to pass through the Soviet Union and Japan.

Visas were unobtainable to most countries in 1940 when Chinue Sugihara served as Japan's consul general in Kaunas. He was ordered by Tokyo to ignore the plight of the Jews. Instead, after a unanimous vote of his family, he decided to continue to issue visas. Thus he guaranteed them safe passage across the Soviet Union to Japan and beyond. He signed papers twelve to sixteen hours a day for one month, causing painful hand cramps. His wife, Yukiko, had to massage the cramps out of his hands at night. He was still issuing handwritten visas out the window of the train as he left with his family. This heroic action allowed people to pass through Japan to other countries.

An able linguist, he was a kind and gentle family man who persuaded the Soviet officials to let the Jews through. He cabled Tokyo for permission three times and was refused each time. Sugihara's disobedience, defying the Japanese government and issuing transit visas, meant possible disgrace and retribution.

Sugihara's defiance of orders from Tokyo eventually cost him his diplomatic career, and he died in relative obscurity in 1986. Sometimes called the "Japanese Schindler," only in recent years have his deeds been honored by the Japanese government. But Holocaust survivors reject any comparison with Oscar Schindler or Raoul Wallenberg. Sugihara did not have a "profit motive," nor did he have the backing of his government. The 10,000 people Sugihara saved were second in number only to the tens of thousands of Jews rescued in similar manner by Swedish businessman Raoul Wallenberg. Professor Hillel Levine, a Holocaust scholar at Boston University, wrote: "Sugihara was the lonely man of decision. His love of life enabled him to form a conspiracy of goodness."

When everyone else was shutting the doors, Sugihara was the only hope. Dr. Sylvia Smoller, then a seven-year-old girl and now a leading New York epidemiologist, insists it was a miracle: "We would have ended up in the ovens, I have no doubt." Benjamin Fishoff, a Manhattan electronics importer, whose parents and siblings stayed behind in Poland and perished in the Treblinka concentration camp, said: "He took us out from hell and put us in heaven."

Solly Ganor was eleven years old when he met Sugihara and his family in Kaunus. He will always remember "this consul of an enemy country, and the only one who was sacrificing himself by issuing visas to total strangers. He was a giant of moral strength." Ganor survived the Dachau concentration camp where he was sent notwithstanding Sugihara's efforts.

Unlike countries such as Bulgaria and, for a time at least, France, members of the Italian government ministries and army personnel made every effort to protect the Jews. To ensure that no Jews under their government fell into German hands they schemed and procrastinated. They resorted to all types of strategies that irritated the Nazis. Berlin was naturally bitter over this intransigence.

There were telegrams from Bureau IV of the Reich Security Head Office—command post for the final solution—inquiring as to when Italy could be expected to begin sending its Jews. Their refusal was based on a full awareness of what awaited any Jew deported for resettlement. "Never," was the silent and unbending response from the Italians. So long as Fascist Italy remained independent, the answer was always the same.

Reflecting the popular attitude of the citizenry at large, not only would the Italian government resist deportation, but its army and consuls also undertook extraordinary efforts to rescue Jews in their zones of occupation.

Fifty years after execution in Dachau, Giovanni Palatucci received the "Medaglia d'oro"—the Gold Medal of Italy—for having saved the lives of 5,000 Jews. At the suggestion of the National Association of Italian Jews, the chief of the police department and the Comune di Montella (Avellino), it was presented May 19, 1995, in the historic Palazzo Pitigliani by the president of the Italian Republic. Addressing the audience, Oscar Luigi Scalfaro stated: "Italy has not forgotten this illustrious son, a martyr for freedom who, like so many others, sacrificed his life as a precious heritage for our youth to emulate."

Palatucci had already been given the gold medal from the Jewish community and was included among the "Just of Israel." A forest in Jerusalem and a street between Ramat Gan and Tel Aviv were also dedicated to Palatucci.

Giovanni Palatucci, born in Irpina, Montella, was the last police commissioner in the area known as Italian Fiume. On September 13, 1944, he was arrested by the Nazis, imprisoned and tortured in Trieste, condemned to death, and deported to the extermination camp of

Dachau. He was number 117826. He died February 10, 1945, as a result of exhaustion and cruelty. Palatucci was thirty-six years old.

As a young commissioner, Palatucci, exposing himself to every risk, remained faithful to his moral formation and to his policeman's oath to serve. He was one of Fiume's heroes. For six years he defended the rights and freedom of citizens and refugees. People of all walks of life have testified to the spirit of religious fraternity that animated him. Innumerable are the testimonials of survivors whose lives were saved by him.

Italians call their struggle to free Italy from German domination "La Guerra di Liberazione." During World War II, Charles T. O'Reilly, Dean Emeritus at Loyola University in Chicago, was an interpreter for the Italian Service Units. In the National Italian American Foundation Newsletter of May/June 1995, he states that "an estimated 600,000 Italian soldiers fought alongside the Allies to drive the Germans from Italy. Other Italian soldiers joined partisan groups to fight the Germans in Nazi-occupied France, Greece, and Yugoslavia. Italian naval units served with the Allies in the Mediterranean and the Atlantic. The Italian Air Force flew combat missions and dropped supplies to Yugoslavia's partisans. About 70,000 Italian soldiers in ISUs served in North Africa and Europe, while 32,000 served in these Italian Service Units in the United States."[37]

When Italy announced the Allied-Italian Armistice on September 8, 1943, the Germans swooped down on unsuspecting units in Italy. By the end of November 1943, more than 20,000 Italian military died fighting the Germans. Another 20,000 Italian POWs drowned when ships taking them to German prison camps were torpedoed or hit mines.

Tens of thousands of Italian soldiers fought the Nazis. More than 42,000 died in battle. An estimated 73,000 of the more than 700,000 Italian soldiers who became German prisoners did not survive the brutal treatment they received in prison camps.

Italian soldiers on the Greek island of Leros defied the Germans for almost two months. After they surrendered, 430 officers were shot. More than 5,000 men on the island of Cephalonia were also shot, as were other Italian soldiers in Montenegro and Yugoslavia. The surrender of the German forces in northern Italy on May 2, 1945, marked the end of the war in Italy. The sacrifices Italian soldiers made, those of the 70,000 Italian partisans who were killed, and the 89,000 Allied soldiers who died in Italy, saved Italy from the Nazis and placed the country on the road to democracy.

In 1943, Pope Pius XII already had ten years' experience of Hitler's reactions when opposed. The German Concordat had been a profound disappointment to the Church. His predecessor's encyclical on the way the Nazis were behaving intensified the anti-Catholic activity of the Third Reich. By publicly challenging Hitler over Jewish atrocities, he could easily make things worse. He knew that not only would he expose the Catholics to grave danger, but he would also fail completely to help the Jews.

In Rome C. E. Heathcote Smith was representative of the Inter-Governmental Committee on Refugees. On August 5, 1944, he reported to his chief in London that Myron Taylor, the U. S. representative to the Vatican, had already taken up the matter of saving Jewish lives with Pope Pius XII. Smith acknowledged that he himself had a highly satisfactory audience with the Holy Father.

Smith also reported that Pope Pius XII requested the German ambassador to stop all further deportations and to communicate to him the number of Jews, including Italian Jews and others in northern Italy, still awaiting deportation. He further suggested that the Axis should permit these people eventually to reach some haven of refuge.

Pope Pius XII did his best to pave the way and gain time for any steps the American and British governments might initiate in regard to internees in Europe. He declared that neither history nor his conscience would forgive him if he made no effort to save at this psychological juncture further threatened lives.

The Germans ignored Pope Pius XII's appeal for justice and charity. The papal nuncio in Switzerland reported on July 31st that fifty Jewish internees in the German concentration camp at Fossoli (Modena) had been recently murdered. Meanwhile all young Jews had been deported to Germany.

Sir Francis Osborne had taken up the matter with the Curia at the request of the British high commissioner in Rome. On September 9th, he reported to the Foreign Office that the issue had by now reached deadlock. Berlin's reaction to the Pontiff's appeal was only to point out that the Italian Social Republic was a sovereign state and that the problem of the Jewish internees in Italy was an Italian domestic affair in which Germans had no business to interfere. Since the Holy See had no relations with the Fascist Republican government, Pius XII had no *locus standi* for intervention in the matter.

Through the Jewish Foundation for Christian Rescuers/ADL, many survivors have provided financial aid for those who helped them. Presently they are repaying a moral obligation to 1,200 unique individuals, in twenty-six countries, who risked their lives to save Jews. These rescuers need assistance to live their remaining years in dignity.

One of the early postwar statements on anti-Semitism was made in Seelisberg (Switzerland), overlooking the lake of Four Cantons, at an international conference in 1947. It was made by Father Calliste Lopinot, a French Capuchin who had been chaplain at the Ferramonti-Tarsia concentration camp in Calabria from 1941 to 1944. Having witnessed the events of the Nazi occupation in Italy, he reported on the extraordinary measures taken by the Catholic Church, as well as on the remarkable work of religious who opened their doors to protect Jews. In Rome, 400 took refuge with the Franciscan Fathers at St. Bartholomew's on the Tiber; 80 were lodged at Holy Cross parish; for seven months Father Volpini had 65 living in his parish of Notre Dame de la Providence. The list of those who helped the Vatican is unending.

Father Lopinot quoted Pius XII's discourse to the cardinals on June 2, 1944, and spoke about the hospitality of the Holy See and the financial assistance given. He included organizations: San Raffaele—the Pallottines with Father Anthony Weber as secretary general assisted over 25,000 Jews to emigrate to the Americas; Ruppen-Ambord—Colonel Ulrico Ruppen and Father Beato Ambord directed this group from the Jesuit generalate of Borgo S. Spirito; DELASEM—the Capuchin Father Marie-Benôit de Bourg d'Iré, with Settimio Sorani, coordinated the rescue operations that saved the lives of innumerable Jews.

According to Father Lopinot, the apostolic visitor in Rome who had charge of 200 female convents wrote: "I recommended to the superiors of religious houses that they accept the Jews with charity and make every effort to hide those in danger of being arrested by the Germans." His recommendation included cloistered convents where he had placed 99 Jews. He said he came to this decision after having reread Proverbs:

> Rescue those who are being dragged to death,
> and from those tottering to execution withdraw not.
> If you say, "I know not this man!"

does not he who tests hearts perceive it?
He who guards your life knows it,
and he will repay each one according to his deeds.[38]

Father Lopinot's presentation at the international conference concluded with the following statement: "These are our sentiments. Ours is the spirit of Pius XII that radiates in his discourses and his example....Let us therefore work assiduously, with confidence. May the spirit of Pius XII save humanity, heal the wounds that are still open, and reunite all races."

Most members of the Catholic Church opposed Nazism. The Holy See responded with action, not words only. Whenever Catholic bishops protested, the Nazis retaliated with more deaths. Although warned not to speak about the deportation of Dutch Jews, the archbishop of Utrecht publicly protested. The Nazis retaliated by increasing the deportations. If the Pope had denounced and publicly protested Hitler's inhumanity, would more lives have been saved? Whichever course he would have taken, terrible consequences were inevitable.

Unable to stop Hitler's fury and stem the tide of evil, the Pope endeavored to alleviate, appeal, petition, and save many lives. Despite his efforts to intervene on behalf of persecuted Catholic priests, more than 3,000 were put to death by the Nazis. Alfred Rosenberg stated in his diary that propaganda moves of the Catholic Church against Hitler's Reich would have hastened the execution of still more Jews and priests.

Eminent rabbinical leaders made special appeals to the Holy See: Grand Rabbi of Jerusalem, Dr. Isaac Herzog; Grand Rabbi of the British Empire, Dr. Joseph Hertz; Rabbi Abraham Kalmanowitz, of Mir, in Lithuania; and Rabbi Safran of Bucharest, among others.

The Talmud teaches that "whoever saves one life, it is as though he had saved a whole world." Pius XII received the commendations and gratitude of worldwide Jewry for his noble efforts on behalf of thousands of them.

The excellent collaboration between the nuncios and the leaders of the Jewish communities demonstrates that the Holy See carried out its humanitarian mission "without distinction of nationality, religion, or race."

On learning of a possible public protest, Joachim von Ribbentrop, who issued deceptive answers to Vatican protests, sent guidelines on silencing the Vatican to the German Ambassador, Ernst von Weizsäcker: "Should the Vatican plan to make a political or propagandist statement against Germany, it should be made clear to them that any worsening in relations would by no means work one-sidedly to Germany's disadvantage. It should be made clear that the Reich government has no lack of effective propaganda material and certainly could take adequate steps to counter effectively any strike against Germany attempted by the Vatican."[39]

Throughout his pontificate, Pius XII's fatherly concern extended to all the victims of World War II, regardless of race or creed. His humanitarian efforts during the last stages of the war were directed toward alleviating suffering and protecting human life and human rights. His diplomacy and direct humanitarian works made him a champion of peace, of compassion, and of human dignity.

No honest seeker of truth will question Pope Pius XII's integrity, charity, and commitment to humanity. To have a balanced view of his efforts and accomplishments, one must consult the many volumes of Vatican documents where the true story unfolds. Details of what was done and what was not done are clearly stated. According to the Jesuit historian Father Robert Graham, "A study of the Vatican documents is the only way to understand the truth and to do justice to those who stretched a helping hand to the Jews in those tragic days."[40]

Daniel Counihan reached Rome as a correspondent for the *Catholic Herald* in 1944. He had ample opportunities to report the conversations and interviews he had with Christians, Jews, agnostics, and atheists—people in the Vatican and out of it. They had experienced the agony of Rome under Nazi occupation and terror, and knew how the Pope, the Vatican, and the clergy and religious of Rome had comported themselves in those dreadful days.

Criticisms about Pius XII's policies had redoubled after his death. In 1958, Daniel Counihan was again in Rome as a correspondent. What astonished and disturbed him was that critics concentrated mainly on one theme—an allegation "that the Pope had done too little to denounce and oppose the crimes of Nazi Germany, and especially, that he was indifferent to the Nazi persecution of the Jews, and had, for example, shown no concern for their fate during the Nazi reign of terror in Rome."

As his predecessor's Secretary of State, Pius XII had played a vital part in framing the encyclical *Mit brennender Sorge*, which was directed at Hitler's Germany, and condemned, among other things, the "myth of blood and race."

Counihan's article of October 23, 1981, commemorated the forty-second anniversary of Pius XII's first encyclical, *Summi Pontificatus*. The encyclical was a clear, if implicit, condemnation of the political and religious policies of the German and Soviet governments. In it, the Pope denounced totalitarianism as being opposed to the principles of natural and international law. The French propaganda services were so pleased that they dropped, by air over Germany, thousands of copies in miniature. So anti-Nazi was the encyclical that Nazi authorities restricted its publication in Germany.

Because of military censorship during the war, Daniel Counihan could not publish the extraordinary escapades of Monsignor Hugh O'Flaherty, an Irish citizen with headquarters in the German college, who ran a famous organization for looking after escaped British prisoners in Rome. The reporter was reminded that the fighting was still going on, and that nothing must be written to endanger people still under German occupation.

However, O'Flaherty was recognized for his efforts after the Liberation. He was honored by Italy, Australia, and Canada and given the United States Medal of Freedom. His story was told in the 1983 motion picture *The Scarlet and the Black* with Gregory Peck as O'Flaherty and Christopher Plummer as the Nazi Herbert Kappler. The film was based on *The Scarlet Pimpernel of the Vatican* by J. P. Gallagher.

Monsignor O'Flaherty is credited for having devoted all his time and energy to hiding refugees and Allied POWs from the Nazis. He built a network of hundreds of people to help him with his efforts and saved thousands of innocent people from death.

In his book *The Papacy in the Modern World*, J. Derek Holmes describes how the Vatican sheltered myriad Jews from deportation by the Nazis. The Pope, helped by two German diplomats, carefully concealed what was being done so that similar work could continue. Father Holmes says: "The Pope's own work on behalf of the Jews might have been endangered by a public denunciation of the Nazis, even though such a denunciation might have justified his moral reputation in the eyes of mankind."

Representing the Hebrew Commission, Dr. Joseph Nathan addressed the Jewish Community: "We express our heartfelt gratitude to those who protected and saved us during the Nazi-Fascist persecutions. Above all, we acknowledge the Supreme Pontiff and the religious men and women who, executing the directives of the Holy Father, recognized the persecuted as their brothers and, with great abnegation, hastened to help them, disregarding the terrible dangers to which they were exposed." (*L'Osservatore Romano*, September 8, 1945.)

Dr. William F. Rosenblum, in his sermon at Temple Israel in New York City on October 12, 1958, spoke about Pope Pius XII who made it possible for "thousands of Jewish victims of Nazism and Fascism to be hidden away in monasteries and convents of the various Catholic orders and for Jewish children to be taken into Catholic orphanages." He paid tribute to the Pope as "a great religious leader whose works for brotherliness and peace in a time of crisis in our history should remain as an example to emulate."

The senior Rabbi, Dr. Julius Mark, delivered another tribute from the pulpit of Temple Emanu-El on Park Avenue: "We mourn the passing of a great religious statesman and spiritual leader, Pope Pius XII. Possessed of a brilliant mind, a compassionate heart and a dedicated spirit, His Holiness gave of himself generously and self-sacrificingly to the sacred task of world peace founded on justice. May his soul be bound up in the bond of everlasting life."

5. Epilogue

On February 4, 1995, *The Tablet* published a letter to the editor by Father Robert Graham, S.J., entitled "Pius XII and the Jews." The letter follows in its entirety.

"Sir: The recent BBC documentary on Pope Pius XII and the Jews, which *The Tablet* extensively reported, illustrates how easy it is for the media to present loaded versions of a particular theme and set the unsuspecting viewer off on the wrong track.

"There was a glaring omission which would have made a difference: the real record of Jewish-Vatican relations during the war. The Vatican has published four volumes on its work for the victims of the war and, in particular, its correspondence with the world Jewish organizations appealing to it for help.

"This assistance was readily given and earned the spontaneous appreciation of the Jewish leaders in Britain and the United States. They found that Pope Pius XII was one of the few on the Continent from whom they could expect understanding and help. There ensued an uninterrupted series of appeals, with corresponding action on the part of the Pope on behalf of the stricken Jews in Nazi-occupied Europe. Never before in history had there been such regular and cordial communication between a Pope and the world Jewish leadership. I submit that this bright chapter has been most undeservedly and shamefully ignored, for it did not fit into the image one wanted to convey.

"Is all this revealing documentation irrelevant? As one of the editors of that series, *Actes et documents du Saint Siège relatifs à la Seconde Guerre Mondiale*, allow me to express my astonishment at the systematic blindness in evidence. The BBC 2 producers let loose an avalanche of cruel imputations of motives, while ignoring, with an air of objectivity, substantial evidence in conflict with their thesis. Is this fair?

174

"The Jewish rescue agencies at that time (1939–1945) knew better than did the Pope how fruitless and harmful would be the kind of melodramatic cries that Pius XII is now reproached for not uttering. Like the Pope they too worked in silence. They asked instead for the pontiff's intervention in the innumerable cases (recorded in the four volumes mentioned) where some successful action to save lives was possible. Why did BBC 2 choose to ignore this body of evidence and deny it the weight it deserves?

"Fifty years later, we like to tell the Pope not only what to do but how to do it; not only what to say but how to say it. And this so often out of the depths of ignorance. This is ignoble second-guessing. Is that not a bit too much?"

A second letter to the editor appeared in *The Tablet* on March 11, 1995, entitled "The Church and the Jews."

"Sir: A short letter of mine to *The Tablet* (February 4, 1995) triggered a four-page article by Jonathan Lewis, the producer of the BBC 2 documentary on Pius XII, the Nazis and the Jews. I am surprised he should say that 'one letter stands out from the others.' Mine. I hope I am not expected to reply with a blockbuster of my own. But I do think I am called to develop further my earlier brief criticisms of what is now more clearly seen to be a 'loaded' TV documentary.

"I wrote of the 'bright chapter' in the history of Jewish-Vatican collaboration during these awful years. Is it wrong to search for and preserve what is positive in an otherwise tragic time? The local Jewish communities and the world rescue organizations looked for, and got, hope and help from the Pope. The producer scoffs at my characterization and tries to run it back to 1944. That is a bit late in the tragedy. In reality, this relationship developed with the beginning of the war and increased with experience in the successive stages.

"From the first days in 1939, Pius XII set among his priorities to come to the help of all the war's victims, as he said often, 'without distinction of nationality, religion or race.' And he pursued his goal consistently and persistently despite contradictions and obstacles. For the Jews of Nazi-occupied Europe, the Vatican in those venomous years represented a beam of hope. They learned that the Vatican was able, and ready, for instance, through its influence at strategic points, to facilitate their emigration from the danger zone. The fall of France in 1940 was a disaster for the refugees, but the work of rescue went on nonetheless, through the Balkans, through Italy, and through Spain.

But the spectre of deportation soon loomed. In Slovakia the threat of deportation of Slovak Jews, under the cover of the war in Russia, shocked the Vatican and it reacted strongly. This was in the spring of 1942, a few weeks after the Wannsee Conference, and many months before the Geneva-based World Jewish Congress (Gerhardt Riegner) learned of the plan to exterminate all Jews.

"Jonathan Lewis does not go into the question as to whether in the Pope's mind a public protest might have done no good and might in fact have cost lives. This was nevertheless a consideration that weighed heavily on Pius XII who had to reckon with the possible consequences, in terms of human lives and sufferings, of an ill-advised move on his part. This is not a secondary aspect but goes to the root of the wartime conduct of the Pope.

"Pius XII expressed publicly on several occasions this very concern. His words reflected, of course, the insistent appeals that came to him, in the first place from the Poles and indeed through a concerted *démarche*, in the end of 1942, of the governments-in-exile located in London. The Pope felt that he could not assume the responsibility for what might ensue had he launched into the course urged upon him.

"It is certain that an open protest—and not only about the fate of the Jews in Hitler's hand—would have had no effect on the Nazis. Does anyone doubt this? Perhaps for some that should have made no difference. This was not enough for Pius XII. He had to look farther and ask if he was not putting innocent lives at risk by an open, foreseeably ineffectual, declaration of protest. In all respect for a great religious and humanitarian leader living at the peak of the greatest war in history, as man's inhumanity to man found its highest and most brutal expression, the awful dilemma facing him deserves more understanding, in the name of justice."

Pius XII exemplified his dilemma in particularly dramatic and explicit terms when he gave an audience, in 1942, to Don Pirro Scavizzi, an old friend and fellow-Roman. As chaplain of the hospital train of the Order of Malta, he brought to the Pope what he had learned through his mission in the East. Scavizzi had not seen any concentration camps but he had seen enough, and heard enough, to give a gruesome picture of the treatment of the Jews.

The Pope, distressed by the shocking revelation, stated: "Perhaps my solemn protest might have obtained for me the approval of the civilized world, but it would have brought to the Jews a most implacable persecution, even greater than the one they are now suffering."

Father John Jay Hughes, a Church historian and professor in the archdiocese of St. Louis, Missouri,[41] recently wrote an article entitled "The Dilemma of Pius XII." He recalls that Dino Alfieri, Italy's wartime ambassador in Berlin, visited Pope Pius XII in 1940. During their conversation, the Pope stated: "The Italians know all too well the horrible crimes that are being committed in Poland. We would have denounced them in searing words but for the knowledge that to do so would worsen the fate of the victims....Whatever happens in the future, even if they come and take me off to a concentration camp, I have absolutely nothing with which to reproach myself. Every man will be answerable to God for his own actions."

A devout Catholic and an anti-Nazi, Ambassador Alfieri was a participant in the events he describes. A man who was not a participant, the Belgian historian Léon Papeleux, is critical of wartime Vatican policy in his book, *Les silences de Pie XII,* published in 1980. Yet he writes: "It is indisputable; Pius XII felt himself impaled on the horns of a terrible dilemma: to speak out with no certainty that this would halt the crimes, and with the risk of worsening the victims' fate; or to remain silent and risk the impression that the highest authority was covering the crimes with his silence."

In 1941, Bishop von Galen courageously condemned Nazi killing of the mentally ill. The slaughter of these Jews was carried out in close proximity to the next of kin. The Nazis had systematically isolated the victims by transporting them to Poland. In strictest secrecy, with their next of kin, they were murdered.

In July 1942, the Dutch bishops publicly protested these actions. Their protests resulted in an immediate intensification of the persecution. The Carmelite nun Edith Stein was among the deported and killed. Pope Pius XII expressed his deep concern for the victims and their families.

An article by Father Hughes is compelling: "What about the Vatican's failure in June 1944 to publicize the eyewitness report of an escaped Auschwitz prisoner about the mass killings there? This seems inexcusable—until we know that leaders of the Dutch Resistance movement and even members of the Jewish Council in Amsterdam (who cooperated with the Nazi deportations in the hope of saving as many as possible, themselves included) flatly refused to credit not just one but numerous eyewitness reports from Auschwitz starting in 1942."

In 1969, this incredible story was recounted in detail by the Dutch historian Louis de Jong.[42] He concluded that "both in its methods and scope the Holocaust was so horrible, and so unprecedented, that most people were able to accept it as reality only when it had ceased to exist."

Even today denial continues in some quarters. The widespread belief that Pius XII remained silent also continues. His protests did not satisfy the Western Allies or the postwar critics. However, they were well understood by the Nazis, who were furious.

The Jewish writer Pinchas Lapide in his book *Three Popes and the Jews* quotes a Jew who, like thousands of others with Vatican help, was able to escape the roundup of Roman Jews in October 1943, as saying twenty years later: "None of us wanted the Pope to speak out openly. We were all fugitives, and we did not want to be pointed out as such. The Gestapo would only have increased and intensified its inquisition....It was much better the Pope kept silent. We all felt the same, and today we still believe that."[43] Thanks to secret Vatican efforts, Pope Pius XII's silence saved Dr. Marcus Melchior, Chief Rabbi of Denmark, with almost his entire community.

Pius XI's 1937 encyclical did not have any effect on the Nazis. Undoubtedly, it had been prepared under the direction of his Secretary of State, Eugenio Pacelli, who became Pope Pius XII in 1939. Would the Nazis have been more open to another encyclical amidst the passions of wartime Europe? The evidence says, "No!"

The wartime Resistance movements that showed great concern for the Jews were in Italy, Belgium, and Denmark. Some countries were indifferent. Certainly they could have offered refuge. Others, including the United States, refused to liberalize their restrictive immigration policies.

In Germany, where listening to Vatican Radio was a capital offense, how could a papal appeal to conscience have an effect? This was a country with a controlled press, where priests were subject to Gestapo surveillance (almost 2,600 were imprisoned in the Dachau concentration camp and 1,072 died there).

Count von Moltke, the leader of the German Resistance to Hitler, was killed on January 23, 1945. The American diplomat George Kennan called him "the greatest person, morally, and the largest and most enlightened in his concepts that I met on either side of the battle-lines in the Second World War."

In 1943, Von Moltke wrote a friend in England about conditions in wartime Germany: "We now have 19 guillotines working at considerable speed without most people even knowing this fact, and practically nobody knows how many are beheaded per day. In my estimation there are about fifty daily, not counting those who die in concentration camps.... The worst is that this death is ignominious. Nobody takes much notice; the relatives hush it up because they would suffer the same fate at the hands of the Gestapo if they dared telling people what had happened."[44]

Maria Chiara Bonazzi in an article in *La Stampa* dated August 23, 1995, describes the anti-Semitism of the BBC: "Between 1939 and 1945 news about the Nazi atrocities was not divulged. It was the BBC's opinion that the public detested the Jews and was not disposed to accept the anti-German propaganda of those who swore that the gas chambers existed. The legendary Radio London accepted the tendentious skepticism of the Foreign Office about the concentration camps and made sure the microphones were closed.

"This revelation comes from the archives of the BBC and of the government papers disclosed for the first time by reporters of Radio 4. The newspaper *Independent on Sunday* anticipates the scandalous results of this research in the first segment of a program entitled "Document: The Unspeakable Atrocity."

Among these papers there is proof that the high-ranking members of the State Radio had little consideration for the Jews, and they maintained that the nation at large shared this opinion. The BBC never spoke about the Holocaust. While the British newspapers in 1942 referred to Hitler's massacre of one million Jews, the radio pretended it did not exist. The only exception was the discourse by Anthony Eden to Parliament in December. The prime minister denounced Germany for "implementing its intention to exterminate the Jewish population of Europe." Public opinion, far from refueling anti-Semitism, answered with an urgent appeal to the government to do more to help Hitler's victims. But the politics of the State Radio did not change.

When Richard Dimbleby transmitted the first historical reports from Bergen-Belsen, he did not mention that the victims were Jews. The shock provoked by his report was such that the BBC officials kept them in a drawer until confirmation was given by the newspapers.

Critics ask: "What could have been worse than the slaughter of 6 million Jews?" The answer is clear: "The slaughter of hundreds of thousands more." It is doubtful that even the most flaming papal protest would have slowed the Holocaust.

What is certain is that such a protest would have risked the lives of countless Jews hidden in Church institutions from Rome to Belgium and the clergy as well. Could things possibly have been made any worse? Of course. And, in this fickle world, Pope Pius XII would be blamed for it.

"The world cares about Holocaust survivors," was Pope John Paul II's message as he addressed AMCHA, marking the fiftieth anniversary of the victory over the Nazis. President Manfred Klafter, accompanied by Italian-born AMCHA therapist Dina Wardi, presented the Pope with an original painting by artist Miriam Neuberger, a hidden child whose entire family was killed in the Holocaust. Both Klafter and Wardi were among the survivors. They represented Israel's 300,000 survivors, some of whom were children saved by Catholic families and the Church during World War II.

Rabbi Leon Klenicki, director of interfaith affairs of the Anti-Defamation League of B'nai B'rith, stated that Catholic-Jewish relations have gone "from argument to dialogue, from conflict to a situation of meeting, from ignorance and alienation to encounter."

There is an ongoing and permanent sacred bond between the Church and the Jewish people. Israel's history and covenant are also ours. The New Testament cannot be understood in depth unless in relation to the Hebrew Scriptures. The best apologia is not in the realm of reasoned debate, but will be found in what Catholics and Jews do in the present for the sake of the future.

Eugene Fisher, director of Catholic-Jewish relations for the National Conference of Catholic Bishops, said that "until *Nostra Aetate*, the Second Vatican Council's 'Declaration on the Relationship of the Church to Non-Christian Religions,' there were no official teachings on Jewish-Christian relations." (*See* Part III, Section B, "Catholic-Jewish Relations," pp. 199–203.)

The Catholic Church recognizes the spiritual patrimony common to Christians and Jews. Documents now reflect the understanding of St. Paul that the Church cannot forget "she received the revelation of the Old Testament through the people with whom God, in His inexpressible mercy, made the ancient covenant."

Fifty years after the Holocaust, testimonials of living witnesses give insight to the mental, physical, and spiritual sufferings endured by the Jews. Pope John Paul II invites all to share their memories and to help others understand: "To keep alive the memory of what happened is not only an historical necessity but a moral one. We must not forget!"[45]

Clearly, in the face of more than 11 million Jews and non-Jews murdered by the Nazis, no one can claim that enough was done. To claim, however, that nothing was done by the Pope and the Church— or that the failure to do more was the result of indifference, cynicism, or cowardice—is grave historical falsification.

Time is the unfolding of truth. One reads in Ecclesiasticus (3:1–8) that "there is an appointed time for everything, and a time for every affair." After fifty years of misrepresentation of Pope Pius XII's role during the Holocaust, it is now time to tell the true story and acknowledge his leadership.

Dossiers, letters, related documents of war prisoners in the Vatican Bureau for Research.

Requests for information were received from every country in the world.

Vatican staff kept in touch with families of war prisoners.

Pope Pius XII at prayer.

Portrait of Shmuel del Arizza, an Italian Jew who disguised himself as a priest and lived in the Vatican from October 16, 1943, to June 6, 1944.

Part III

Leone Bondi and Virginia Piperno with three of their six children. The entire family was deported to Auschwitz, where they all perished.

A. Testimonials

---

1. Frank Tammera

*F*rank Tammera, a U.S. citizen, lived in Rome during the German occupation of World War II.

Frank was very young when, with his parents and two brothers, he went to Italy to visit relatives. Shortly after, his mother died and the family decided to remain there while retaining American citizenship. To support the family, his father opened a grocery store on Via Ostiense across from the Monastery of San Paolo.

During the war Frank and his brothers refused to join the Italian army. They had received instructions from the American embassy that, as American citizens, they had to obtain permits to remain in Rome. Provided they did not leave Rome before 8 A.M. and would return home before 6 P.M., their American citizenship would be respected. They were given a document that bore the seal of the Italian and Swiss governments.

Rome had been declared an "Open City." Frank recalls that, according to Bishop Ildebrando Vannucci of the Monastery of San Paolo, the Holy Father ordered all churches, monasteries, and convents to open their doors and to protect the Jewish refugees. In an agreement with General Kesselring, the Pope insisted that Vatican vehicles be respected. They were no longer subject to inspection by the German soldiers.

The bishop told Frank and six other young American seminary students to go to the Jewish synagogue to help gather the refugees. They were given cars with Vatican plates and Vatican flags. The Jews were hesitant about leaving their homes in the Trastevere ghetto, but soon word spread that they would be safe in the monastery. There they worked in the tailor shop and made outfits that they wore to disguise

189

themselves as monks and nuns. Their children attended classes with the Italians.

General Kesselring was suspicious about the Monastery of San Paolo. When he insisted on an inspection, he was told he would not be allowed to speak to anyone there. During his inspection tour of the monastery, everyone was working in silence. All the residents were dressed as monks and nuns. The general could not find fault.

Walking on Via Ostiense one day, Frank Tammera witnessed what happened when two women and a man were crossing the street. One woman was pregnant. For no apparent reason, German soldiers killed the three of them with bayonets.

Mr. Tammera, Frank's father, who had spent sixteen months in prison after the Fascists confiscated his store, invited two Jewish families to live with him. In all there were ten; they were told not to leave the premises. One young member of the Jewish family, whose name was Renato, decided to take a walk along Via Ostiense.

Unfortunately, Renato did not return from his walk. He was captured by the Germans and was either killed or sent to a concentration camp. The family never heard from him.

Camped across the way from the Tammera home was a platoon of German soldiers. Their task was to go from house to house to locate Jews who then would be sent to the concentration camps.

One day two German soldiers went to the Tammera house to investigate why Frank and his brothers were not in the Italian army. Since their father spoke very little German, the soldiers began to speak English. They soon discovered that all were American citizens.

The two German-Americans had been forced to join the army while visiting their homeland. They were originally from Brooklyn! During the conversation the soldiers learned that the Tammera family was harboring refugees in the house. The soldiers assured the Italian-Americans that they would arrange protection for the entire household. They immediately placed a sign on the door of the house in Italian and in German stating that no further inspection was needed. Later they returned with food and other necessities. In fact, throughout the war, they remained friendly and faithful to the Italians.

In the monastery of the Basilica of Saint Paul Outside-the-Walls, where Frank rendered service to the Vatican, there was a German monk, Fra Pietro, who was a master tailor and worked with the Jews.

One day, he invited Frank and the six Americans who were helping the Vatican protect the Jews to remain at the monastery for a game of chess and poker. They accepted his hospitality and went to bed at 1 A.M. When they separated, Fra Pietro told them that he had night duty and would have to sleep in the janitor's quarters near the gate.

Around 3 A.M., there was a great deal of commotion. The guard had opened the gate for a man disguised as a priest. Soon after, about 300 Nazi and Fascist soldiers entered and began rounding up the Jews. In the meantime, Swiss Guards arrived, forcing the soldiers to leave. The soldiers had succeeded in capturing only a few Jews.

When the Americans realized what was happening, they ran to the courtyard where they found three trucks covered with hay. They got under the trucks and waited patiently while the soldiers searched the vehicles, sticking their bayonets into the hay. They later learned that Fra Pietro was found dead along the roadside.

The Americans were now in danger. Soon after this incident, the friendly German-American soldiers invited Frank and his friends to go north where they would be safe. On the way American airplanes bombed the truck caravan. The Germans rushed them into a nearby church. That night the Americans pretended they were sleeping. In the morning everyone was forced to dig holes and prepare graves for the dead. The Americans were alerted to the fact that the Germans intended to kill them too.

At the suggestion of their soldier-friends, who took them to the railroad track going south, they reached Rome walking about ninety kilometers. The group consisted of Frank, his brother, one woman, and three other men.

Around this time, a new law was passed in Rome. Young men— American, English, French—had to surrender to the German officers or they would be killed on the spot. On hearing this, Frank and his friends took some clothing and went toward Anzio. They stopped at Cacciarella Reale where they joined shepherds who lived in a hut and tended their sheep. They killed rabbits and pigeons for food.

When the Nazis came, they were obliged to hide in the woods for three months. The Americans were on one side of the woods and the Germans on the other. Frank was shot in the face during a skirmish. The six friends were finally saved by the Americans who gave them uniforms and a Jeep to return to Rome. Only three survived.

[March 25, 1995, Interview with Frank Tammera, President, Purt Tech IND, RES, INT (Industry, Research, International), 177 E. McClellan Avenue, Livingston, NJ 07039.]

2. Fernando G. Giustini

In 1942, life in Rome became daily more and more difficult. There was an atmosphere of restlessness and unhappiness because of the war. Italian family life had been disrupted. The bread, milk, and foodstuff lines were becoming longer and longer. My family decided, therefore, to return to Corchiano, a little village of some 800 inhabitants, about seventy-two kilometers northeast of Rome. It consisted of small tufo buildings perched atop large tufo cliffs, so typical of this region of Italy. The village was surrounded by a small gorge at the bottom of which ran a tributary of the Tiber River.

The only access into the village was a small bridge. Visitors rarely passed through Corchiano. The population had not been touched by the war with the exception of some men who had been called to duty in the armed services. There was a lukewarm interest in the war and people hoped it would end soon.

My grandfather, a sturdy farmer whose allegiance was to the Allied cause, had spent fifteen years in the United States in the early part of the century. When war was declared he commented: "OK, now the Axis is really in trouble; Pittsburgh alone, with its steel mills, can win the war against Italy and Germany."

My father, an admirer of the Risorgimento, was a teacher and a student of Italian history. He was a man who still looked upon Germany and Austria as enemy countries. Obviously he loved the United States and often spoke of his childhood in an elementary school in McKees Rocks, Pennsylvania.

In 1940, Helen and Oscar Deutsch, a Jewish couple, after unsuccessfully trying to obtain visas for Switzerland, went to Albania and obtained permission to go to America. En route to Naples, their car broke down and they missed the boat and the opportunity to relocate in the United States. Instead they were sent to the Ferramonti internment camp. When the Italian government decided that the camp was needed for Yugoslavians, the Jewish families at the camp were sent to live in villages where they were allowed to circulate. They were required to report to the police daily.

My grandmother allowed the Deutsch couple to occupy my bedroom. A strong, genuine friendship developed immediately between my father and Oscar Deutsch. They spent time together speaking English and reviewing the classic works of Lord Byron, Longfellow, and Shakespeare. In addition, my father had a good collection of American magazines that he shared with Oscar. In November 1942, my father left for Yugoslavia to teach Italian in a public school.

When the Fascists and Nazis started a systemized canvassing for Jews to take to Germany, the Giustini family began hiding the Deutschs. My father, who had returned to Corchiano, responded with great enthusiasm to the invitation of Radio London to join the Resistance. He became the leader of the activity that covered the territory between Prima Porta, just on the outskirts of Rome and Orte. Thirty-five to forty Allied prisoners and airmen who were shot down from the skies over Italy were rescued by my father and his friends, and our little house in the country became the headquarters of this rescue operation.

In the meantime my father had become a member of Monsignor Hugh O'Flaherty's organization in Rome. Allied soldiers were smuggled into Rome by my father in small groups and sheltered in the various hiding places made available by the Vatican.

I was thirteen years old when the Germans invaded our village searching for my father and anyone who was connected with him. My father was able to escape. My mother, brother, sister, and I left Corchiano on foot in the middle of the night and walked thirteen to fourteen miles to the next town to get a train to Rome where we were hidden until the Allied troops entered the city.

Although the people of our community did not know about the atrocities that were taking place north of the Alps, they were well aware of the local sabotage against the Germans. Yet everyone acted as though nothing was happening. They had a profound respect for human life and would have helped any person in danger of persecution.

In Rome, my father continued his activity, and it was at this time that he had the opportunity to help another Jewish family. Monsignor O'Flaherty introduced him to a young man named Neerman, who was hiding with his brother in the Plaza Hotel in the center of Rome. Their mother had been arrested by the Germans. Monsignor asked my father to go to the hotel, pay their bill, and take the two young men into a more secure hiding place.

Both Gestapo and Fascist police became more and more aggressive. Raids on religious institutions increased. There were many arrests and the Rome organization had to stop operations. As my father was trying to help two POWs, he was arrested. Fortunately, after several days of torture in the basement of the Czechoslovakian embassy, he was able to escape. (*See* Appendix, Document V, pp. 224–230.)

Hiding Jewish newlyweds and fleeing in the middle of the night are some of the memories I shall never forget. The issue of the Holocaust has to be told time and time again, so that it doesn't happen again.

[Fernando G. Giustini, M.D., F.A.C.O.G., F.A.C.S. Diplomate of the American Board of Obstetrics & Gynecology, 30 Medical Park, Suite 230, Wheeling, West Virginia 26003-6391.]

3. Joseph S. Frelinghuysen

The Frelinghuysen family included a vice-presidential candidate, four United States senators, and a university president. Hanging on the walls of Joseph S. Frelinghuysen's home in Far Hills, New Jersey, were the portraits of his great-great-grandfather who had commanded a company of artillery at the Battle of Princeton in 1776, of his grandfather who had commanded a detachment of troops in the War of 1812, and of his father, a United States senator from 1917 to 1923, who was a Spanish-American War veteran.

Joseph Frelinghuysen was a first lieutenant in the United States Reserves. He went on active duty in July 1941. Fifty years later he wrote *Passages to Freedom*, the stirring story of his flight from captivity. His book tells a story of hope and enriches the annals of World War II.

As a captain, Frelinghuysen was part of the Allies' heavily armed troops that landed on the shores of northwestern Africa. These were the first steps of the assault that would permit the Allies to roll through Algeria to Tunisia, eventually gaining control of the Mediterranean from Nazi Germany and Fascist Italy.

He describes the inevitable, chilling experience: American infantrymen were "sprawled out at the side of the road, their faces a grayish green, the ground around them pooled with drying blood." Within a few weeks, about twelve miles from Tunis, his artillery reconnaisance party was ambushed by German paratroopers.

Fortunately, Joseph Frelinghuysen was among the Americans and the British captured by the Nazis to be turned over to the Italians. The prisoners were sent first to Capua near Naples, and then to Chieti in the Abruzzi region. He realized that he must learn to speak Italian. Determined to escape, he began his studies immediately and became a fluent speaker. He also realized that in order to escape it was necessary to follow a routine of strenuous physical exercise and arranged a schedule of calisthenics.

By September 1943, the Italian Prime Minister, Pietro Badoglio, had secretly surrendered to the Allies. After ten months of prison life, Frelinghuysen, aware that he was to be shipped to Germany, planned to escape. On September 23rd, accompanied by Captain Richard M. Rossbach—and with the blessing of their superior officer—they crawled through wire fences, under the eye of a German machine gun.

Shirley Horner wrote about Frelinghuysen's book in *The New York Times* (January 6, 1991), and described how the two men slept wherever they could, be it a shack or a cave, "too exhausted to worry about hunger or the jagged rocks." They moved across "all of Italy's heavily guarded rail and highway arteries, which were carrying supplies and ammunition to the German divisions fighting in the south." Their only hope lay in crossing the rest of the Apennines and reaching the British Eighth Army.

Frelinghuysen explains that what really saved them was the "humanity" of many of the people of the Italian mountain ranges, who took pity on the starving soldiers and risked their lives to give comfort to the Americans.

In particular, he could not forget the DiGiacomantonio family. They lived in a remote valley of the Apennines and provided shelter to many seeking refuge from the Germans. They cared for the New Jersey soldier as if he were one of them, and a warm friendship developed between him and the thirty-year-old Bernardino and his wife Letizia.

Captain Frelinghuysen describes how in 1956 he and his wife— by then the parents of four—drove "up from Rome to Abruzzi, past snowbanks ten feet high, to a place where the road ended" in cobblestones. Smiling townspeople greeted the Italian-speaking American with "Ben arrivato, Giuseppe." His friend Bernardino welcomed him and sadly revealed that the Germans had murdered many of the Abruzzesi who had helped the escapees.

[Joseph S. Frelinghuysen, *Passages to Freedom*, Manhattan, Kansas: Sunflower University Press, 1991.]

4. Massacres in Tuscany

Only when Friedrich Andrae's book *Auch gegen Frauen und Kuder Kinder (Even against Women and Children, The War of the Wehrmacht against Civilians in Italy 1943–45)* appeared did German culture take cognizance of the barbarisms committed by the Nazis on the Italian peninsula during World War II.

One of the most appalling and abominable massacres perpetrated by the Nazis occurred in Via Porrettana, Marzabotto, a small town along the Reno River located in the Appenines of Emilia. It was drizzling and very cold toward dawn on the morning of September 29, 1944, when the SS Panzer Grenadier 16th Division Reichsführer, under the command of Major Walter Reder, entered Marzabotto, a picturesque town encircled by huts and farming villages with small churches and cemeteries.

Rushing from one house to another the Germans shot and killed whomever they encountered—including women and children—and set fire to the barns and stables. The massacre lasted until October 5th. In many homes people were piled in one room and killed with a hand grenade. The total number executed in this manner—1,830 men, women, children, and defenseless invalids—is appalling even after the passage of half a century.

Just as their forefathers had sought sanctuary during the invasions of the Middle Ages, the inhabitants of the hamlet of Casaglia took refuge in the church. Don Ubaldo Marchioni exhorted them to remain calm and to pray. A man who was paralyzed and sitting in a wheelchair at the entrance of the church was machine-gunned by the SS. When the pastor tried to explain that these people had nothing to do with the anti-Fascist partisans, the blast of a machine gun struck him at the altar. Young and old were herded to the cemetery where they were massacred with machine guns. Similar episodes took place in the villages of

Cadotto, Prunara, Steccata, Casone di Rio Moneta, in the oratory of Cerpiano, and others.

When it seemed that the bloody fury of the Germans was placated, the pastor of Sperticano, Don Giovanni Fornasini, went to the San Martino Cemetery on October 13th to give Christian burial to the corpses that had been burned. The stench of decomposing bodies that had been covered with gasoline and set on fire filled the air. The SS were still lingering in the area. At the sight of the terrible spectacle, unaware that he was being observed by an SS Captain, Don Fornasini commented: "These were not partisans; only the elderly, women, and children." The Captain responded, "Pastor kaput." The blast of a machine gun ended his life.

Nazi cruelty against civilians was manifest in all Tuscany. Testimonials about the massacres were provided by a few survivors who, pretending to be dead, had been buried under the corpses or had hidden in tombs. At Civitella della Chiana, in the Province of Arezzo, 168 persons were massacred on June 29, 1944.

A few days later on July 4th, the SS arrived in Castelnuovo del Sabbioni, in the municipality of Cavriglia, Arezzo. Lignite mines and an electrical plant, considered war industries of primary importance, were in this area.

When employees of the mine industry of Valdarno arrived at work, 82 persons were captured by the SS. These hostages were laborers of the war industry; they were not partisans. The defenseless civilians were herded to the church where the pastor, Don Ferrante Bagiardi, was given permission to distribute Communion. He tried to intercede for the prisoners and offered his life in exchange for them. In response to his request, the Nazis machine-gunned Don Ferrante and the poor unfortunate prisoners as they stood in front of the church. The corpses were covered with gasoline and burned.

That afternoon Nazi cruelty shifted to the valley, in the village of Meleto. Ninety-three persons were rounded up. Don Giovanni Fondelli voluntarily joined his parishioners: the dead, who were killed and burned as in the neighboring Castelnuovo, numbered 94. Similar atrocities were committed in various other localities—Gubbio in Umbria and, in Tuscany, Vallucciole and Stazzema.

[These episodes were related by survivors of Nazi terrorism in Tuscany. They are indicative of the sufferings of countless Italians during the German occupation of Italy.]

B. Catholic-Jewish Relations

*I*n *Crossing the Threshold of Hope* (1994), Pope John Paul II dedicated a chapter on Judaism: "Through the amazing plurality of religions, arranged as it were in concentric circles, we come to the religion that is closest to our own—that of the people of God of the Old Testament."

Catholic-Jewish relations were clearly defined by the Second Vatican Council in 1965 by *Nostra Aetate* (Section 4). This Declaration on the Relationship of the Church to Non-Christian Religions states: "As this Sacred Synod searches into the mystery of the Church, it recalls the spiritual bond linking the people of the New Covenant with Abraham's stock."

The Catholic Church makes no distinction between men or peoples in the matter of human dignity and the rights that flow from it. She rejects any discrimination against human beings or harassment of them because of their race, color, condition of life, or religion. Mindful of her spiritual patrimony with the Jews, the Church deplores the hatred, persecutions, and displays of anti-Semitism directed against them.

The following statement was issued on November 14, 1942, by the Administrative Board of the National Catholic Welfare Conference (a forerunner of the National Conference of Catholic Bishops): "Since the murderous assault on Poland, utterly devoid of every semblance of humanity, there has been a premeditated and systematic extermination of the people of this nation. The same satanic technique is being applied to many other peoples. We feel a deep sense of revulsion against the cruel indignities heaped upon the Jews in conquered countries and upon defenseless peoples not of our faith....We raise our voice in protest against despotic tyrants who have lost all sense of humanity by condemning thousands of innocent persons to death in subjugated countries as acts of reprisal; by placing thousands of innocent victims in concentration camps, and by permitting unnumbered persons to die of starvation."

With the advantage of hindsight in the aftermath of World War II, Christians everywhere questioned whether enough had been done to aid their fellow human beings, the persecuted Jews. Charges were made that Pope Pius XII remained silent in the face of what was happening to Jews across Nazi-occupied Europe.

Dr. Joseph L. Lichen, then director of the Intercultural Affairs Department of the Anti-Defamation League of B'nai B'rith, commented in a pamphlet: "There is considerable documentation in support of Pope Pius' fear that a formal statement would worsen, not improve, conditions for the persecuted." (See *A Question of Judgment: Pius XII and the Jews,* published by the National Catholic Welfare Conference.)

In 1936, as Vatican Secretary of State, Eugenio Cardinal Pacelli set up an organization for aiding Jewish refugees from Nazism. As Pope he continued to support this rescue mission group operated by Father Anton Weber in Lisbon. The Portuguese government would grant transit visas, for passage principally to Brazil, but only to refugees with steamship tickets. The cost to help each emigrant was about $800, with much of the funding coming from the Vatican. Father Weber's organization helped about 25,000 Jews, of whom some 4,000 were able to flee safely overseas.

On March 11, 1940, the Pope granted a formal audience to Joachim von Ribbentrop, German foreign secretary, who spoke of "the futility of papal alignment with the enemies of the Führer. Pius XII heard von Ribbentrop out politely and impassively. Then he opened an enormous ledger on his desk and, in his perfect German, began to recite a catalogue of the persecutions inflicted by the Third Reich in Poland, listing the date, place, and precise details of each crime. The audience was terminated; the Pope's position was clearly unshakable."

In 1942, efforts by the Vatican failed. The Pope agreed to a plan devised by a Capuchin priest, Father Marie-Benôit, that entailed getting the help of the United States and Great Britain to move some 50,000 French Jews to North Africa. The plan, which was based on the priest's persuasive powers with Italian authorities in occupied France and his "factory" in a Marseilles monastery for turning out forged papers, failed when German troops entered the Italian zone of France.

In his Christmas message of 1942 and on June 2, 1943, Pope Pius XII deplored the treatment of "hundreds of thousands of persons who, through no fault of their own and by the single fact of their nationality or race, have been condemned to death or to progressive extinction. It is a consolation for us that, through the moral and spiritual assistance of Our representatives and through Our financial assistance, we have been able to comfort a great many of the refugees, homeless, and emigrants, including non-Aryans."

After Pope Pius XII's death, Rabbi Elio Toaff said: "More than anyone else, we have had the opportunity to appreciate the great kindness, filled with compassion and magnanimity, that the Pope displayed during the terrible years of persecution and terror, when it seemed that there was no hope left for us."

According to Pope John Paul II, there should be a complete eradication of anti-Semitism "in its ugly and sometimes violent manifestations." He also stated during the twelfth meeting of the International Catholic-Jewish Liaison Committee held on October 28–30, 1985: "The Catholic Church is always prepared, with the help of God's grace, to revise and renew whatever in her attitudes and ways of expression happens to conform less with her own identity, founded upon the Word of God, the Old and the New Testament, as read in the Church. This she does, not out of any expediency nor to gain practical advantage of any kind, but out of a deep consciousness of her own *mystery* and a renewed willingness to translate it into practice."

Other statements by Pope John Paul II in promotion of dialogue between Catholics and Jews include: June 7, 1979, at Auschwitz, he called the infamous concentration camp the "Golgotha of the Modern World"; October 3, 1980, in a homily on the Hill of Martyrs in Otranto, Italy, he said: "The Jewish people, after tragic experience connected with the extermination of so many sons and daughters, driven by the desire for security, set up the state of Israel"; November 17, 1980, in an address to the Jewish community in Mainz, he spoke of "the meeting between the people of God of the Old Covenant...and the people of the New Covenant"; March 6, 1982, in addressing representatives of episcopal conferences gathered in Rome, he called for a renewal of catechesis that "will not only present Jews and Judaism in an honest and objective manner, but will also do so with a lively awareness of our common spiritual heritage...taking into account the faith and religious life of the Jewish people as professed and lived now as well"; March

22, 1984, at an audience with members of the Anti-Defamation League of B'nai B'rith, he commented on "the mysterious spiritual link which brings us close together, in Abraham and through Abraham, in God who chose Israel and brought forth the Church from Israel."

Pope John Paul II has underscored the importance of good relations between Jews and Catholics. In his apostolic letter *Redemptionis Anno* (1984) which dealt with Jerusalem, he wrote: "For the Jewish people who live in the state of Israel, and who preserve in that land such precious testimonies to their history and their faith, we must ask for the desired security and the due tranquillity that is the prerogative of every nation and condition of life and of progress for every society."

On February 14, 1985, in receiving a delegation of the American Jewish Committee, Pope John Paul II reconfirmed the meaning of *Nostra Aetate*. In meeting with Australia's Jewish leaders in Sydney on November 26, 1986, the Pope said: "No valid theological justification could ever be found for acts of discrimination or persecution against Jews. In fact, such acts must be held to be sinful."

On April 13, 1986, Pope John Paul II became the first Pope since St. Peter to pay a recorded visit to a synagogue. He met and prayed with Chief Rabbi Elio Toaff in Rome's central synagogue, the place of worship for what is believed to be the longest established Jewish community in Europe. Their vocal prayers were selections from the Psalms, which the two faiths have in common.

"The Jewish religion is not 'extrinsic' to us, but in a certain way is 'intrinsic' to our own religion," the Pope said. "With Judaism therefore we have a relationship which we do not have with any other religion. You are our dearly beloved brothers, and in a certain way it could be said that you are our elder brothers." In his address he recalled the "high price in blood" paid by the Jewish community in Rome during the war. "And it was surely a significant gesture that in those dark years of racial persecution, the doors of our religious houses, of our churches, of the Roman seminary, of buildings belonging to the Holy See and of Vatican City itself were thrown open to offer refuge and safety to so many Jews of Rome being hunted by their persecutors."

Pope John Paul II listed his 1986 visit to the synagogue as an event to be remembered for "centuries and millenniums in the history of this city and this church." On the tenth anniversary of that memorable visit, the Pope told Rabbi Toaff: "The climate of sincere friendship between us and the feelings of fraternal concern for each other

that motivate us are essential prerequisites for that process of reciprocal acceptance that will lay the foundations for a more serene future for
everyone."

[Adapted from the souvenir booklet, *Welcome* (Pope John Paul II's Pastoral Visit to the
United States), published by Magee Publications, 1987. See: *Spiritual Pilgrimage:
Texts on Jews and Judaism 1979–1995,* edited by Dr. Eugene J. Fisher and Rabbi Leon
Klenicki, Crossroad Publishing, New York, 1995. Further information can be obtained
from the Secretariat for Ecumenical and Interreligious Affairs, National Conference of
Catholic Bishops, 3211 Fourth Street, NE, Washington, DC, 20017.]

C. Notes

PROLOGUE

1. See Andrea Riccardi's letter dated October 7, 1995, to Margherita Marchione: "The text regarding Vatican instructions was published in the article, "Roma città sacra? Dalla Conciliazione all'operazione Sturzo," *Vita e Pensiero*, Milan, 1979. See also: "La Chiesa a Roma durante la Resistenza: l'ospitalità negli ambienti ecclesiastici," in *Quaderni della Resistenza laziale*, 1977, pp. 87–150.
2. See Father Robert Graham's letter of March 19, 1995, to M.M.
3. Robert Graham, *The Vatican and Communism in World War II. What Really Happened?* p. 184.
4. Pope John Paul II's statement during a meeting with Jewish leaders at the start of his 1987 visit to the United States.

PART I
A. INTRODUCTION

1. Interview with Margherita Marchione, July 1995.
2. Martin Gilbert, *Atlas of the Holocaust*, p. 11.
3. "Bien que le gouvernement de Vichy ait donné l'ordre de laisser ignorer une protestation du Pape, elle a été rapidement portée à la connaissance de la population, grâce à la courageuse attitude du clergé catholique….Le gouvernement britannique a dans les mains une instruction de Vichy à le presse française ou l'on peut lire: 'Dans aucune circonstance il ne doit être fait allusion à la protestation du Vatican auprès du maréchal Pétain en faveur des Juifs de France'."
4. Nechama Tec, *When Light Pierced the Darkness*, p. 150.
5. *Ibid.*, p. 180.
6. Nechama Tec, *In the Lion's Den, The Life of Oswald Rufeisen*, 1990.
7. Susan Zuccotti, *The Italians and the Holocaust*, pp. 225–226.

8. *Ibid.*, pp. 285–286.
9. Carol Rittner and Sondra Myers, *The Courage to Care*, pp. 74–77.
10. *Ibid.*, p. 144.
11. "The Rescuers," *The New York Times*, May 5, 1993.
12. Jewish Foundation for Christian Rescuers/ADL, New York.
13. "Benvenuti a parco Perlasca," *Il Mattino*, December 20, 1993.
14. Alexander Stille, *Benevolence and Betrayal*, p. 193.
15. Saul Friedländer, *Pius XII and the Third Reich*, p. 228.
16. *Ibid.*, p. 230.
17. Eva Fogelman, *Conscience and Courage.* p. 36.

B. THE HOLOCAUST

1. *The Jewish Monthly*, May 1989.
2. John Patrick Carroll-Abbing, *But for the Grace of God*, p. 47.
3. Annual U.S. Bishops' Meeting, Washington, D.C., November 1942.
4. William L. Shirer, *The Rise and Fall of the Third Reich*, 1950.
5. December 16, 1984.
6. "Britain and the Vatican during the Second World War."
7. May 6,1985. David Wyman, *The Abandonment of the Jews.*
8. John F. Morley, *Vatican Diplomacy and the Jews during the Holocaust*, 1980.

PART II

A. ITALIAN JEWS

1. "Abbiamo in questo modo potuto sentir palpitare vicino al nostro migliaia di cuori con il commosso tumulto dei loro più intimi affetti o nell'anelante tensione e nell'incubo grave della incertezza nell'esultante gioia della ricuperata sicurezza nella profonda pena e pacata rassegnazione sulla sorte dei loro cari."
2. Cesare De Simone, *Roma città prigioniera*, 1994, p. 257.
3. See Appendix 3. Also, Renzo De Felice, *Storia degli ebrei italiani sotto il fascismo*, p. 685.
4. Letter of Carlo Sestieri to Margherita Marchione, January 1995.
5. Giulio Andreotti, *The U.S.A. Up Close.* Foreword, p. vii.
6. Letter of Giulio Andreotti to Margherita Marchione.
7. Giulio Andreotti, *A ogni morte di Papa*, p. 42.
8. April 3, 1943.
9. Pietro Palazzini, *Il clero e l'occupazione di Roma*, 1995.
10. *Ibid.*, p. 21.
11. *Ibid.*, p. 28.
12. *Ibid.*, p. 16.

13. In Hitler's *Tischgesprache* (Conversations), April 7, 1942.
14. In *Figaro,* Paris.
15. April 27, 1986.
16. Interview with Sy Rotter in *"A Debt to Honor,"* 1995.
17. Nicola Caracciolo, *Uncertain Refuge* [trans. of *Gli ebrei e l'Italia durante la guerra 1940–45,* Rome, 1986], p. 102.
18. Renzo De Felice, *Ebrei in un paese arabo,* pp. 261–262.
19. Caracciolo, *op. cit.,* p. 108.
20. *Ibid.,* p. 116.
21. *Ibid.,* p. 120.
22. Primo Levi, *The Drowned and the Saved,* p. 11.
23. Alexander Ramati, *The Assisi Underground,* pp. 181 ff.
24. Interview with Sy Rotter, *op. cit.*
25. Caracciolo, *op. cit.,* Prologue, xli.
26. *Ibid.,* p. 133.
27. *Ibid.,* p. 138.
28. *Ibid.,* pp. 6–8.
29. Emanuele Pacifici, *Non ti voltare,* pp. 103–109.

B. MEMORIES

1. Cardinal Mark Anthony Barbarigo (1640–1706) and Saint Lucy Filippini (1672–1732) founded the Religious Teachers Filippini in 1692. They established schools for the Christian education of youth and promoted the dignity of womanhood. Under the direct jurisdiction of the popes, the first nucleus of Teachers embarked on a revolutionary innovation. They taught reading and writing to the poor and conducted conferences for women. The social apostolate was an extension of the classroom; and, at a time when there were socioeconomic problems, their efforts helped influence a healthy family life. This legacy has continued over 300 years.
2. "Ha inizio l'esodo delle donne ebree rifugiate nella nostra casa. Erano con i bambini oltre 60, e occupavano l'ambiente dell'educandato più qualche camera."
3. Giuliana Lestini, *S. A. S. G.,* p. 7.
4. Archivio Storico Ispettoria Romana, *Corrispondenza.*
5. Andrea Riccardi, *La Chiesa a Roma durante la Resistenza,* p.102.
6. *Ricerche Storiche Salesiane,* January–June 1994, Vol. 24, XIII, 1.
7. *Ibid.,* July–December, 1994, Vol. 25, XIII, 2.
8. *Catholic Herald,* October 23, 1981.
9. Interview with Sy Rotter, *op. cit.*

C. THE CATHOLIC CHURCH

1. Pascalina Lehnert, *Pius XII. The Privilege of Serving Him,* p. 53.
2. August 6, 1938.
3. De Felice, *op. cit.,* pp. 335–341.
4. Zuccotti, *op. cit.,* pp. 126–135.
5. *"Bekanntmachung! Dieses Gebäude dient religiösen Zwecken und gehört dem Vatikanstaat Haussuchungen und Beschlagnahmungen sind verboten. Der Deutsche Kommandant General Stahel."*
6. Robert A. Graham, *Pius XII's Defense of Jews and Others,* p. 1.
7. Letter to Margherita Marchione.
8. "Eugenio Zolli," *Civiltà Cattolica,* March 1981, p. 346.
9. Giorgio Angelozzi Gariboldi, *Pio XII, Hitler e Mussolini,* p. 5.
10. Arthur D. Morse, *While Six Million Died,* p. 335.
11. October 20, 1939.
12. Luke xxii, 53.
13. Matthew xxiv, 8.
14. See translation of *Summi Pontificatus* in "The Unity of Human Society," New York: America Press, pp. 39–40.
15. June 2, 1943.
16. Alexis Curvers, *Pie XII, Le Pape outragé,* Paris, Laffont, 1964, p. 139.
17. Saul Friedländer, *op. cit.,* p. 35.
18. *Der Papst und die Verfolgung der Juden,* pp. 103–104.
19. Galeazzo Ciano, *Mussolini segreto,* p. 308.
20. Kirkpatrick to Vansittart, August 19, 1933, DBFP, 2nd Ser. v. 524.
21. Guenter Lewy, *The Catholic Church and Nazi Germany.* "The attitude of the Roman Catholic Church toward National Socialist anti-Semitism must be seen in the context of the still partially unresolved 2,000-year-old conflict between Church and Synagogue" (p. 268).
22. Pius XII's niece.
23. Robert Katz, *Death in Rome,* p. 242.
24. *Ibid.,* p. 245.
25. Angelozzi Gariboldi, *op. cit.,* p. 148.
26. October 20, 1939.
27. For 250 years the Religious Teachers Filippini were under the jurisdiction and protection of the Secret Almoner of the Pope and were listed in the directory of the Pontifical Family. This changed with Vatican II. Today they assist the Vatican by preparing meals for the Papal Guards at Castelgandolfo, the Pope's summer residence. Pope Benedict XV addressed the Sisters in 1915: "We remember well, dearest daughters, your enthusiasm and generosity in assisting the little refugees, left orphans by the earthquake that devastated Marsica....With maternal love, you opened your schools as a safe refuge for almost five hundred

children to whom you gave not only food for their bodies, but also religious instruction." Pope Pius XII expressed his appreciation by personally approving their revised Rules: "Having examined the present Rules of the Pontifical Institute of the Religious Teachers Filippini, We willingly give Our approval. From the Vatican, 13 October 1951. Pius pp. XII."

28. *Lettere a Suor Margherita*, p. 157.
29. William O. Chadwick, "The Pope and the Jews in 1942," p. 469.
30. *Ibid.*, p. 470.
31. *Civiltà Cattolica*, March 18, 1995.
32. *The Tablet*, May 11, 1963.
33. Pope John Paul II, *Crossing the Threshold of Hope*, p. 97.
34. *Corriere della Sera*, Milan, April 16, 1996.
35. *Gli Ebrei a Venezia, 1938–1945*, Venice, Il Caro, 1995.
36. Kristeller's letter of April 25, 1995, to Sister Margherita Marchione.
37. O'Reilly, NIAF *Newsletter*, Washington, D.C.
38. Proverbs 24:11, 12.
39. Telegram No. 181, dated January 24, 1943.
40. Graham, *op. cit.*, pp. 1–46.
41. Hughes, "The Dilemma of Pius XII," in *The Catholic Answer*, July–August, 1995, Vol. 9, No. 3, pp. 32–37.
42. "Die Niederlande und Auschwitz," in *Vierteljahreshefte fur Zeitgeschichte* 17, pp. 1–16.
43. Hughes, *op. cit.*, p. 34.
44. *Ibid.*, p. 37.
45. Pope John Paul II, 50th Anniversary Mass, St. Peter's Basilica, June 11, 1995.

[To study relations between the Jews and the Vatican, see the eleven-volume series of records and documents of the Holy See relating to the Second World War: *Actes et documents du Saint Siège relatifs à la seconde guerre mondiale;* vols. 9–10: *Le Saint Siège e les victimes de la guerre.* Roma, Libreria Editrice Vaticana, 1980. See also, Andrea Riccardi, *Pio XII,* 1985, and *Il potere del Papa da Pio XII a Giovanni Paolo II,* Bari, Laterza, 1993.]

D. Glossary

AMCHA—National Israeli Center for Psychosocial Support of Survivors of the Holocaust and the Second Generation.

Aryan—Originally the term "Aryan" referred to peoples speaking Indo-European languages. The Nazis perverted its meaning to support racist ideas. They considered the typical Aryan as blond, blue-eyed, and tall. The Nazis blamed the Jews for Germany's defeat in World War I, for its economic problems, and for the spread of Communism in Europe. The Poles, Russians, and other Slavic peoples were destined to serve as slave labor for the Germans. Others were persecuted, imprisoned, and often killed on political and behavioral (rather than racial) grounds.

DELASEM—Delegation for Assistance to Jewish Emigrants—was funded mostly by the Joint Distribution Committee in the USA. In 1942 the organization rescued forty-two Jewish children (ages eleven to nineteen) in Italian-occupied Yugoslavia who were hiding in a castle at Lesno Brdno. With the help of the Red Cross, they acquired a villa in the town of Nonantola, near Modena. All survived.

Ferramonti-Tarsia was the largest concentration camp built in Italy. It was for 2,000 refugees in a malaria-ridden section of Calabria.

GAP—The "Gruppi Azione Patriottica" was responsible for the bombing of Via Rasella in Rome.

Genocide—The Nazis killed thousands of handicapped Germans by lethal injection and poisonous gas in the late 1930s. In 1941 the German army began killing Jews and Roma (Gypsies) in open fields and ravines on the outskirts of conquered cities and towns. Eventually the Nazis began a more organized method of killing civilians—six extermination centers were established in occupied Poland where murder by gas and body disposal through cremation were conducted. Victims had been deported from Western Europe and from the ghettos in Eastern Europe which the Nazis had established. Millions died in the ghettos and concentration camps as a result of forced labor, starvation, exposure, brutality, disease, and execution.

209

Ideology—The Nazis believed that Germans were "racially superior." Jews, Roma (Gypsies), and the handicapped belonged to an "inferior race." They were seen as a threat to the purity of the "German (Aryan) Race" and had to be exterminated.

ISU—Italian Service Units during World War II.

Liberation—German concentration camps were liberated by Allied soldiers in 1945. Those who survived tried to locate family members. Others learned that they were the sole survivors of once large extended families. The future was uncertain. They owned nothing and belonged nowhere. Many refugees left Europe and, with assistance provided by immigrant aid societies or sponsorship from relatives abroad, they emigrated to the United States, South Africa, or Palestine which became the State of Israel after 1948. They developed new lives in their adopted countries.

Mishnah—Second-century law code compiled by Judah HaNasi.

Nazi—A short term for the National Socialist German Workers' Party. It was a right-wing political party formed in 1919 primarily by unemployed German veterans of World War I. The Nazi party ideology was strongly anti-Communist, anti-Semitic, racist, nationalistic, imperialistic, and militaristic.

Republic of Salò—Benito Mussolini's Fascist Republican Government after the Italian Armistice.

Shoah—The Hebrew word for "Holocaust."

Talmud—The Talmud is composed of either the Mishnah and the Palestinian commentary, or the Mishnah and the Babylonian commentary. Thus, there are two Talmuds: Palestinian and Babylonian.

Torah—Torah refers to the totality of Jewish learning: the Biblical Five Books of Moses (Genesis, Exodus, Leviticus, Numbers, Deuteronomy); and the sacred scroll used in the synagogue which contains the Five Books written in Hebrew on parchment. It is read on every Sabbath and Holy Day.

Vatican City—An independent state, with the Pope as its absolute ruler. It comprises 108.7 acres (44 hectares) within Rome, on the west bank of the Tiber River and west of the Castel Sant'Angelo. It consists of the Basilica of St. Peter, the administration buildings, the papal residence, and the Vatican Gardens. The Italian government extends the rights of extraterritoriality and tax exemption to the basilicas of St. John Lateran, St. Mary Major, and St. Paul Outside-the-Walls, as well as to the palace of San Callisto at the foot of the Janiculum and the papal residence at Castelgandolfo in the Alban Hills.

E. Bibliography

Actes et documents du Saint Siège relatifs à la Seconde Guerre Mondiale. Vatican City: Libreria Editrice Vaticana, 1965–81, Vols. I–XI, edited by Pierre Blet, Robert A. Graham, Angelo Martini and Burkhart Schneider.

Andreotti, Giulio, *A ogni morte di Papa.* Milan: Rizzoli, 1980.

————,*The U.S.A. Up Close.* New York: New York University Press, 1992.

Angelozzi Gariboldi, Giorgio, *Pio XII, Hitler e Mussolini.* Milan: Mursia Editore, 1988.

Archives of the Religious Teachers Filippini. Villa Maria Regina, Rome, Italy.

Archives of the Religious Teachers Filippini. Villa Walsh, Morristown, New Jersey.

Archivio "Renato Maestro." *Gli Ebrei a Venezia, 1938–1945.* (Una comunità tra persecuzione e rinascita).

Caracciolo, Nicola, *Uncertain Refuge.* Chicago: University of Illinois Press, 1995.

Carroll-Abbing, John Patrick, *But for the Grace of God.* Delacorte Press, 1965.

Chadwick, William Owen, "The Pope and the Jews in 1942," in *Persecution and Toleration, Studies in Church History,* Vol. 21, edited by W. J. Sheils, The Ecclesiastical History Society. Oxford: Blackwell, 1984.

Ciano, Galeazzo, *Diario.* Milan: Rizzoli, 1950.

————, *Mussolini segreto.* Bologna, 1958.

De Felice, Renzo, *Storia degli ebrei italiani sotto il fascismo.* Giulio Einaudi editore, 1961.

————, *Ebrei in un paese arabo.* Bologna: Il Mulino, 1978.

De Lubac, Henri, *Christian Resistance to Anti-Semitism: Memories from 1940–1944.* San Francisco: Ignatius Press, 1990.

De Simone, Cesare, *Roma città prigioniera.* Milan: Mursia Editore, 1994.

Falconi, Carlo, *The Silence of Pius XII.* Boston: Little, Brown and Company, 1970.

Fisher, Eugene J., "Jews, Catholics and the Holocaust," in *The Priest.* Our Sunday Visitor Press. Part I: August 1995, pp. 10–15. Part II: September 1995: pp. 34–38.

Fogelman, Eva, *Conscience and Courage.* New York: Anchor Books, Doubleday, 1994.

Friedländer, Saul, *Pius XII and the Third Reich.* New York: Alfred A. Knopf, 1966.

Gilbert, Martin, *Atlas of the Holocaust.* New York: William Morrow and Co., 1988.

Graham, Robert, *Pius XII's Defense of Jews and Others.* Milwaukee: Catholic League for Religious and Civil Rights, 1987.

———, *The Vatican and Communism in World War II. What Really Happened?* San Francisco: Ignatius Press, 1996.

Greenberg, Gershon, "American Catholics during the Holocaust," in *Peace/Shalom after the Holocaust: First Scholars' Conference on Teaching the Holocaust.* Greensburg, Pa.: Seton Hill College, 1989, pp. 37–51.

John Paul II, *Crossing the Threshold of Hope.* New York: Knopf, 1994.

———, *Spiritual Pilgrimage: Texts on Jews and Judaism 1979–1995,* edited by Eugene J. Fisher and Leon Klenicki, New York: Crossroad Publishing, 1995.

Lapide, Pinchas E., *Three Popes and the Jews.* New York: Hawthorn Books, 1967.

Lehnert, Pascalina, *Pio XII. Il privilegio di servirlo.* Milan: Rusconi, 1984.

Lestini, Giuliana, *S. A. S. G.* Rome: Il Ventaglio, 1993.

Lewy, Guenter, *The Catholic Church and Nazi Germany.* New York-Toronto, 1964.

Lichten, Joseph, A *Question of Judgment: Pius XII and the Jews.* Washington, D.C.: U.S. Catholic Conference, 1963.

Marrus, Michael R., *The Holocaust in History.* Hanover and London: University Press of New England, 1987, pp. 179–183; and "French Churches and the Persecution of Jews in France 1940–1944," in Otto Dov, *et al.,* eds, *Judaism and Christianity under the Impact of National Socialism.* Jerusalem: Historical Society of Israel, 1987, pp. 305–326.

Montini, Giovanni Battista, "Pius XII and the Jews," in *The Tablet,* June 29, 1963, pp. 714–715.

Morley, John F., *Vatican Diplomacy and the Jews during the Holocaust.* New York: KTAV Publishing House, 1980.

Morse, Arthur D., *While Six Million Died.* New York: Random House, 1968.

Motto, Francesco, "L'Istituto Salesiano Pio XI durante l'occupazione nazi-fascista di Roma" in *Ricerche Storiche Salesiane,* No. 24, January–June 1994 and No. 25, July–December 1994, pp. 315–359.

O'Carroll, Michael, *Pius XII: Greatness Dishonored, A Documented Study.* Dublin: Laetare Press, 1980.

Pacifici, Emanuele, *Non ti voltare.* Florence: La Giuntina, 1993.

Palazzini, Pietro, *Il clero e l'occupazione di Roma.* Rome: Apes, 1995.

Pawlikowski, John T., "The Vatican and the Holocaust: Unresolved Issues," in M. Perry, ed., *Jewish–Christian Encounters over the Centuries.* New York: Peter Lang, 1994, pp. 293–312.

Prezzolini, Giuseppe, *Lettere a Suor Margherita*. Rome, Edizioni di Storia e Letteratura, 1992.

Ramati, Alexander, *The Assisi Underground: Priests Who Rescued Jews*. New York: Stein and Day, 1978.

Riccardi, Andrea, "La Chiesa a Roma durante la Resistenza," in *Quaderni della Resistenza laziale,* Rome, 1977, pp. 89–150.

Rittner, Carol and Sondra Myers, *The Courage to Care*. New York: New York University Press, 1986.

Stille, Alexander, *Benevolence and Betrayal*. Summit Books, 1991.

Tec, Techama, *When Light Pierced the Darkness*. New York, Oxford University Press, 1986.

————, *In the Lion's Den*. New York: Oxford University Press, 1990.

Uffreduzzi, Marcella, *Il Viale dei Giusti*. Rome: Città Nuova Editrice, 1985.

Wiesel, Elie, *Night/ Dawn/ Day*. New Jersey: Jason Aronson Inc., 1985.

Woodruff, Douglas, "Pius XII and the Jews," in *The Tablet,* May 11, 1963, pp. 504–506; June 29, 1963, pp.714–715.

Yerushalmi, Yosef Hayim, "Response to Rosemary Reuther." in Eva Fleischner, ed., *Auschwitz: Beginning of a New Era?* New York: KTAV/ADL/St. John the Divine Cathedral, 1977, pp. 97–107.

Zuccotti, Susan, *The Italians and the Holocaust*. New York: Basic Books, Inc., 1987.

F. Appendixes

·

DOCUMENTS

I. Pontificio Collegio dei Sacerdoti per l'Emigrazione Italiana: Refugees in the Vatican compiled by Cardinal Pietro Palazzini (1995)

Almagià, Comm. Nino, Generale
    d'Armata
Almagià, Prof.sa Amalia
Ascoli, Comm. Gino, Comandante di
    Marina
Ascoli, Prof. Ing. Enrico, Tecnico del
    Governatorato di Roma
Ascoli, Severino
Ascoli, Signora e 3 Figli
Balbino, Senatore Giuliano
Balbino, Signora
Bontempelli, Ing. Mino
Bontempelli, Prof. Massimo,
    Accademico d'Italia
Bontempelli, Signora
Castelnuovo, Prof. Comm. Enrico,
    Regia Università di Roma
Castelnuovo, Signora
Citoni, Armando
Citoni, Signora e Figlio
Coen, Avv. Prof. Giovanni e Figlio
Fiorelli, Avv. Giulio
Fiorelli, Signora
Fiorentini, Prof. Dott. Ruggiero
Fiorentini, Signora

Fioretti, Cav. Ing. Giosué e Figlio
Grandi, On. Achille
Grandi, Signora
Monti, Sereno
Romanelli, Prof. Romano,
    Accademico d'Italia
Salimebi, Conte Giuseppe
Salimebi, Signora
Sammartino, Dott. Comm. Ubaldo
Sammartino, Signora e Figlia
Sipari, On. Prof. Comm. Erminio
Sipari, Signora e Figlia
Sonnino, On. Angelo
Sonnino, Signora
Spaventa, Comm. Siro, Prefetto
    di Pavia
Spaventa, Signora
Stheiner, Carlo
Stheiner, Rag. Giuseppe
Stheiner, Signora
Tomasetti, Ing. Conte Zaccaria
Toscano, Cav. Giuseppe
Toscano, Signora e 2 Figli
Tucinei, Nobile, Avv. Augusto

II. Pontificio Seminario Romano Maggiore: Refugees in the Vatican compiled by Cardinal Pietro Palazzini (1995)

Albertario, Luigi, Studente
Almagià, Edoardo, Ingegnere
Almagià, Roberto, Studente
Amienna, Salvatore, Capitano
Arcieri, Giulio, Avvocato
Baldaloni, Giuseppe, Capitano
Baldaloni, Luigi, Maestro
Baragli, Ernesto, Ragioniere
Bartolini, Ecc. Domenico, Ministro
    Finanze
Bellino, Enzo, Studente
Beltramo, Silvio, All. Uff.
Bertani, Bernardo, Guardia
Bertozzini, Ermanno, S. Ten.
Bifulco, Ottorino, Studente
Bigi, Giuseppe, CapitanoVascello
Biscatelli di Ruffia, Marchese Paolo,
    Prof. Università
Boldrini, Alberto, Sergente
Boldrini, Anselmo, Allievo Guardia
Bonamico, Giulio, Capitano Navetta
Bonamico, Giulio, Studente Univer.
Bonamico, Raoul, Studente Univer.
Bonomi, Ecc. Ivanoe, Capo Comit.
    Liberazione
Boz, Angelo, Operaio
Bucco, Tommaso, Ten. Medico
Buongiovannini, Operaio
Bureca, Domenico, Studente
Buti, Ecc. Marcello, Ambasciatore
Calamari, Enrico, Guardia Palatina
Caraffa, Mario, S. Ten.

Caraffa, Vittorio, S. Ten. Medico
Casati, Conte Alessandro, Senatore
    Partito Dem. Lib.
Casetto, Alessandro, Capo
Cassisa, Aldo, Geometra
Cattaneo, Raffaele, Studente
Chiechi, Venanzio, Carabiniere
Ciamarra, Ugo, Oper. Militare
Ciuffa, Diego, Studente
Colonna, Don Aspreno, Capitano
Colozza, Edoardo, S. Ten. Artigl.
Cortese, Alessandro, Guardia
Cosentino, Cosimo, Oper. Militare
Cristina, Girolamo, Studente
D'Andria, Carlo, All. Uff. Caval.
D'Andria, Pietro, All. Uff. Artigl.
D'Avanzo, Aspirante Guardia
D'Inzillo, Conte Amedeo,Cavalleria
Dal Monte, Gino, Studente
De Angelis, Dott. Renzo, Tenente
De Courten, Eugenio, Studente
De Riso, Domenico, Studente
De Rossi, Giovanni, Studente
De Silia, Comm. Silvio, Referendario
    Corte Conti
De Vita, Alberto, Guardia
Del Vecchio, Prof. Giorgio, ex Rettore
    Univ. Roma
Di Carlo, Adriano, Studente
Di Gregorio, Nobile Carlo, Prof.
Di Loreto, Giuseppe, Tenente
Di Segni, Angelo, Commerciante

Di Stefano, Comm. Mario, Ministro
Ecobar, Pietro, Studente
Ena, Nello, Architetto
Enriques, Federico, Professore
Fares, Giovanni, Stud. Università
Farnese, Mario, Avvocato
Ferretto, Rag. Filippo, Agricoltura
Ferti, Ivo, Studente
Flaudrin, Coriolano, Guardia
Franchini, Mario, Studente
Gabbianelli, Rolando, Capitano Aer.
Gaetani, S.E. Conte Alfonso, Prefetto di
    Firenze
Galata, Giorgio, S. Ten. Artigl.
Galata, Gerardo, Cap. Vascello
Gentilini, Lanfranc, Guardia
Gessini, Massimo, Studente
Gheradini, Gabriele, Guardia
Giovannetti, Tullio, Ten. Col. Pilota
Giusti, Giorgio, Studente
Glori, Licinio, Capitano RR.CC.
Gregorio, Giuliano, Studente
Guidi, Giovanni, Tenente
Hopps, Antonio, Impiegato
Iannelli, Ettore, Studente
Ilari, Aldo, Studente
Impiombato, Alberto, Possidente
Impiombato, Francesco, Possidente
Isalberti, Arturo, Avvocato
Ischudi, Aldo, Studente
La Rosa, Pasquale, Prof. Chimica
Lancellotti, Francesco, Capitano
Lancellotti, Massimo Paolo,
    Addetto Consolare
Latorre, Luigi, Guardia
Lorenzini, Walter, Soldato
Luzzi, Alberto, Ingegnere
Luzzi, Alberto, Studente
Luzzi, Riccardo, Guardia
Malaguti, Federico, Impiegato
Mandetta, Silvio, Studente
Mangani, Nicola, Guardia Marina
Marabotto, Pasquale, Allievo Uffic.
Marchetti, Vitaliano, Impiegato
Marignoli, Francesco, Studente Univer.
Massenzio, Aldo, Studente

Menasci, Raffaele, Commerciante
Mendoni, Remo, Sergente Aviaz.
Mercanti, Gian Maria, Studente
Migliorini, Luigi, Allievo Guardia
Moscardelli, Giuseppe, Ten. Col.
Murri, Enrico, Ingegnere
Nenni, On. Pietro, Partito Socialista
Notari, Gen. Amerigo, Gen. Aerea
Odescalchi, Don Livio, Industriale
Olivetti Rason, Pier Ettore, Industr.
Oliviero, Mario, Tenente
Oreffice, Giorgio, Avvocato
Oreffice, Roberto, Avvocato
Ottaviani, Gaetano, Impiegato
Padoa, Ruggero, Studente
Padovani, Massimo, Studente
Padovani, Paolo, Studente
Panzarasa, Silvano, Studente
Panzieri, Raniero, Studente
Paolicelli, Franco, Guardia
Papi, Antonio, Studente
Papi, Mario, Studente
Pascoli, Paride, Impiegato
Pecci, Nicola, Studente
Pedde Lai, Giuseppe, Cap. Veterin.
Peirce, Giovanni, Dir. Navigazione
Pellegrini, Alvaro, Guardia
Pelosi, Giulio, Impiegato Banca
Pelosi, Serafino, Dott. Commerc.
Permegiani, Leonardo, Studente
Perrone, Comm. Mario, Direttore
Persano, Aldo, Tenente
Petricca, Luigi, Guardia
Piccolomini, Alfredo, Guardia
Pignatti di Morano, Giulio,Studente
Piperno, Rag. Pellegrino, Commer.
Piscopo, Guido, Tenente
Porretti, Salvatore, Soldato
Prefetto, Renato, Ten. Col. Medico
Provenzano, Vitaliano, Pilota
Pucci, Sergio, Studente
Quadrini, Pietro, Studente
Ramelli, Giancarlo, Impiegato
Ramelli, Luciano, Impiegato
Rapanotti, Nicola, Guardia Palatina
Ravasini, Sergio, Farmacista

Rey, Riccardo, Guardia Palatina
Ricci, Dott. Mario, Tenente
Ricci, Ecc. Umberto, Ministro
Ricci, Francesco, S. Tenente
Ricci, Ugo, Impiegato
Ricciulli, Enrico, Avvocato
Riello, Giorgio, Studente
Righini, Desiderio, Tenente R.E.
Righini, Stefano, Tenente Aer.
Rio, Giuseppe, Capitano R.E.
Romano, Alfonso, S. Ten. Genio
Romano, Ubaldo, Studente
Ronchetta, Walter, Studente
Rossetti, Enzo, Soldati
Rossetti, Rolando, Soldati
Rovigatti, Sergio, Impiegato
Ruini, Ecc. Bartolomeo, Capo
    Part. Democr. Lavoro
Ruini, Prof. Carlo, Prof. Univer.
Sabino, Francesco, Operaio
Santoro, Francesco, Soldati
Selvaggi, Giovanni, Avvocato
Serventi, Francesco, Studente
Severi, Ecc. Leonardo, Ministro
Siciliano di Rende, March. Francesco,
    Magg. R.E.
Sistopaoli, Fulvio, Studente
Soleri, Ecc. Marcello, Ministro
Sonnino, Angelo, Commerciante

Sonnino, Pacifico, Commerciante
Spina, Eugenio, S. Ten. Genio
Staderini, Giorgio, Capitano R.E
Stefanelli, Raffaele, Studente
Tagliacozzo, Michele, Impiegato
Terzi, Carlo, Studente
Terzi, Ettore, Studente
Tesoro, Alberto, Commerciante
Tesserini, Paolo, Studente
Tirozzi, Alfonso, Maggiore Pilota
Torlonia, Don Alessandro, Studente
Torlonia, Princ. Giovanni, Senatore
Trinchiero, Mario, Prefetto Cremona
Trocchi, Fernando, Studente
Trocchi, Vittorio, Ten. artiglieria
Urbani, Giovanni, Studente
Valenti, Aldo, Operaio
Valenti, Fernando, Operaio
Vannini, Dino, Soldato
Veneziano, Benedetto, Commercio
Veneziano, Carlo, Studente
Veneziano, Giacomo, Studente
Verdura, Sergio, Studente
Vernesi, Vezio, Maggiore R.E.
Villa, Alessandro, Ingegnere
Zeitun, Comm. Giacomo, Cambio
Zippel, Adolfo, Studente
Zippel, Guido, Studente

III. Institutions in Rome with Number of Jewish Refugees: Compiled by the Italian historian, Renzo De Felice (1963)

Figlie della Carità 7
Suore Agostiniane 7
Suore Sacramentine di Bergamo 7
Suore della Carità di Nevers 6
Madri Pie di Ovada 6
Clarisse di San Bernardino 6
Suore Povere Bonaerensi di San Giuseppe, via dei Fienili, 45a...............................6
Suore Ospitaliere del Sacro Cuore di Gesù, via Castelfidardo, 45 5
Suore della Dottrina Cristiana 5
Suore della Sacra Famiglia, salita Monte del Gallo, 19 5
Domenicane Annunziatine 5
Suore Riparatrici, via de' Lucchesi, 9 5
Retraite d'Angers 4
Maestre Pie Venerini..3
Suore della Resurrezione (Polacche) 3
Suore Turchine del Corviale 3
Orfanotrofio Antoniano 3
Monastero Visitazione 2
Suore Armene di Monteverde 2
Clarisse di San Lorenzo 2
Suore della Divina Provvidenza 2
Suore del Rosario Perpetuo 2
Suore Orsoline di Parma 2
Suore di Sant'Orsola della Beata Vergine 2
Suore dell'Addolorata...1
Suore San Giuseppe di Cluny 1
Ancelle del Sacro Cuore 1
Clarisse Riformate 1

Jews with male religious:

Reverendi Padri Francescani San Bartolomeo all'Isola 400
Reverendi Padri Stimmatini Parrocchia Santa Croce......................................100
Parrocchia della Trasfigurazione 100
Fratelli delle Scuole Cristiane 96
Società Salesiana di San Giovanni Bosco 83
Parrocchia Santa Croce...80
Parrocchia della Divina Provvidenza 65
Pontificio Seminario Lombardo 63
Fratelli Ospitalieri della Immacolata Concezione..52
Pontificio Seminario Francese...50
Pontificio Seminario Romano Maggiore..48
Fatebenefratelli 46
Reverendi Padri Gesuiti in case diverse 43
Parrocchia di Santa Maria della Pace..40
Parrocchia di Santa Maria in Campitelli 38

IV. *Partial List of Jewish Refugees:*
Guests of the Religious Teachers Filippini
(1943–1945)

Anticoli, Angelo
Anticoli, Marco
Anticoli, Silvia
Conigliani, Fernanda
Conigliani, Mario
Conigliani, Nando
Di Castro, Elisa
Di Segni, Cesira
Di Segni, Emma
Di Segni, Giacomino
Di Segni, Giovanni
Di Segni, Maria
Di Segni, Rubino
Di Segni, Silvana
Di Segni, Viviana
Di Veroli, Chiara
Di Veroli, Errico
Di Veroli, Fernanda
Di Veroli, Gianni
Di Veroli, Giulia in Piperno
Di Veroli, Giuliana
Di Veroli, Grazia
Di Veroli, Graziella in Pavoncelli
Di Veroli, Michele
Di Veroli, Mirella
Di Veroli, Olga
Di Veroli, Tina in Sonnino
Di Veroroli, Attilio
Di Veroroli, Costanza
Di Veroroli, Debora
Di Veroroli, Ida
Di Veroroli, Michele

Di Veroroli, Rosina
Fatucci, Alberto
Fatucci, Angelo
Fatucci, Costanza
Fatucci, Ernesta
Fatucci, Giacomo
Fatucci, Giuseppe
Fatucci, Lazzaro
Fatucci, Rosa
Greco, Bruno
Greco, Donato
Greco, Giuseppe
Greco, Grazia
Greco, Luciana
Greco, Mariella
Greco, Marietta
Greco, Ombretta
Pall Corrado, Emma
Pall Corrado, Errica
Pall Corrado, Natio
Pall Corrado, Raffaele
Paoncello, Adele
Paoncello, Cesare
Paoncello, Clorinda
Paoncello, Emanuele
Paoncello, Michele
Pavoncelli, Celeste
Pavoncelli, Elisa
Piperno, Ermelinda in Di Veroli
Piperno Leda
Piperno, Rosetta
Piperno, Virginia

Piperno, Wilelma
Sermoneta, Delia
Sermoneta, Pacifico
Sermoneta, Rosa
Sonnino, Amedeo

Spagnoletto, Fortuna
Spagnoletto, Rosetta
Zarfati, Wanda in Anticoli
Zarfati, Yolanda

V. Rescue Network Report

A. THE ALLIED MILITARY COMMAND

Collaborating with the Vatican and Pope Pius XII, Catholic institutions in Rome were an integral part of a rescue network of the Allied Military Command. With members of the persecuted Jewish community in Italy and in the world, countless refugees, political prisoners, and escaped prisoners of war were assisted by the Italians who risked their lives to save them.

Monsignor Hugh O'Flaherty recommended the leader of one of the partisan bands from the Province of Viterbo: "During the German occupation of Rome, Antonio Giustini did everything possible to help British and American prisoners of war who had escaped. Several times he risked his life, bringing American aviators through the German cordons to the City. Arrested by the Germans, he refused to betray anyone of our organization and cleverly managed to escape after his wife was hidden. His home was destroyed and everything he had was lost. Any help that can be given will be greatly appreciated."

At the request of the Allied Screening Commission, Antonio Giustini, known locally as the "Schoolmaster," prepared an official report of the partisan activities in the Corchiano (Viterbo) district under the jurisdiction of Colonel Giuseppe Pironti.

Having lived in the United States as a child, Giustini was encouraged by the September 8, 1943, Armistice. Sergeant Gordon Bennett was the first Allied prisoner of war who sought refuge in Corchiano. Delighted to hear Giustini speak English, Bennett described his flight from Fara Sabina, his arrest by the Fascists, his arrival in the concentration camp near the Lake of Bracciano, and his flight from the train that would have taken him to Germany.

Father Clancy, an Irish priest, worked with Monsignor O'Flaherty in the Vatican. He was director of the Collegio Marcantonio Colonna. Through the Vatican offices, he provided Giustini with funds and clothing for the escapees. He also arranged to send future supplies to help the people of Corchiano care for them. Giustini was able to hide many refugees on his own large estate, or in grottos, abandoned tunnels, and homes of local peasants. He arranged for their personal and medical needs, regulated their food supply and cigarettes, advised them when there was danger of spies and Nazi raids, directed them as they joined the local band for sabotage activities, and delighted in singing their favorite song, "It's a long way to Tipperary."

Giustini's band of partisans had a two-fold purpose: a) Promote propaganda against the Nazi-Fascists and resist every kind of collaboration with the Germans; b) Accomplish acts of sabotage against the military enemy organization and eventually perform true warlike actions.

Propaganda favoring the Allies resulted immediately in helping and protecting Allied prisoners of war who had escaped from the Nazis. Instead of joining the German Army as ordered by the Nazis, young Italians joined the partisans in the grottos which were inaccessible to the enemy. They sabotaged German military telephone lines along the Rome-Corchiano-Civitacastellana route, as well as Via Flaminia, Cassia, Vetralla, Soriano, and Borghetto. On the night of February 28, 1944, hiding in the hills as an enemy division was passing by, they showered bombs on the Germans and, being in a superior position, they were able to kill the entire division. Activities were often in the middle of the night when fires were started and nails and glass spread on the roads to damage the tires of German vehicles.

The following excerpts regarding the situation in Italy during the Nazi occupation are gleaned from official reports:

1. Letter of August 16, 1944, from the Allied Screening Commission, Largo dei Lombardi, 21, Rome, to Antonio Giustini:
"Major Derry wishes to convey his heartiest personal thanks for the exceptionally fine work which you did on behalf of the escaped Allied Prisoners of War during the German Occupation.... He is insistent that you should realize how we appreciate the service you rendered, at such great personal risk to yourself.

"We should very much like to have a statement from you, regarding the work you did, the names of the prisoners who were sheltered on your property and the respective periods for each prisoner (as far as possible). Any other relevant information concerning your work will be useful to us."

2. On March 2, 1945, Colonnello Conte Giuseppe Pironti, Commander of the Gruppo Bande Col. Pironti, communicated to Lieutenant Colonel Antonio Giustini that he had been nominated as a recipient of the Silver Medal for Military Valor:
"As the Commander of an Armed Band, with ingenuity and with example, rendering extraordinary service to the national cause, he succeeded in organizing an organic unity for combating the enemy. He not only protected

numerous Allied prisoners, but succeeded in leading them in actions of sabotage and warfare against the Germans.

"Persecuted by the Nazis, he hurriedly settled the Allied prisoners before his arrest by the SS and endured cruel torture both moral and physical, but he kept the secret of his affiliation and in every circumstance gave proof of intelligence, valor, and spirit of sacrifice.

"On this occasion we express our most cordial felicitations. Colonel Giuseppe Pironti."

3. On August 17, 1946, Antonio Giustini (Via Rosa Raimondi Garibaldi, 14, Scala G., Int. 16, Rome), the holder of Passport No. 163425 issued by the Repubblica Italiana, requested a visa for entry to the United States of America where he wished to reside permanently. The Consulate Section of the American Embassy in Naples sent this information to the American Embassy in Rome and the American State Department, Washington, D.C.:

"Mr. Giustini gave magnificent assistance to the Allied cause during the period following the Italian Armistice. As the leader of an Italian partisan band in Viterbo Province, he, in company with escaping British and American PsW, committed acts of sabotage against the Germans. He contacted the "Rome Organization" and placed himself and his band at the disposal of Lt. Col. (then Major) S.I. Derry for the purpose of collecting, sheltering, clothing, and feeding escaped PsW in the Corchiano (Viterbo) area. As a result of his activity dozens of PsW were assisted.

"On 16 January 1944, an American plane of the 320th Bomb. Group, 444 Bomb Squadron, was shot down in the area. Mr. Giustini and some followers immediately searched for the crew who had baled out. They met a German patrol, also in search of the crew.

"They misdirected the patrol; and other members of the partisan band contacted some of the crew; namely, O.727717 Lt. Green J., O.670657 Lt. Stewart J.B., and Sgts. De Lisle, Gardner and Harrison for whom they arranged lodging. Later they contacted O.789187 Major MacCrory J. and arranged for his removal to Rome to the American Pontifical College.

"By this time Giustini's activities were well known to the Germans, so that he was forced to flee from his home and proceed to Rome, where he continued to act as an agent for the "Rome Organization." On 9 May 1944, he was arrested by the Germans, and underwent severe torture to force him to give information regarding the hiding places of PsW, both in Rome City and in Viterbo Province. Despite this, Giustini refused to talk. Later, by use of his ingenuity, he escaped and was forced to remain in hiding until the liberation of Rome.

"Mr. Giustini lived in the United States for 10 years in his boyhood and has a deep admiration for the country and the people. He is well educated and a good citizen. He has been an efficient employee of this Commission for two years.

"We respectfully request that every consideration be given to Mr. Giustini's application for a visa, in view of his courageous service to the Allied Cause, at great risk to himself. We have no hesitation in recommending him most highly." Signed: Major J.H. Aiken for Lt. Col. C.S., Commanding Allied Screening Commission (Italy).

4. H.R. Alexander, Field-Marshal, Supreme Allied Commander, Mediterranean Theatre, gave the folowing Certificate of Patriot:

"IN THE NAME OF THE GOVERNMENTS AND PEOPLES OF THE UNITED NATIONS, WE THANK GIUSTINI ANTONIO LATE FAUSTINO, FOR HAVING FOUGHT THE ENEMY IN THE BATTLE FIELDS ON SERVICE IN THE PATRIOT RANKS, AMONG THESE MEN, WHO HAVE USED THE ARMS FOR THE TRIUMPH OF LIBERTY, DEVELOPING OFFENSIVE OPERATIONS, DOING ACTS OF SABOTAGE, GIVING MILITARY INFORMATIONS.

"WITH THEIR COURAGE, AND THEIR PLUCK, THE ITALIAN PATRIOTS HAVE GREATLY CONTRIBUTED TO THE LIBERATION OF ITALY AND THE GREAT CAUSE OF ALL FREE MEN.

"IN THE RE-BORN ITALY, THE OWNERS OF THIS CERTIFICATE WILL BE CONSIDERED AS PATRIOTS, WHO HAVE FOUGHT FOR THE HONOUR AND FOR THE LIBERTY." Date: 9 January 1947.

5. The Allied Screening Commission letter of March 5, 1947, summarizes Antonio Giustini's contribution:

"It is with great regret that this Commission loses your valuable services. For the past 2-1/2 years you have occupied a position of trust and importance in this Unit, and you have always given your best, with enthusiasm, which has been an example to younger members of the Staff.

"Before that, during the dark days of the Nazi/Fascist occupation, your work was even more valuable and gallant. Your activities proved a great thorn in the side of the enemy, and what you did for the Partisans and escaped Allied PsW, is well known to all in this Commission.

"Now that you are leaving, it is desired to thank you for everything, and wish you the very best of luck in the future."

B. PRISONERS OF WAR

Many American and British Prisoners of War escaped from the Nazis and Fascists and were saved by the "Corchiano" partisans. Collaborating with the Allied Military Command, they joined the Italians and participated in sabotage efforts. On September 17, 1944, Antonio Giustini submitted the following information to Colonnello Giuseppe Pironti in Rome, Monsignor Hugh

O'Flaherty in Vatican City, and United States Army Major J.R. Aiken, Allied
Screening Commission for Italy:

1. 0789187- James McCrory - U.S.A. A.C.
   320 G.P. 444 Bomb. Squ.
   Goodman, Mississippi, U.S.A.
2. 0727717- Joseph Green - 1st Pilot Lt. U.S.A., A.C.
   320 G.P. 444 Bomb. Squ.
   San Francisco, California, U.S.A.
3. 0670657- J.B. Stewart - Lt. U.S.A., A.C.
   320 G.P. 444 Bomb. Squ.
4. 32388039- J.W. Gardner - S/Sgt. U.S.A.
   320 G.P. 444 Bomb. Squ.
   461 Henry Street, Elizabeth, N.J.
5. 32276519- H.W. De Lisle - S/Sgt. U.S.A.
   320 G.P. 444 Bomb. Squ.
6. 32176519- W.G. Harrison - S/Sgt. U.S.A., A.C.
   320 G.P. 444 Bomb. Squ.
7. 1063396- Gordon Bennett - Sgt. R.A.F.
   19 Cedar Crescent Newton, Le Willows, England
8. 16010254- Clyde Everett - C.O. "I" 168 Inf., U.S.A.
   1000 N. London Street, Grand Rapids, Michigan
9. 88097- Robert P. Rossignol (French) - 1 Coy - D.C.B.
   Div. A.M.L.S.C. 4
   38 Rue de l'Horloge, Madagascar
10. 267804- John McBride - C.D.S.M. - Unit B.N.A.F.
    145 Merchiston Street, Carntyne, Glasgow, Scotland
11. 5955910- A. Watkins, Pte - Unit Army
    Jackman's Place, Letchworth, Herts, England
12. 5502919- Arthur Allan, Pte - Inf.
    116 Pendragon Road, Bromley Kent, England
13. 5503883- Arthur F. Groundsell, Pte - Inf.
    2 Rose Cott. Yaverland, Sandown, I.O. Wight
14. 89742- A.E. Hartshorne, Pte - Unit Art. - U.D.F.
    96 Greyling Street, Pietermatzburg, S.A.
15. 11688- Theremis Jacobus Botha, S.A. Inf.
    3 Beach Nahoon, East London, S.A.
16. 88853- Joseph William Southam, Sgt. R. Artil.
    19 Alderson Street, Bishop Aukland, c/o Durham
17. R91186- Joseph Anthony Gordon, Fl/Sgt. R.A.F.
    147 Stanley Avenue, Mimico, Ontario, Canada

18. 82029- Lazar Epstein, S/Sgt. U.D.F.
164 Seventh Avenue, Mayfair
Johannesburg, S.A.
19. 106115- Jean Louis De Villiers, Sgt/Inf. S.A.
Dekomme, P.O. Toutelbos, Calvinia, C.P.S.A.
20. 887562 - Robert Bell Smith, Gnr-Artil.
Victoria Street, Lanchester, Durham
21. 1485513- John Morrow, Gnr-R.A.
Ballyatwood-Ballywalter, c/o 1 Down-Eire
45 Durham Avenue, Salisbury R.D.
22. 5631238- Douglas Haughey, 2/C.A.M.H.
19 Grd'es Plymouth, Devon, England
23. 854739- Cyril Victor Bensley, Sgt. R.A.
32 Gainsford Crescent, Bestwood Estate, England

The following have incomplete identification:

24. Eddie Giardino, 1138-78th Street, Brooklyn, N.Y., U.S.A.
25. Tou Tou (Algerian)
26. Aincoros Mohamed, 2 R.T.A. 10 G.
27. Benhouda Alidiaziz, 2 R.T.A. 10 G.
28. ZiZi Mohamed, Sgt. 2 R.T.A. 10 G.
29. Florimon Riviere (French)

C. RESCUERS

Italian Rescuers in the Province of Viterbo distinguished themselves for their intelligence, fidelity, and valor. The Allies and the Italian government recognized their contribution in fighting the Nazis and the Fascists:

1. Ferruccio Nardoni
2. Loreto Capitoni
3. Elio Spiriti
4. Ludovico Lilli
5. Alberto di Majo
6. Tenente Dottor Aldo Lucchetti di Rignano Flaminio
7. Fabio Polinari di Castelnuovo di Porto
8. Francesco Pettinari di Faleria
9. Maresciallo dei RR. CC. Angelo Filippi di Borgocolleferato
10. Angelo Fiorentini di Canepina
11. Maresciallo dei RR. CC. Giuseppe Prandini di Canina
12. Tenente Emanuele di Vittorio di S. Oreste
13. Faustino Giustini

14. Ezer Cianca
15. Studente di Medicina Oliviero Crescenzi
16. Carabiniere Lauro Montanini
17. Dottor Domenico Signoriello
18. Francesco Orlandi
19. Adriano Pastori
20. Dottor Girolamo Capece
21. Gasperino Gasperini
22. Aida Mastrogiovanni
23. Silvestro Fiaschetti
24. Settimio Ortenzi
25. Luigi Ortenzi
26. Luciano Maffucci
27. Ampelio Spiriti
28. Eraldo Massucci
29. Roberto Laurie
30. Bastiano il Siciliano
31. Luciano il Siciliano
32. Ercole Todini
33. Francesco Cioccolini
34. Francesco Berto
35. Luigi Berto

VI. Statistics on the Holocaust
(The Holocaust Museum, Washington, D.C.)

A. NUMBER OF JEWISH VICTIMS BY COUNTRY

The minimum and maximum figures from Hilberg, Reitlinger, Wellers, *Encyclopedia of the Holocaust* and other sources specific to individual countries have been used in reaching estimated figures.* All statistics are estimates. The lowest figure for Jews killed in the Holocaust is 5,100,000 (Hilberg, Reitlinger) and the highest 5,700,000 (Benz).

ALBANIA: 591 deportees; mortality not known.

AUSTRIA: ca. 65,459 Jews killed. March 1938 (Anschluss): 185,246 Jews living in Austria. December 1939: 70,000 Jews living in Ostmark.

BULGARIA: 11,393 Jews deported from Bulgarian occupied territory (all native Bulgarian Jews were rescued).

CZECHOSLOVAKIA (Protectorate plus Slovakia): 143,000 Jews killed (lowest estimate in Benz) to 260,000 Jews killed (highest figure in Hilberg). The discrepancy involves whether you calculate Slovakian mortality in part with Hungarian Jewish mortality, since Hilberg's figure is lower for Hungary and larger for Slovakia than the norm.

DENMARK: 116 Jews killed (Yahil, Benz).

FRANCE and BELGIUM: (linked as one territorial zone under German occupation) France: ca. 65,000 Jews killed (including Jewish aliens and stateless Jews). Belgium: ca. 26,000–28,500 Jews killed (including Jewish aliens and stateless Jews). Only 32,200 of these Jews held French or Belgian citizenship.

GERMANY: ca. 145,000–160,000 Jews killed. June 1933 census of Jews in Germany: 499,682 Jews (ca. 500,000). 1939 census: 215,000 Jews and October 1, 1941 census by the Reichsvereinigung: 163,696 (this is the last census before the first deportations of Jews from Germany).

*Bibliographic citations for sources mentioned on this page and in the following pages are provided at the end of this Appendix.

231

GREECE: ca. 60,000 Jews killed.

HUNGARY: ca. 550,000 Jews killed.

ITALY: 6,513 Jews killed (Fargion) to 9,000 Jews killed (high estimate Hilberg).

LUXEMBOURG: ca. 1,000–1,200 Jews killed. December 1935 census: 3,144 Jews registered (consisting of 870 Luxembourg nationals and 2,274 of foreign nationality).

NETHERLANDS: ca. 102,000 (out of 140,000) Jews killed.

NORWAY: 762 (low estimate in Hilberg) to ca. 1,000 Jews killed (Hilberg's highest figure).

POLAND: ca. 2,700,000 to 3,000,000 Jews killed (Hilberg, Benz, and Yad Vashem have the same range).

ROMANIA: ca. 211,000 Jews killed (Reitlinger and Benz); highest estimate of 270,000 with Hilberg.

SOVIET UNION: ca. 1,000,000 Jews killed (lowest realistic estimate in Hilberg; Reitlinger gives only 750,000 Jews) to 2,000,000 Jews killed (highest estimate in Wellers and Benz).

YUGOSLAVIA: ca. 60,000–65,000 Jews killed (Benz). The total number of Jews based on adding the minimum mortality of Jews in the above compilation is rounded off to: 5,658,000, which is a safe compromise between the changing low and high figures in the statistical literature. This is very close to Gilbert's figure of 5,700,000 victims. Recent publicity about new unpublished Soviet statistical work has given rise to unsubstantiated rumor that the larger figure of 2,000,000 Soviet Jews killed may be correct.

B. VICTIMS BY CONCENTRATION CAMP

AUSCHWITZ-BIRKENAU: Mortality rate

1,082,000 to 1,100,000 Jews	94.4 percent
21,000 Gypsies	93.5 percent
70,000 to 75,000 Poles	58.1 percent
15,000 Soviet POWs	99.2 percent

Source: Franciszek Piper, "Number of Victims of Auschwitz-Birkenau," *Yad Vashem Studies* 21 (1991): p. 98; the mortality rates were calculated in Georges Wellers, "Essai de détermination du nombre des morts d'Auschwitz," *Le Monde Juif* 112 (1983).

BELZEC: Killing center in eastern Poland. Opened in March 1943 and closed in December 1944. More than 600,000 persons, overwhelmingly Jews, and several hundred Gypsies were murdered there, initially in gas vans and later in gas chambers.

CHELMNO: Killing center opened in late December 1941 in incorporated western Poland (the Wartheland), where the SS—using special mobile gas vans—killed more than 320,000 Jews from Lodz (including Jews from Poland, Germany, Austria, the Protectorate of Bohemia and Moravia, and Luxembourg) and Poznan provinces as well as about 5,000 Austrian Gypsies incarcerated in the Lodz ghetto. It operated from December 1941 to March 1943 and resumed operation between April and August 1944 during the liquidation of the Lodz ghetto.

MAJDANEK: Established in the outskirts of Lublin along the Lublin-Zamosc-Chelm highway in October 1941. Initially a Soviet prisoner-of-war camp under the Waffen-SS Lublin District. Like Auschwitz, Majdanek included a concentration camp, labor camp, and killing center. More than 360,000 of the ca. 500,000 prisoners from twenty-eight countries perished at Majdanek; nearly 60 percent died from malnutrition, exposure, epidemics, and labor conditions, and 40 percent were executed (lethal phenol injections, shooting, and hanging) or killed in the seven gas chambers (with carbon monoxide or Zyklon B). In 1943, thousands of Jews from the Warsaw and Bialystok ghettos were gassed at Majdanek. The largest prisoner groups included 100,000 Poles, 80,000 Jews, and 50,000 Soviet prisoners of war. One of the satellite camps of Majdanek was the Gesia Street camp in the ruins of the Warsaw ghetto that existed from June 1943 to October 1944. Liberated by the Soviet army on 23 July 1944, the first trial of German war criminals was held by a Polish court at Lublin in November–December 1944.

SOBIBOR: Killing center in Lublin district in eastern Poland. Opened in May 1942 and closed one day after rebellion by Jewish prisoners on 14 October 1943. At least 250,000 Jews were killed there.

TREBLINKA: Killing center on Bug River in the General Government. Opened in July 1942. It was the largest of the Operation Reinhard killing centers. Between 700,000 and 850,000 persons, mostly Jews and a few hundred Gypsies, were killed there. A revolt by the inmates on 2 August 1943 destroyed most of the camp; it was closed in November 1943.

SAN SABBA: Killing center in Trieste (Adriatic Coastal Zone after the occupation of Italy), ca. 5,000 Jews and Italian and Slovenian partisans killed there. The only killing center with gas chamber and crematoria not on Polish soil and run by the staff of T4 (euthanasia) and the Operation Reinhard camps. Opened October 1943; liberated 2 May 1945.

Zyklon B was used only at Auschwitz-Birkenau and Majdanek; all others used carbon monoxide in gas vans and gas chambers. The latter method of killing was introduced in the so-called euthanasia institutions after 1940 (Hartheim, Grafeneck, Hadamar, Bernburg, Brandenburg, Sonnenstein).

234 *Yours Is a Precious Witness*

C. STATISTICS FOR OTHER VICTIM GROUPS

ROMA and SINTI (GYPSIES): Low figure 250,000 (Puxon in the 1970s) to highest estimate 500,000 (Zimmermann, Roma and Sinti Center Heidelberg, Koenig) in Europe. The 500,000 figure is probably a better estimate based on growing information of mortality in various occupied countries.

SOVIET PRISONERS OF WAR: 2,200,000–3,300,000 killed (Strelm and Krausnick).

JEHOVAH'S WITNESSES: Arrested after 1935 in Germany and after 1938 in Austria and 1939 in Czechoslovakia, 1940 in Belgium, Netherlands, Norway, and Poland. About 10,000 Witnesses were imprisoned in the concentration camps (Dachau, Belsen, Buchenwald, Ravensbruck, Auschwitz, Mauthausen, Sachsenhausen, and many others) and about 2,500 died in the camps.

HANDICAPPED ("EUTHANASIA," T4): Includes physically disabled and psychiatric patients as well as deaf, blind, mute children, and later, after 1942 (14f13 program) concentration-camp prisoners too ill to work (including Jews) and some healthy part-Jewish children from Jewish mixed marriages in Germany (ca. 50 killed in Hadamar in 1943). In all of Europe 1940–45: ca. 200,000–250,000 including 70,000 in the first phase in Germany and Austria (1940–41). This includes 3,000 Jews killed in the spring of 1940. In France ca. 160,000 are the lowest estimates and patients in Polish and Soviet hospitals killed as part of the program were simply taken out and executed. It is likely that as research on this grows in all of German occupied Europe (e.g., Netherlands, Yugoslavia) that this figure will increase. For reasons that are not yet clear in the literature, Bohemia-Moravia was exempted from the "euthanasia program," even though it was incorporated in Reich territory after 1939. After the so-called stop in the euthanasia program in 1941, euthanasia became more secret and even higher numbers of victims were recorded.

HOMOSEXUALS: Arrest statistics range from a low of 5,000 to a high of 12,000 (Stumke, Lautmann, etc.) sent to concentration camps after 1935 under the revised par. 175 of the German penal code. Mortality rate unknown, but believed to be at least 2,200 (Percy, German report by Dr. Wuth for mortality rate 1940–43). The literature also indicates that ca. 50,000 to 63,000 men were convicted in courts of homosexual offenses (Johansson and Percy). In Warren Johansson and William Percy, "Homosexuals in Nazi Germany," *Simon Wiesenthal Center Annual* 7 (1990): p. 252 f., there is an excellent summary of the problems of figures for this group. Thus, only three categories of homosexual victims of the Nazi regime can be identified with any accuracy: (1) those arrested, sentenced, and executed for homosexual acts; (2) those who were sent to forced labor or concentration camps and died there; and (3) those put to death as part of the program of euthanasia because they had been committed to institutions as homosexual. All others—for example, those who committed suicide—can never be statistically identified or calculated. Also falling outside this figure are those who were permanently mutilated—castrated or sterilized against their will.

D. OTHER STATISTICS

DACHAU: The first concentration camp, near Munich, Germany. The opening of the camp was announced on 20 March 1933. When the camp opened, only known political opponents were interned. Gradually, more and more groups were incarcerated there. In Dachau there was no mass extermination program with poison gas. But out of the total number of 206,200 registered prisoners there were 31,591 registered deaths. Prisoners too ill to work were deported to the euthanasia institution of Hartheim and killed there. However, the total number of deaths in Dachau, including the victims of individual and mass executions and the final death marches, will never be known. On 29 April 1945, the camp was liberated by units of the United States Seventh Army.

BUCHENWALD: One of the first major concentration camps, opened in 1937; located on the Ettersberg hillside overlooking Weimar, Germany. The first German and Austrian Jewish prisoners arrived in 1938; German and Austrian Gypsy prisoners were deported there after July 1938. During the war, political prisoners came to dominate the camp's internal administration. In the summer of 1941, Jewish and other prisoners too ill to work were sent under the 14f13 program to the euthanasia institution at Bernburg and killed there. Buchenwald also included the Little Camp, an enclosure for prisoners evacuated from camps in the East; shortly before it was liberated by the United States Army on 11 April 1945, the prisoners themselves seized control of the camp. Buchenwald developed more than 130 satellite labor camps, including Langeinstein-Zwieberge, also known as "Malachit." More than 65,000 of the approximately 250,000 prisoners perished at Buchenwald.

MAUTHAUSEN: A camp for men opened in August 1938 near Linz in Austria. Established to exploit the nearby quarries, it was classified by the SS as a camp of utmost severity, and conditions there were brutal even by concentration-camp standards. Many prisoners were killed by being pushed from 300 ft. cliffs into the quarries. Liberated on 5 May 1945 by the U.S. Army. Prisoners included political prisoners, Spanish republicans, Jews from Czechoslovakia and the Netherlands (1941), Gypsies from Austria (1938–40), Soviet POWs, and in January 1945 more than 9,000 prisoners evacuated from Auschwitz. Major subcamps at Ebensee and Gusen held nearly 100,000 additional prisoners by the last years of the war. Nearly 30,000 Polish prisoners (including Jews) were in Mauthausen; several thousand Czech prisoners (including Jews) especially during 1941–1942 (including those later murdered at the camp in reprisal for Heydrich's assassination); thousands of Soviet prisoners of war; large numbers of Italian, French, and Yugoslavian political prisoners. Of 7,500 Spanish republicans, nearly 4,200 died at Mauthausen. The total number of prisoners who passed through Mauthausen is ca. 200,000. It is believed that 119,000 of them perished there; of these nearly 38,000 were Jewish prisoners. This includes those who were regularly killed—under the 14f13 killing of prisoners unable to do labor—at the euthanasia institution at Hartheim (near Alkoven and Linz).

SACHSENHAUSEN: Concentration camp for men opened in 1936. Located in Oranienburg, a suburb of Berlin and site of an earlier "wild" concentration camp, it was adjacent to the Inspectorate of the Concentration Camps. It held about 200,000 prisoners, of whom 100,000 perished. It was liberated by the Soviet Army in late April 1945.

RAVENSBRUCK: Concentration camp for women opened in May 1939. More than 132,000 women prisoners from twenty countries were incarcerated at Ravensbruck and in the more than seventy subsidiary camps; after April 1941, more than 12,000 male prisoners passed through the newly erected men's subcamp of Ravensbruck known as Uckermark, where elderly and ill female prisoners unable to perform forced labor were killed by gas, poison, or shooting early in 1945. Very few of the 800 children born at Ravensbruck survived. Of the women, more than 2,000 Gypsies were imprisoned there and ca. 7,500 female Jewish prisoners. The camp also held Soviet female prisoners of war, Jehovah's Witnesses, 170 Lidice women, and Resistance prisoners from many nations. In December 1940, about 1,200 prisoners were deported from Ravensbruck to the euthanasia institution at Bernburg for gassing under "14f13," the program for killing prisoners unable to work; many of those killed were Jews. The largest prisoner groups at Ravensbruck were Polish (26 percent of the prisoners), German and Austrian (20 percent), Russian and Ukrainian (19 percent), Jewish (15 percent), French (7 percent), and Roma and Sinti Gypsies (ca. 5.5 percent). Unusually brutal medical and sterilization experiments on Polish, Gypsy, and Jewish women prisoners were conducted at Ravensbruck. It is estimated that more than 60,000 of these women prisoners perished at Ravensbruck and its subsidiary camps. In April 1945, just before liberation, approximately 7,500 women were evacuated via Denmark to

Sweden through the Swedish Red Cross. The camp holding ca. 3,000 prisoners not evacuated on the death march was liberated on 30 April 1945 by units of the 2nd Belorussian Front. Ravensbruck also served as the training headquarters for ca. 3,500 SS female overseers (SS-Aufseherinnen), who were then sent to staff Auschwitz and other concentration camps.

BERGEN-BELSEN: Originally Stalag 311, where 16,000–18,000 of 20,000 Soviet prisoners of war died of starvation, exposure, and epidemic between 1941 and 1943. Several estimates of Soviet POW deaths in literature by the Memorial at Bergen-Belsen list 50,000 dead Soviet POWs. March 1944 Bergen-Belsen became a detention camp for Jewish prisoners with foreign passports to be used for exchange and ca. 4,000–6,000 Jewish women prisoners transferred from Birkenau. In 1945, more than 60,000 prisoners (including about 1,000 Gypsies) transferred from the eastern camps about to be liberated by the Russian army to Bergen-Belsen. Prisoners died of malnutrition, exposure, and disease; there were no gas chambers and no forced labor. The very high mortality rate at Bergen-Belsen prior to liberation includes 18,000 for the month of March 1945 of starvation and epidemics; from January to mid-April 1945, ca. 35,000 mostly Jewish prisoners died at Bergen-Belsen. The best-known prisoner who perished there in these last months of the war was Anne Frank. An additional 14,000 prisoners died of starvation and disease at Bergen-Belsen after liberation, despite British medical efforts to save the prisoners.

SOURCES:

Benz, Wolfgang, ed., *Dimension des Völkermords: Die Zahl der Jüdischen Opfer des Nationalsozialismus.* Munich: Oldenbourg, 1991.

Hilberg, Raul, *The Destruction of the European Jews.* 3 v. , New York and London: Holmes and Meier, 1985.

———, "The Statistic," in François Furst, ed. *Unanswered Questions: Nazi Germany and the Genocide of the Jews.* New York: Shocken, 1989.

Piper, Franciszek, "Estimating the Number of Deportees to and victims of the Auschwitz-Birkenau Camp," *Yad Vashem Studies* 21, 1991.

Reitlinger, Gerald, *The Final Solution: The Attempt to Exterminate the Jews of Europe, 1939–1945.* New York: A.S. Barnes-Perpetua, 1961.

Wellers, George, "Essai de détermination du nombre des morts d'Auschwitz," *Le Monde Juif* 112, 1983.

Other published sources: The Blue Series of the International Military Tribunal at Nuremberg and facsimile documents reproduced in the 18-volume series *The Holocaust* (edited by John Mendelsohn) and the 19-volume facsimile series *Archives of the Holocaust* (edited by Sybil

Yours Is a Precious Witness

Milton and Henry Friedländer); the 1941–42 Einsatzgruppen situation reports, the January 1942 Wannsee protocol, and the March 1943 report by the SS statistician Richard Korherr (NO 5193097). Also Klarsfeld's memorial books for France and Belgium and the German *Gedenkbuch* published by the Bundesarchiv and Yad Vashem for statistics on mortality rates.

G. Index*

* Appendixes are not indexed.

Ganor, Solly, 165
GAP (Gruppi Azione Patriottica),
    127–128, 209
Gariboldi, Giorgio Angelozzi, 145,
    152–153
Gas chambers, 99, 163
Gazzaniga, 78
Geiser, Arthur, 159
Genio Navale, 72
Genoa, 75, 85, 87–91
Genocide, 209
Gensano, 47
Gentile, Father, 100–101
Gentile, Giovanni, 163
Gentiles, 49
German Catholics, 149
German Church, 137
Germany, 17, 19 ff.
Gestapo, 39, 123, 178
Giamarini, Antonio, 96
Gianaroli, Alberta, 25
Gianaroli, Sisto, 25
Gilbert, Martin, 19
Ginnasi Palace, 109
Ginzburg, Leon, 127
Giordana, Anna , 88
Giordana, Maria, 88
Giorgi, Don Fernando, 126–128
Girelli, Sister Luisa, 131
Girotti, Father Giuseppe
    (Dominican), 75
Gistron, Ines, 73–74
Giulio, Father, 100
Giustini, Fernando G., 192–194
Giustini Family, 192–194
Globocnick, Gruppenführer Odillo,
    99
Gloria, 129
God, 54, 181, 206
Goldoni, Nori, 162
Goldoni, Renato, 162
Goldschmidt, Samuele, 103

Golgotha, 201
Gonella, Professor, 68
Gorizia, 75
Gradassi, Don Giulio, 94
Graham, Father Robert, S.J., iv, 6,
    152, 154, 159, 171, 174–176
Granada, 123
Grassi, Mr. and Mrs., 71
Grassini, Lello, 102
Grasso, Bernardo, 87
Great Britain, 41, 53, 200
Greco Family, 115
Greece, 28, 76
Gregorini, Don Giovanni, 111
Gregory XVI, Pope, 109
Greiser, Arthur, 159
Grigolato, Sister Maria, 43
Grini, Mauro (Spy), 99
Gubbio, 115, 198
Guerra di Liberazione, La, 167
Gundlach, Professor Gustave, 154
Gyor, 147
Gypsies: Austrian, 40; German, 40;
    Roma, 39

H

Herskovic, William, 17
Hertz, Joseph (Grand Rabbi), 170
Herzer, Ivo, 29
Herzog, Isaac (Grand Rabbi), 56,
    170
Heuss, President of Western
    Germany, 57
Heydrich, Reinhardt, 54
Hill of Martyrs, 201
Himmler, SS Chief Heinrich, 3, 33,
    54, 99
Hiroshima, 5, 56
Hitler, Adolf, 13, 15, 17, 19, 20, 44,
    50, 53, 55, 71
Hochhuth, Rolf, 15, 127, 149–150,
    159–160

H. Illustrations

BOOKS BY MARGHERITA MARCHIONE

CLEMENTE REBORA:

L'Imagine Tesa, Edizioni di Storia e Letteratura, Rome, 1960, 300pp.;
   reprinted and enlarged, 1974, 410pp.
Lettere, Vol. I, 1976, 680pp.; Vol. II, 1982, 450pp.
Clemente Rebora, Twayne's World Author Series, Twayne Publishers,
   1979, Boston, 183pp.

CORRESPONDENCE OF GIOVANNI BOINE:

Carteggio Boine-Prezzolini (1908-1915), Vol. I, Edizioni di Storia e
   Letteratura, 1971, Rome, 264pp.; reprinted, 1981.
Boine-Cecchi (1911-1917), Vol. II, 1972, 233pp.; reprinted, 1982.
Boine-Amici del "Rinnovamento" Tome 1 (1905-1910);
   Tome 2 (1911-1917), Vol. III, 1977, 1130pp.
Boine-Amici de "La Voce" (1904-1917), Vol. IV, 1979, 690pp.

PHILIP MAZZEI:

Jefferson's "Zealous Whig," American Institute of Italian Studies,
   Morristown, NJ, 1975, 352pp.
My Life and Wanderings, American Institute of Italian Studies,
   Morristown, NJ, 1980, 438pp.
The Comprehensive Microform Edition of His Papers, 1730- 1816,
   nine reels and clothbound *Guide and Index,* Kraus International
   Publications, 1982, 172pp.
Selected Writings and Correspondence, Cassa di Risparmi e Depositi,
   Prato, 1983, Vol. I - Virginia's Agent during the American
   Revolution, XLVIII - 585pp.; Vol. II - Agent for the King of
   Poland during the French Revolution, 802pp.; Vol. III - World
   Citizen, 623pp.
Scritti Scelti e Lettere, (Italian Edition, same as above, 1984).
The Constitutional Society of 1784, Center for Mazzei Studies,
   Morristown, NJ, 1984, 49pp.
Istruzioni per essere liberi ed eguali, Cisalpino-Gogliardica, Milan,
   1984, 160pp.
Philip Mazzei: World Citizen (Jefferson's "Zealous Whig"),
   University Press of America, Lanham, MD, 1994, 158pp.
*The Adventurous Life of Philip Mazzei—La vita avventurosa di
   Filippo Mazzei,* University Press of America, Lanham,
   MD, 1995, 215pp.

GIUSEPPE PREZZOLINI:

Un secolo di attività, Rusconi, Milan, 1982, 160pp.
Carteggio Angelini-Prezzolini, Edizioni di Storia e
  Letteratura, Rome, 1982, 394pp.
Ricordi, Saggi e Testimonianze, Edizioni del Palazzo, Prato,
  1983, 300pp.
L'Ombra di Dio, Rusconi, Milan, 1984, 200pp.
Incontriamo Prezzolini, Editrice La Scuola, Brescia, 1985, 210pp.
Giuseppe Prezzolini: Lettere a Suor Margherita, (1956-1982).
  Introduction by Margherita Marchione, edited by Claudio
  Quarantotto, Edizioni di Storia e Letteratura, Rome, 1992, 378pp.

BIOGRAPHY:

From the Land of the Etruscans, (Lucy Filippini) Edizioni di
  Storia e Letteratura, Rome, 1986, XIV-68pp.
Cardinal Mark Anthony Barbarigo, Religious Teachers Filippini,
  Rome, 1992, 220pp.
Prophet and Witness of Charity, (Tommaso Maria Fusco),
  edited by Margherita Marchione. Daughters of Charity,
  Paterson, NJ, 1993, 170pp.
Peter and Sally Sammartino (Biographical Notes), Cornwall Press,
  Cranbury, NJ, 1994, 305pp.

HISTORY:

A Pictorial History of the Saint Lucy Filippini Chapel, Edizioni
  del Palazzo, Prato, 1992, 130pp.
*Yours Is a Precious Witness (Memoirs of Jews and Catholics in
  Wartime Italy)*, Paulist Press, Mahwah, NJ, 1996, 300pp.

POETRY:

Twentieth Century Italian Poetry: A Bilingual Anthology, Fairleigh
  Dickinson University, Rutherford, NJ, 1974, 302pp.

PROFILES:

*Contemporary Profiles: National Italian American Foundation
  Awardees*, NIAF, Washington, DC, 1993, 265pp.
Americans of Italian Heritage, University Press of America,
  Lanham, MD, 1995, 39 photographs, 246pp.